CONTEM
EVILS

Edited by David Utting

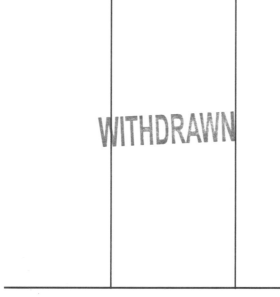

JOSEPH ROWNTREE
FOUNDATION

This edition published in Great Britain in 2009 by The Policy Press for the
Joseph Rowntree Foundation

The Policy Press
University of Bristol
Fourth Floor, Beacon House
Queen's Road
Bristol BS8 1QU, UK
t: +44 (0)117 331 4054
f: +44 (0)117 331 4093
e: tpp-info@bristol.ac.uk
www.policypress.org.uk

North American office:
The Policy Press
c/o International Specialized Books Services
920 NE 58th Avenue, Suite 300
Portland, OR 97213-3786, USA
t: +1 503 287 3093   f: +1 503 280 8832   e: info@isbs.com

British Library Cataloguing in Publication Data: A catalogue record for this book is
available from the British Library.

Library of Congress Cataloging-in-Publication Data: A catalog record for this book
has been requested.

ISBN 978 1 84742 408 2 paperback
ISBN 978 1 84742 409 9 hardcover

Cover design by The Policy Press
Front cover: image kindly supplied by www.istock.com
Printed and bound in Great Britain by Hobbs the Printers, Southampton

Contents

Foreword

Nicholas Timmins

History is littered with exhortations from the great and the good to the aspiring to go out and solve problems.

Forty years before he wrote the report that bears his name, William Beveridge was urged by Edward Caird, the Master of Balliol, to go forth 'and discover why, with so much wealth in Britain, there continues to be so much poverty, and how poverty can be cured' (Beveridge, 1953, p 9).

The Joseph Rowntree Foundation (JRF), in setting up the trusts that bear his name, charged them with an even broader remit: to seek out the underlying causes of weakness in society. And it is that duty that has led JRF to re-examine, perhaps redefine, the 'social evils' that need to be tackled a hundred years on.

This book, the results of thousands of contributions from normally unheard voices to those of some of the country's most distinguished social commentators, is the outcome and it is challenging, stimulating reading.

For a country in which religious observation is now a minority sport, the use of the word 'evil' packs a powerful, even disturbing, punch. But from the online consultation and some of the contributions to this book, concerns about the decline of community and family (or at the least, its rapidly changing nature), and worries about rampant individualism, consumerism and a loss of solidarity emerge strongly.

One needs a degree of caution in analysing this.

Opinion polling regularly reveals a sense of pessimism about the present in the British character. Whether one is thinking of society as a whole, or the state of public services for example, Britons tend instinctively to believe in a 'better yesterday', even in the face of the facts – and even if (depending on economic circumstances) they may still believe that a better tomorrow is possible, or even likely. After all, it was in the 1950s – now seen by some as an ideal time of social cohesion, if by others as a period of social repression – when the composer and lyricist Lionel Bart struck a powerful chord, although admittedly a humorous one, with 'Fings ain't what they used to be'.

But while this project was conceived in better economic times, now may be the ideal time to publish it. Recession will, for the time being at least, reduce both the public and private resources needed to tackle many of the concerns outlined here. But there is nothing like a crisis to trigger a rethink, both individually and collectively, about society's values, goals and directions.

There is not – unsurprisingly – entire agreement within this book about how modern social evils should be tackled, but there is a fair element of agreement over how to define them.

History suggests that major reform tends to follow major disruption – whether great wars or the Great Depression, with modern welfare states and institutions emerging from the ashes such events create. How bad the current recession will be, nobody yet knows. But it may be that now is the perfect moment, having started the debate, for the JRF to encapsulate it in this book and take the argument onwards. Difficult times may, paradoxically, provide the best moment for framing difficult solutions.

Reference

Beveridge, W. (1953) *Power and influence*, London: Hodder & Stoughton.

Acknowledgements

The Joseph Rowntree Foundation (JRF) first would like to thank all the people who took part in the public consultation, without whom there would have been no project. This includes the participants in the 'unheard voices' research and the 3,500 website respondents who gave up precious time to provide us with their detailed and often heartfelt thoughts.

We are also indebted to numerous other individuals who have contributed to the project as it has developed: the Hartrigg Oaks residents who responded so enthusiastically to the initial idea; the participants in the three events we held to discuss the initial findings from the consultation; the staff and fellows of the Royal Society for the encouragement of Arts, Manufactures and Commerce (RSA), who have been so supportive over the course of the whole project; and Beth Watts and Chris Creegan who, although employed to undertake work on the project, became closely involved in its development over and above the call of duty.

Finally, thanks are due to Charlie Lloyd, Rosie Knowles and other staff in the policy and research and communications departments at the JRF, who worked hard on the project and enabled this book to be produced.

Notes on contributors

Shaun Bailey is co-Founder of MyGeneration, a youth and community charity.

Zygmunt Bauman is a philosopher and sociologist. He is Emeritus Professor of Sociology at the University of Leeds.

Anthony Browne is Policy Director to the Mayor of London, Boris Johnson, and a former director of the Policy Exchange.

Chris Creegan is Deputy Director of the Qualitative Research Unit at the National Centre for Social Research.

A.C. Grayling is Professor of Philosophy at Birkbeck, University of London.

Jose Harris is Emeritus Professor of Modern History at the University of Oxford, and a fellow of St Catherine's College.

Rachel Kinsella is a researcher in the Qualitative Research Unit at the National Centre for Social Research.

Neal Lawson is Chair of Compass and a research fellow at the Global Policy Institute, London Metropolitan University. He is the author of *All consuming* (2009, Penguin).

Anna Minton is a writer and journalist. She is the author of *Ground control: Fear and happiness in the twenty-first-century city* (2009, Penguin).

Ferdinand Mount is a prolific author who has been both a political columnist of *The Spectator* and Head of the No 10 Policy Unit under Margaret Thatcher.

Alice Mowlam is a senior researcher in the Qualitative Research Unit at the National Centre for Social Research.

Julia Neuberger is a rabbi, social reformer and member of the House of Lords.

Jeremy Seabrook is an author and journalist specialising in social, environmental and development issues. His most recent book is the *Refuge and the fortress: Britain and the flight from tyranny* (2009, Palgrave Macmillan).

Matthew Taylor is Chief Executive of the RSA.

Stephen Thake is Reader in Urban Policy at London Metropolitan University.

Nicholas Timmins is Public Policy Editor of the *Financial Times*, author of *The five giants: A biography of the welfare state* (2001, HarperCollins), Visiting Professor in Public Management at King's College, London, a senior associate of the Nuffield Trust and President of the Social Policy Association.

Julia Unwin is Chief Executive of the Joseph Rowntree Foundation.

David Utting is an author, researcher and policy analyst specialising in issues concerning children, young people and families. He was Deputy Director of the Policy Research Bureau until March 2007 and previously Associate Director (Public Affairs) of the Joseph Rowntree Foundation. He is currently Secretary to the Independent Commission on Youth Crime and Antisocial Behaviour.

Martha Warrener is a researcher in the Qualitative Research Unit at the National Centre for Social Research.

Beth Watts is a research associate at the Young Foundation and a former researcher for the Joseph Rowntree Foundation.

1

Introduction

Julia Unwin

When Joseph Rowntree set up the trusts that bear his name in 1904, he urged them to "search out the underlying causes of weakness or evil in the community". Strikingly, he also advised the trustees of his considerable wealth to keep alert to the "changing necessities of the nation" and ensure that they continued to focus on investigating the underlying causes of evil, rather than the superficial manifestations. He was clear that, while there were "scourges of humanity" that plagued his own times – including poverty, war, slavery, intemperance, the opium trade and gambling – times were bound to change. He wanted his trusts to be "living bodies, free to adapt themselves to the ever changing necessities of the nation". It was in this spirit of inquiry that the Joseph Rowntree Foundation (JRF), a century on, decided to investigate the nature of 'social evil' in the 21st century.

To gather contemporary perspectives, we launched a national debate that proved to be more wide-ranging and more challenging than we dared hope. While allowing us to revisit our original mandate, it also prompted a large number of people across the UK to consider fundamental questions about the nature of society. The term 'social evils' can feel rather uncomfortable. As a Foundation we are used to considering the administrative improvements that can make a difference to the lives of people living in poverty and disadvantage. However, a discussion about 'social problems' would be unlikely to have prompted the same level of impassioned public engagement as our general invitation for people to send us their views on social evils. The concept of 'evil' appears to have led many people to look beyond commonly discussed social problems such as drugs, poverty or social exclusion, to express more fundamental, less tangible fears about the nature of society and how it is changing. It brought valuable urgency to the debate, and a palpable moral sense.

The national discussion engaged the thoughts and interests of more than 3,500 people who responded to an online consultation exercise initiated through JRF's website, as well as those who took part in a number of public meetings and in radio phone-ins. It also gained the interest and enthusiasm of people whose voices are not usually heard in these discussions. Through focus groups and workshops run by NatCen (National Centre for Social Research), the work was enriched by the views of people with learning disabilities, ex-offenders, carers, unemployed people, vulnerable young people, care leavers and people with experience of homelessness. Their perspectives, and the results of the online consultation, are described in Section 1. Discussion of the major themes identified, both abstract and concrete, is augmented in Section 2 by 11 leading thinkers and writers from contrasted political and ideological perspectives who were asked to contribute their own viewpoints. We also invited Matthew Taylor, Chief Executive of the RSA to read the resulting wealth of material and set down his own, consequent thoughts (Section 3).

However, to begin with – and in order to place these contemporary views in perspective – we asked Jose Harris, Emeritus Professor of Modern History at the University of Oxford, to contribute a preliminary essay tracing the ways in which understandings of social evil have shifted and changed in the last 100 years. As she points out in the next chapter, Joseph Rowntree and other social investigators were active at a time when deep anxieties about the problems facing their society were matched by impressive optimism. They believed that scientific progress and rational thinking could bring solutions, and that the great scourges of want, disease and ignorance could be resolved by expanding wealth, as well as the growing abilities of people of goodwill. A belief in progress, and a courageous desire to recognise the value of all individuals, informed their view that society could be improved, and social evil eliminated.

Do people today believe that an Edwardian sense of optimism has in any sense proved justified or been maintained? Judged by the responses JRF received to its consultation on contemporary social evils, the answer is mostly, although not wholly, positive. People talked about the enormous advances and freedoms we now have that would have been considered impossible 100 years ago. The freedom for self-expression, the much greater tolerance of individual lifestyles and the ability to make choices, as well as the greater wealth available to us, were all seen as having brought huge advantages. So too was our ability to order information, to analyse material and to understand social trends.

This combination of freedoms and assets, as well as capabilities, is seemingly well designed to enable us to understand and address the social problems of our own age with relative rapidity and ease. Yet these advances, welcome though they are, were seen as having been achieved at a price that many considered we have yet to understand sufficiently or calibrate. The debate about contemporary social evils did not reveal any strong discomfort with modernity, or nostalgic desire to go back in time. There was little sense of a pre-lapsarian past; indeed, there was a delight in the benefits of progress, and recognition that freedom has brought vast benefits. There was, nevertheless, concern that in embracing these freedoms we have not sufficiently reflected on what we might have lost, and have not troubled to compensate for them. For example, as Anthony Browne points out (Chapter 7), growing sexual equality has made it possible for more women to leave abusive and unhappy homes. If this has resulted in different patterns of family life, we do not largely regret the freedom that has made this possible. But we are prepared to note the challenges that this now poses.

Similarly, the greater mobility of individuals, and their ability to exercise choice and freedom, makes communities different, and in some senses unrecognisable. Welcome interventions, such as greater protection for vulnerable people, have also brought new challenges. Julia Neuberger (Chapter 9) describes how gains in child protection and the protection of older people have also, paradoxically, contributed to a stifling of the impulse of kindness. The human and humane response of compassion is all too frequently tempered nowadays by concerns about regulation and hostile perceptions.

Yet it will be seen that this was by no means an entirely negative or pessimistic debate. The urgency and enthusiasm with which people responded to the challenge of defining contemporary social evils suggested a willingness to get engaged, and a desire to effect change. Even the lament of people who felt they had little connection or control within their communities implied a deeper desire for involvement. Commentators like Stephen Thake (Chapter 14) talk about an entirely new approach to the development of civil society, recognising that its form and shape in the 21st century will be different from the institutions that Joseph Rowntree knew in 1904. Equally, Jeremy Seabrook (Chapter 17), with his interest in sufficiency as a defining feature, highlights the need for new models that will allow people to contribute to a fairer, more just and ultimately freer society.

While this book was being prepared, Barack Obama was elected as President in the US, acclaimed by crowds shouting "Yes, we can!". JRF's social evils debate strongly suggests that this slogan has a powerful resonance in the UK as well as the US. We have learned that in the diagnosis of social evil, as well as in prescriptions and remedies, there is more common ground than many would imagine. Respondents to the website, those at the meetings, the 'unheard voices' and the eminent commentators, focused on many of the same issues, even if they sometimes used different language and expressed contrary views.

Concerns about individualism and greed, and anxieties that individual preferment has become valued over common good, were to be found across the respondents. So, too, was a conviction that inequality is damaging for all. The nature of community, and the strength of the ties that bind us, were frequently raised as issues. Thus, a study that shone a light on a more fragmented, more stratified society, also — paradoxically — drew attention to an array of common, and commonly shared, concerns.

Inviting contemporary views of social evil risked, as one commentator put it, "swimming in a sea of social pessimism". There was a danger of producing a false dichotomy in which the apparent gains of recent decades were contrasted with the gloom and doom of the present day. But to dismiss the voices raised as simply 'miserable' would be to misread the findings. Those who responded did so with a real desire to look at the underlying causes of today's social ills, motivated by a powerful sense that so much of the way we are currently living is not sustainable.

These are voices to which we all need to listen, as we work together to design and build a good society. We might also agree that this is increasingly true as people experience the consequences of a global downturn that rapidly developed from a distant cloud at the start of this project into potentially the most severe economic storm in 60 years. Notwithstanding the additional difficulties that the recession has created in people's lives, JRF's inquiry into the nature of social evil demonstrates a desire to grapple with difficult issues, a commitment to identify the common good in shaping a better society and a passionate conviction that our unsustainable present offers an unreliable route map for our future.

2

'Social evils' and 'social problems' in Britain since 1904

Jose Harris

Definitions of 'social evil'

What is meant by a 'social evil', and how does it differ from the more familiar and less dramatic concept of a 'social problem'? A working definition might be that a '*social problem*' suggests an undesirable state of affairs for which people hope to find a practical cure. A '*social evil*', by contrast, suggests something more complex, menacing and indefinable, and may imply a degree of scepticism, realism or despair about whether any remedy can be found. In everyday speech, both terms are often used rhetorically and interchangeably. At a deeper, more technical level, however, the language of social problems may be seen as linked to the Anglo-French 'positivist' tradition, endorsed over the past century by many prominent British social reformers. The language of social evils is more difficult to pin down. But it is used by people from a variety of traditions – radical and conservative, secular and theological – who see individual and social action as, in some sense, shaped and constrained by moral, natural or transcendental laws.

Questions also arise about the meaning of the term 'social'. For much of the 19th century, 'social' responsibilities in Britain were largely thought of as civic, voluntary or 'associational' ties, to be discharged by local agencies of the Poor Law, by charity or by self-governing friendly societies that insured their members against sickness, old age and death. It was only in the early 20th century that social evils and the responsibility for dealing with them came to be identified as 'national'. A hundred years later, that perspective has shifted again, as social relations, obligations and the mysterious entity of 'society' itself are increasingly reconceived as cross-national, or even 'global', in their scope. A further complication arises from the fact that some perceived social evils of the present time were seen in the past as quintessentially private. Thus, addiction to opium (casually smoked by Sherlock Holmes), supplying cocaine (sold over the counter by Edwardian pharmacists) and the physical chastisement of children (a routine adjunct of parenting) were scarcely viewed as social offences at all, let alone as criminal.

Likewise, most 19th-century economists believed that 'artificial' public strategies to counteract unemployment, however well intentioned, would inevitably exacerbate the social evil they were trying to prevent. Many Victorian reformers and moralists felt the same about hunger and destitution: it was a moral duty to assist the victims of these conditions, but unthinkable to expect such evils ever to go away. Charles Dickens, for example, dramatically highlighted a series of appalling social evils, including death by starvation, child cruelty and paedophilia, sexual exploitation, compulsive gambling and environmental filth. Yet he and other literary figures rarely pointed to practical solutions, other than calling for greater personal generosity and the softening of human hearts.

Such attitudes provide a backcloth and a clue to the philosophy of Joseph Rowntree. As a largely self-made Quaker chocolate manufacturer, Rowntree reflected many of these Victorian beliefs. He fully endorsed public scepticism about treating 'social diseases' by applying 'worse remedies' (a charge famously levied by T.H. Huxley against the 'Darkest England' policies of the Salvation Army in 1891). But he also shared the commitment of other philanthropists to a moral, spiritual and personal element in promoting social reform. There was, however, a distinctive third element in Joseph Rowntree's approach. This was his belief in the possibility of transforming certain social evils into defined, measurable social problems, by subjecting them to systematic research. One of the long-term results of this new approach was a gradual shift of public attitudes away from the fatalism of earlier epochs. Over the course of the 20th century, many dire social conditions that earlier generations had accepted as unavoidable facts of life were to be either eliminated or transferred to the domain of remedial social policies. Malnutrition, mass unemployment and the treatment of many fatal diseases were among them. Nevertheless, the lurking notion of amorphous but intractable social evils, beyond the reach of constructive intervention, never entirely went away. Instead, it ebbed and flowed at different moments of the 20th century. Most strikingly and recently, something akin to the ill-defined sense of unease and social disintegration that pervaded the late-Victorian and early-Edwardian epochs has resurfaced during the present decade. For evidence of this, it is only necessary to turn to a daily selection of newspapers or the results of the Joseph Rowntree Foundation's (JRF) online consultation on contemporary social evils described in the next section of this book.

Both the causes and the content of surges in collective anxiety remain, to some extent, conjectural. But the present chapter will seek to offer a brief history of such concerns over the course of the 20th century, and to pose questions about the social realities behind them. How far did the periodic resurgence of public anxieties accurately reflect objective conditions? Should they be seen as indices of more indefinable factors, such as changing moral, religious, behavioural and gender norms and adaptation to 'advanced modernity'? To what extent have such moments of malaise been not just socioeconomic in character, but also political and moral, reflecting some kind of breakdown in 'public trust'? Why have some social difficulties that were thought to have been 'consigned to history', re-emerged? How far has the widespread Victorian belief – that certain kinds of remedial social policies inadvertently generate further evils – re-acquired credibility in the early 21st century? How far have such cycles of moral anxiety been peculiarly British concerns, or do they mirror similar concerns in other countries?

As the subject is vast, I shall take as one of my reference points the researches of Joseph Rowntree's youngest son, Seebohm, who eventually succeeded his father as chair of the York chocolate firm, but also pursued a career as Britain's most prominent empirical social scientist throughout the first half of the 20th century. Like his father before him, Seebohm Rowntree harboured a lifelong interest in the moral, cultural and spiritual aspects of social and economic relations, together with a commitment to developing a 'value-free' social science.[1] Although his primary interest lay in analysing different kinds of poverty, the range of Rowntree's inquiries encompassed much of what he saw as the attitudinal and 'communitarian' strengths and weaknesses of the periods he was investigating. His surveys over half a century provide a significant thread of evidence concerning changing social attitudes and values from the 1890s through to the 1960s. As such, they offer an important benchmark from which to contrast earlier perceptions of social evils with those of the present day.

Edwardian Britain: poverty and 'degeneration'

The creation of the Rowntree trusts in 1904 coincided with an unusual moment of malaise and uncertainty in British social history. This was linked to a prolonged fiscal crisis, the after-effects of an expensive and unpopular war in South Africa, and international economic recession. The results were widespread unemployment and the first shrinkage in average real incomes in Britain for more than half a century. One immediate result was to concentrate public attention on certain longstanding social conditions, no longer as matters of merely philanthropic concern, but as dangers to the overall 'health' of the body politic. The central theme was not just mass poverty but, more speculatively and sensationally, a possible link between poverty and social breakdown, economic failure and national decline.

The prevalence of mass poverty in Britain had been identified during the 1890s; first by Charles Booth's survey of 'life and labour' in London, and then, more precisely and scientifically, by Seebohm Rowntree's 1899 survey of York. These studies together concluded that between a quarter and a third of the inhabitants of Britain were living in 'poverty', a condition that both authors diagnosed as harmful to the efficiency and well-being of the whole of society. Both had suggested that at least part of this poverty was caused by expenditure on alcohol. But Rowntree's study also concluded that, even if all poor people were to practise rigorous abstinence and frugality, then 10% of the population would still have incomes below a level necessary for efficient physical health. Both studies also concluded that the direst poverty was heavily concentrated among families with young children and among older people living alone.

These findings caused something of a stir, but it was not until 1904, with the publication of an inquiry into 'physical deterioration' set up by the War Office, that poverty was catapulted into the public arena as a pressing danger to both military security and the nation's health (Interdepartmental Committee on Physical Deterioration, 1904). The inquiry reported that over 60% of recruits to the British army during the Boer war had proved physically unfit for military service (a finding it ascribed to a vast range of precipitating causes, such as malnutrition, overcrowding, low wages, chronic underemployment, contaminated milk supplies, tuberculosis, parental inadequacy, 'working mothers', mental deficiency and sexually-transmitted diseases). Most shocking of all was the disclosure that one sixth of infants born in Britain at the start of the 20th century were dying before the age of one. These bleak findings, coming from the very heart of the military establishment, precipitated a decade of intense enquiry into the terrifying spectre of physical, social and cultural 'degeneration'. Between 1904 and 1914, no less than eight royal commissions investigated these issues. Most important among them was the Royal Commission on the Poor Laws of 1905-09, which launched the most comprehensive review of social, health and environmental conditions ever undertaken in Britain. Many of these enquiries played a seminal role, not just by voicing popular and 'expert' understanding of contemporary social evils, but also by proposing remedies. The report on physical deterioration, for example, inspired major changes in policy on the physical and moral welfare of children. The proceedings of the Poor Law commission likewise led to the 'break-up' of the Poor Laws and their eventual replacement by the more comprehensive services of the welfare state. Landmark legislation, such as the 1908 Old Age Pensions Act and the 1911 National Insurance Act, gave promise of addressing with dignity the problems of 'honourable' poverty and unpredictable 'interruptions of earnings'. The decade also brought rapid expansion in the employment of health visitors, midwives and social workers, together with major developments in the 'voluntary' sector, including the setting up of 'Social Service Councils' in cities throughout Britain.

It is striking, however, that, despite much sensationalist news reporting, the overall impact of Edwardian public inquiries turned out to be cautiously optimistic, reassuring and anti-alarmist in tone. Very little credence was given to panic-stricken fears about hereditary degeneration, breakdown of social and family structures, a hidden army of 'unemployables' or other symptoms of national decay. Indeed, far from suggesting that 'nothing can be done', the attitude of Edwardian experts came close to overconfidence about the long-term prospects for progressive social, economic, industrial and environmental reform. An upturn in real wages from 1905, the introduction of school milk and meals in 1906-07, the payment of the first old-age pensions in 1910 and – above all – a steep decline in infant mortality, helped defuse the oppressive sense of social breakdown that had occurred after the Boer war.

War and mass unemployment

Both the pessimistic and optimistic strands in Edwardian social thought were overtaken from 1914 by far more pressing and apocalyptic anxieties arising from the First World War. The supposed 'War to End all Wars' brought in its trail such diverse trends as escalating food prices, rationing, mass military conscription, an unprecedented absorption of women into the labour market and the enforced break-up of many great aristocratic estates. Not all pre-war concerns were eliminated overnight, with public fears of the 'racial poison' of alcohol growing, if anything, even more vociferous (Central Control Board for Liquor Traffic, 1919). Similarly, anxieties about the supposed moral and biological menace of 'working mothers' were intensified, as young women were drafted into factories to make munitions. But the experiences of the six million young men who faced maiming, shell shock and violent death, pushed anxieties about mere social evils, temporarily at least, into the background.

The aftermath of the war saw a resurgence of anxiety about social relations in Britain; but this was to take a very different form from that of the Edwardian decade. Britain was no longer the world's predominant financial power. Her heavy industries were threatened by world overproduction, and problems of restructuring the economy took precedence for many over the challenge of more amorphous social evils. Many policy experts who had pioneered social reforms before 1914, either became more cautious in outlook, or were attracted by the far more ambitious social experiments taking place in revolutionary Russia. An enormous increase in trades union membership during and after the war also meant that the focus of debate on social issues shifted away from degenerationist concerns of the Edwardian era towards industrial problems affecting many of the most skilled and 'respectable' working class, notably mass unemployment.

One important aspect of this changing focus was that the geographical distribution of pressing social questions changed markedly. An unexpected trend, only partially understood at the time, was that the 1920s and 1930s brought rising real wages for working people in some regions and occupations, while bringing misery, poverty and redundancy even to highly skilled workers in others. A further difference, as Seebohm Rowntree noted in 1936, was that opportunities for working-class domestic consumerism and leisure had greatly increased. Another change was that many of the social services and income-support schemes initiated in the 1900s took off in the inter-war period, with the result that the worst indices of physical privation were never quite so dire as they had been in 1904. Major poverty inquiries of the period, including Seebohm Rowntree's second York survey of 1936, found that, despite the shrinkage of major industries, the proportion of the population living in 'primary' poverty was half what it had been a generation before.[2] Surveys also hinted at an emerging sense of what would later be termed 'relative deprivation' – of 'poverty' interpreted, no longer as just absolute or even relative 'want', but as exclusion from the normal culture of wider society.

Nevertheless, in many respects, the inter-war phenomenon of mass unemployment exactly fitted the notion of a dire social evil – as something felt to be beyond the scope of remedial human action – suggested at the start of this chapter. The 'hunger marches' of the early 1930s seemed to epitomise the notion of a social evil that governments, experts and ordinary people felt helpless to address. Yet in the more radical discourse of the period, the focus was quite different.

Critics from both Left and Right claimed that governments and vested interests were simply failing to implement rational solutions to problems whose nature and causes were well known. This pointed to another aspect of the social evils question that was subtly different from that of the Edwardian decade – namely the emergence of a much wider spectrum of contested political and philosophical convictions. This was particularly so in the early and mid-1930s, before full realisation had dawned about the character of Nazism (and, later, of Stalinism), when significant numbers of normally 'constitutionalist' politicians and social activists dabbled with the possibility of curing mass unemployment by extra-parliamentary direct action or the use of 'emergency' powers (Cripps et al, 1933). From this perspective, liberal capitalism itself came to be seen as the source and summation of social evils, outweighing such merely 'secondary' symptoms as mass unemployment or poverty.

Planning and reconstruction

Despite the attraction of many theorists to more extreme solutions, the later 1930s brought a resurgence of empirical research into social questions. This included the possibility of a 'halfway house' – somewhere between liberal constitutionalism and more authoritarian politics – in the form of social and economic 'planning'. The planning movement included some who continued to favour revolutionary goals, but it also attracted a new generation of young social scientists, less indebted to Stalinism than to the St Simonian 'positivist' and 'public works' tradition. A further important stimulus to planning was J.M. Keynes's (1936) *Theory of employment, interest and money*, which challenged a central premise of earlier British economic thought – namely that 'artificial' investment to counteract unemployment was always counterproductive. These planners had many different 'policy' interests – the economy, the environment, housing, education, income redistribution and national health. But a key theme binding them together was unanimous confidence in the future of applied social science. For this generation, there were no imponderable social evils, other than those artificially fostered by laissez-faire liberalism or fascism. Instead, there was a wide range of practical social problems urgently waiting to be clearly defined, investigated and solved.

Such attitudes came to a head with the outbreak of the Second World War, when Britain's military plight appeared to overturn conventional ideas about the limits to collective action. The impact of bombing and mass evacuation opened the eyes of many politicians, planners and ordinary citizens to the geographical 'two nations' that had been invisibly developing over the inter-war years. Despite much talk of national solidarity, the initial reaction of 'respectable' Britain to the condition of slum-dwelling evacuees was no less moralistic than in former times – the difference being that patriotic citizens now had to swallow their horror and do something about it. Such developments rapidly brought 'expert' social scientists to the fore (Seebohm Rowntree's own recommendations on child poverty, for example, were incorporated into government plans for wartime family allowances before the end of 1939). The next six years were to see a continuous stream of public inquiries into wartime problems and planning for post-war 'reconstruction'. The most celebrated of these was the Beveridge Report of 1942, which recommended final abolition of the Poor Law, and its replacement by universal national insurance, family allowances, a comprehensive National Health Service (NHS) and permanent elimination of unemployment by means of centralised economic planning. Beveridge, like other liberal intellectuals during the inter-war years, had for a time been overwhelmed by the prevailing pessimism of 'nothing can be done'. Yet in the early 1940s, he and many others moved towards the opposite extreme, at times hinting that even a largely 'communist' style of social planning need not be irreconcilable with maintaining personal liberties in a democratic state. Similar views were widely pervasive in the wartime town–planning movement, where privacy, freedom, consumer choice and family life were all portrayed as perfectly compatible with a centrally planned and prefabricated urban environment.

The chronic deficit in national finances after the war prevented many visions of holistic planning from being fully acted on. The immediate post-war period was one of prolonged economic hardship as severe in many respects as during wartime itself. Yet sociological studies of the later 1940s reported renewed strength in family and community life, as women returned from factories into the home, as parents and children took their first holidays together for nearly a decade and as working men enjoyed greater job security, higher wages and more enhanced social status than at any previous period of English history. Infant mortality was found to have fallen dramatically since 1939. Public opinion surveys, likewise, suggested that most people were extremely happy with the new social services. Maintaining full employment became an absolute priority of post-war economic policy, while the NHS, founded in 1948, commanded well-nigh universal support (Harris, 2003). Seebohm Rowntree's final York survey, published in 1951, suggested – overoptimistically – that primary poverty had all but vanished in post-war Britain; its only serious incidence occurring among older people living alone in decrepit dwellings that were too big for them (their 'aloneness' being often more of a problem than a shortfall of income). Many people continued to be apprehensive about incalculable 'evils'; but these were much more closely linked to the aftermath of war, including the implications of the atomic bomb, and the rise of the Soviet Union.

Despite the dread of nuclear war, much of this modest post-war contentment appeared to survive throughout the 1950s. Some commentators even suggested that Britain was living through a 'golden age', marked by full employment, rising living standards, greatly enhanced social equality and close-knit family and community life. Such indicators were coupled with some of the lowest levels of crime, delinquency, drunkenness, public disorder and marital breakdown ever registered. Voluntary and associational life appeared to flourish, with charities, churches, chapels, youth movements, sports clubs and 'special interest' groups all booming in numbers. Later commentators, however, reinterpreted the 1950s more pessimistically. Critics on the Right drew attention to the period's low growth rates, mounting inflation, poor industrial relations, chronic budgetary deficits and a decline in Britain's international competitiveness. Critics on the Left emphasised the persistence of class divisions, social 'deference' and the emergence of new symptoms of social pathology such as juvenile delinquency, landlord exploitation of housing scarcity and prejudice against the new phenomenon of immigration.

The 1950s and early 1960s was also a classic age of sociological surveys into what real people thought about real issues. So it is not difficult to track down feelings of both contentment and unease, often expressed simultaneously by the same people. Such evidence suggested that Britain was seen as a 'fairer' society than in the past; but the 1930s perception of Britain as 'two nations' had by no means disappeared. A recurrent theme was that, although many people perceived themselves as 'better off' than in the past, they nevertheless felt 'less happy'. The reasons given were often vague, but some were linked to side effects of recent policies of which respondents paradoxically acknowledged themselves to be beneficiaries. Higher living standards, better housing and wider educational opportunities were often seen as being achieved at the expense of close contact with families and communities, and a loss of religious and other cultural identities.

Despite the solidarity of family life, there were also premonitions of future disturbance in the domestic sphere. Women who had returned to the labour market to furnish their homes with consumer goods, started to find (often to their own surprise) that paid employment was more rewarding and enjoyable than housework. Many men of the 1950s disliked any suggestion that they should undertake domestic tasks; but a large minority who wanted to share in parenting and home-building found their goals in conflict with the demands of overtime, unsocial hours and a need to earn extra money. In a different sphere, the sense of 'aloneness', noted almost casually among older people by Seebohm Rowntree in 1951, had become a more widespread phenomenon. Indeed, an important but neglected aspect of the period was that, despite almost universal gratitude for the welfare state, other services – such as buses, trains, town halls, community centres, municipal dance halls and dealings with officialdom – were often deemed inferior to those of the pre-war years. This seemed to echo a claim made by the US economist and social commentator, J.K. Galbraith (1958), that the hallmark of the epoch was not communal prosperity, but the rise of 'private affluence' at the price of 'public squalor'. These concerns may be seen as presaging aspects of the more intense sense of unease and social dislocation that was to resurface later in the century.

Sea changes in the later 20th century

The 1960s brought fundamental changes that subtly transformed the ways in which social evils were conceived and understood. One such was that increasing professionalisation of social work, planning and the social sciences meant that there was an increasing divergence between social evils as perceived by policy 'experts' and those encountered by citizens in the street. This became apparent in such varied, complex and conflict-ridden areas of policy as urban redevelopment, and the treatment of problem families, drug addiction and people with mental health problems. Another important trend was that, in contrast to other major European economies, income-support policies in Britain gradually shifted back from the 'universalist' model of contributory insurance pioneered by Beveridge towards the (fiscally much cheaper) means-tested system inherited from the Poor Law. Social benefits were increasingly targeted on the selective relief of social 'need', a shift that disadvantaged the skilled and 'regular' working classes by comparison with more marginal groups (Flora, 1986; OOPEC, 1998; ONS, 2000-04).

These trends coincided with a dramatic and conspicuous revolution in sexual, interpersonal and gender norms that was to transform social attitudes over subsequent decades. It penetrated deeply into relations between childbearing, parenthood and cohabitation, on the one hand, and the state welfare system, on the other. The arrival in Britain of large numbers of immigrants from a diversity of cultural backgrounds, whose family structures ranged from the ultra-conservative to the ultra 'postmodern', likewise challenged longstanding social perceptions and norms. Perhaps more fundamentally, the later 1960s and the 1970s brought a tidal erosion in the post-war consensus of support for the welfare state and mixed economy. As the pound weakened, industrial relations worsened, oil prices tripled and staple industries collapsed in the face of foreign competition, ideologies on both Left and Right mounted challenges. Critics on one side called for a more egalitarian, collectivised 'shift in the balance of power and wealth'; and, on the other, for the freeing up of capitalism and the defusing of industrial strife through monetary stringency and the 'discipline of the market'.

These issues were fought out in a prolonged series of industrial battles, and there can be little doubt that to many Britons at that time the key social evils were not moral or welfare issues, but mutually reinforcing pressures from inflation and bad industrial relations. Conflict culminated in the 1978-79 'winter of discontent', when power stations closed down, rubbish rotted in the streets, dead bodies remained unburied, life-saving operations were cancelled and rats were seen in NHS hospitals. The sequel was the General Election of 1979, which brought to power a government and Prime Minister committed to a fundamental reconceptualisation of what many people understood by the term 'social'. For Margaret Thatcher, a disciple of the liberal economist F.A. von Hayek, 'society' was not a disembodied force or entity in its own right, but the sum of autonomous human individuals (together with 'natural' units such as the family) and their interactions. The actual text of Margaret Thatcher's famous 'no such thing as society' interview with *Woman's Own* in 1987 gave little support to subsequent claims that she opposed all forms of social and collective action. But elsewhere in her thinking, post-war public ownership of the 'commanding heights of the economy' was dismissed as a thinly veiled form of protectionism, while economic inequality, far from being regarded as socially evil, was seen as the indispensable motor of efficiency and higher output. Social welfare services and protection against poverty were by no means deemed unnecessary. But, in stark contrast to the 'universalist' aspirations of the post-war era, they were seen as needing to be targeted on a minority who were unable to share in the overall maximisation of wealth.

Such ideas were to fuel government social and economic programmes in Britain for more than three decades, given that 'New Labour' after 1997 honoured Margaret Thatcher with the sincerest form of flattery. They were never imposed with the thoroughness that many neoliberal theorists hoped for, but they nevertheless transformed many aspects of economic and social relations to an extent unimaginable only a few years before. Despite generating deep and sometimes violent disturbances, they clearly struck a deep chord in British society, as witnessed by Thatcher's victory in three General Elections, and John Major's in a fourth. The full impact of 'Thatcherism' on the values and structures of British society in the later 20th century still awaits serious historical assessment. Yet, since many voices in the current debate about social evils directly invoke (or blame) 'Thatcherite' themes, it is worth trying to pinpoint some aspects of what its impact actually was.

One consequence of 'Thatcherism' (and subsequently 'Blairism') was that trends that had been slowly evolving over the previous quarter of a century now raced forward with unprecedented speed. Thus, the 'commodification' of public services, the shift from a 'social insurance' to a means-tested system of welfare and the castration of the powers of local government (all gestating since the early 1960s) were transformed from changes of degree to changes in kind. At the same time, many aspects of local and national culture appeared to become less cohesive and distinctive than in any earlier period of British history. The closure or foreign takeover of many major industries, the free movement of labour and capital across international boundaries, the disappearance of ancient provincial centres under car parks and shopping malls and the globalisation of banking and finance, were all examples of forces that radically transformed the ways in which people thought and lived. To some degree, they even altered who the British people actually were. Skilled and semi-skilled industrial workers who in 1951 had made up 70% of the adult male employed population in Britain, by the end of the 20th century accounted for little more than 15%; their successors having moved upwards into offices and professions, sideways into marketing and retail or downwards into the ranks of the long-term sick and casually employed. Such a change inevitably entailed major changes in social relations and in the character of popular culture, not least because such workers had played such an important role in the fraternal, voluntarist, sporting, communitarian and even literary culture of Britain earlier in the century (Webb and Webb, 1899; McKibbin, 1998; Rose, 2001). Their transformation into 'consumers', whose main leisure activity (after watching television) was shopping, could scarcely fail to have a far-reaching impact on personal relations and on wider British life and culture.

Diseases of prosperity

Social theorists and moralists from Aristotle and the Old Testament prophets to more recent figures like John Ruskin, R.H. Tawney and Mahatma Gandhi, have warned against the dangers of affluence and acquisitiveness for their own sake, rather than for meeting basic human needs. Many economic theorists have treated such warnings with disdain, as smuggling subjective ethical and spiritual concerns into a 'value-free' social science. Ironically, however, the triumph of market principles during the Thatcher years was to provoke a resurgence of interest in such normative questions not just among social moralists but also among mainstream economists. The separating out of the concepts of 'wealth', 'welfare' and 'well-being' as ways of describing human satisfactions has increasingly figured in economics literature, together with attempts to measure subjective as well as objective indicators of these conditions. Qualitative notions of consumption have also crept back into the discussion, in conscious echo of John Ruskin's maxim, 'there is no wealth but life' (Nussbaum and Sen, 1993; Offer, 1996, 2006; Layard, 2003, 2005).

Moreover, recent research by economists, social psychologists and economic historians has produced some surprising and suggestive empirical results. One unsurprising point (wholly predictable not only from a neoliberal but also from a commonsense perspective) is that some degree of 'inequality' appears to have been more efficient than 'equality' in generating a level of economic growth that initially makes a system of redistributive social welfare possible. Nevertheless, recent case studies have indicated that this may cease to be true when a certain level of prosperity is reached, and where private 'affluence' becomes a strategic device for keeping an economy going, rather than for satisfying real human needs. Mounting evidence has also suggested that affluence for its own sake tends positively to undermine the pleasures of consumption, and to generate secondary disorders, such as boredom, obesity, addiction, antisocial behaviour and even marriage breakdown. It tends in many circumstances to subvert normal rationality and prudence. But, above all, it singularly fails in the utilitarian objective of making people happy (Offer, 2006, pp 138-9, 167-8, 188-90, 270-302, 305-6, 347-56). Thus, cross-national studies of 'subjective well-being' (a concept derived from the pioneering work of Seebohm Rowntree) have found that it varies widely across countries and cultures with only minimal reference to levels of income and wealth (Offer, 2006, pp 28-38, 294-302).

These findings seem directly relevant to the history of the ebb and flow of anxieties about social evils, and to the construction of such evils in contemporary Britain. For example, the JRF's public consultation exercise, detailed in the next section of this book, started in the summer of 2007 at the high peak of unprecedented investment and a housing boom, and more than a year before the precipitate collapse of the world's economies into recession. Real incomes in Britain had risen over the previous quarter-century by nearly 70%, inflation had reached an historic low and standard rates of income tax had fallen by a third. Although public services had stagnated under Thatcher, government spending since 1997 on health services, education and various forms of income support (including the targeting of child poverty) had virtually doubled. How was it, then, that respondents to the consultation exercise voiced such pessimism about social, communal and family issues?

Most economic theorists a short generation ago might have argued that the consultation respondents were simply 'smuggling in' non-economic ethical concerns, and that the discipline of the market would automatically resolve such problems. The new economics of 'affluence' and 'well-being', however, points towards a different conclusion. It suggests that pursuit of 'consumption' as an end in itself may be a powerful generator of personal misery, failure of rational self-discipline, social pathology, and economic disorder and decline. Such reflections throw a highly suggestive light, historical as well as theoretical, on the genesis and character of social evils in the early 21st century.

Some international perspectives

As noted at the start of this chapter, an historical perspective is a useful reminder that anxieties about social evils are by no means unique to the present time. A comparable sense of moral crisis gripped the public imagination in Britain at least twice during the last century. The first occurred in the aftermath of the Boer war (in circumstances uncannily like those of the present time) and the second was generated during the inter-war years by mass unemployment. Both crises were eventually transcended. But this did not happen without a great deal of intellectual effort, serious research, and social controversy and conflict.

Little has been said so far, however, about the comparative and international dimension of such crises, in either the past or the present. The subject is enormous, but a few examples may give an indication of how far anxiety about social evils in Britain reflected wider international experience, or whether it was essentially national in character. Thus, cross-national evidence for the 1900s suggests that the perception of social crisis in Edwardian Britain, although intensely felt, was quite mild by comparison with similar apprehensions in other industrialising countries. In France and Italy, for example, studies of social questions at the *fin-de-siècle* were far more deeply obsessed with visions of a dangerous 'underclass', hereditary degeneration and imminent social breakdown than was ever the case in Britain. Concern with many measurable symptoms of social pathology, such as crime, illegitimacy, prostitution and suicide, were also more muted in Britain than on the continent. Commentators in the US during the 1900s, meanwhile, remarked on the boredom, rootlessness, alienation and estrangement experienced by residents of great US cities, to an extent that was also unknown at that time in Britain (Wallas, 1914; Pick, 1989).

A generation later, Britain, as the most heavily industrialised country, suffered far more prolonged mass unemployment than elsewhere in Europe. Yet by comparison with much of the continent, British society remained a haven of social integration and order throughout the inter-war years. Both in the 1900s and in the 1930s, social relations were glued together by dense networks of voluntary organisations that, despite depression and unemployment, were seen by many as the essential social cement of British national culture. This was often compared with France under the Third Republic, where such organisations were frowned upon unless regulated and licensed by the state. In both decades, Britain also had by far the smallest professional police forces per head of population of any major Western country. The vast majority of Britons, so it was suggested, had little need of 'policing' in the continental sense, since they largely policed themselves, either through their self-governing organisations or through the 'Anglo-Saxon' conscience (von Schulze-Gaevernitz, 1893; Dawson, 1894; Duckershoff, 1899; Peaker, 1910).

Social indicators and other evidence from the most recent decades, however, tell a different story. They do not imply that Britain has become more like other nations, but they do suggest that some distinctively 'communitarian' features of British culture that earlier militated against the more dire social evils experienced on the continent may have declined or been irrevocably lost. Thus, although the British people remain extensive supporters of charities and voluntary movements, this has become a largely passive activity involving donations to organisations run by professional fundraisers. Sport, once the epicentre of local associational life, has been transformed into a largely commercial and 'spectator' pastime. Similarly, although nearly 80% of the population at the start of the 21st century claimed some kind of religious belief, the corporate and associational aspects of religious practice have steeply declined. In outward observance at least, Britain has been transformed from one of the most to one of the least religious cultures in Western Europe (Brown, 2006). Possibly as a consequence, the self-regulating 'Anglo-Saxon conscience' has seemed also to be in steep decline, signalled by a pervasive loss of the 'mutual trust' on which Britain's lightly regulated institutions had so long relied. On the one hand, there has been a loss of popular confidence in public institutions and professional bodies; on the other, governments have expressed their lack of trust in the governed through the escalation of ever more detailed regulatory codes for guiding public and professional conduct – a practice long familiar in many continental countries, but previously rare in traditionally 'self-policing' Britain (O'Neill, 2002).

By a strange paradox, the increasing regulation of public and workplace behaviour has coincided with increasing libertarianism, diversity and instability in personal relations. Such developments have, of course, been common across the Western world. But there have been marked differences in their impact on particular societies. In the 1900s, and again in the 1950s and early 1960s, Britain had the lowest recorded rates of marriage breakdown, family violence and 'illegitimate' births in Western Europe. Yet by the early 21-first century, it had moved close to the top of the league table on all three counts. Moreover, although births of children to unmarried couples rose from the 1980s at a similar rate throughout the continent, Britain at the end of the 20th century had a far higher proportion of children living in single- rather than two-parent families than any other European country (Flora, 1983-87; OOPEC, 1998; ONS, 2004-05). Moreover, although Britain had one of the lowest unemployment levels in Europe, the percentage of British children living in families with no employed breadwinner was much higher than elsewhere (Marlier et al, 2007). Likewise, Britain had the highest rate of teenage pregnancies of any European country. As in the US, where lone motherhood was even more prevalent, this was taken by some as evidence that the structure of benefits and housing provision favoured single parenthood over the claims of married or permanently cohabiting couples (O'Neill, 2005). Among European countries, only Denmark, which like Britain had a very strong tradition of 'premodern' social support, based on needs and means rather than on national insurance, appears to have developed a not dissimilar pattern of 'postmodern' welfare dependency (OOPEC, 1998; Harris, 2002).

Some conclusions

The narrative in this chapter has necessarily been highly selective, particularly in relation to recent decades where the long-term historical significance of changing attitudes, institutions and patterns of human behaviour remains far from clear. Nevertheless, certain tentative conclusions and suggestions may be drawn:

- One fairly obvious observation is that concern about widely perceived but half-understood social evils is by no means unique to the present time. It has erupted for a variety of reasons at earlier moments in both British and European history.
- A less reassuring suggestion is that whereas the highly integrated, historic culture of Britain in past epochs meant that its institutions and policy makers were better able to cope with such crises than their continental neighbours, at the present time they may be less able to do so. In particular, comparison of family structures and welfare policies in Britain and Western Europe appears to lend some support to the claim that Britain's increasingly 'selective' and 'means-tested' income-support policies (introduced with a view to *preventing* family poverty) may have inadvertently contributed both to the long-term *generation* of poverty and to the weakening of family life.
- A third point links the concerns raised by respondents to the JRF's consultation on social evils with developments in social and economic thought concerning human happiness and 'human flourishing'. Such studies have concluded that many aspects of contemporary social evils have come about, not simply because some groups in society have been excluded from recent prosperity, but because the very nature of that prosperity has in certain aspects been corrosive of interpersonal and communal ties, and even pathological in its influence on social relations and human behaviour.

A concluding proposal might be for a closer reassessment of the social philosophies of Joseph and Seebohm Rowntree. Both father and son were committed to the view that social ills could be moral, cultural and spiritual, as well as measurable and material, in character. But they were also clear that the techniques used to assess these two dimensions should not be confused. Seebohm Rowntree's poverty studies, in particular, went to great lengths to separate out the 'quantitative' aspects of social need from those associated with psychological factors and disorderly lifestyles, and to distinguish the material prerequisites of prosperous communities from more intangible ones. Over the course of 100 years, this dual approach has regularly fallen foul of critics on both these counts. On the one hand, humanitarians have accused Rowntree of employing an inhumanly detached and 'Spartan' definition of 'primary poverty', while quantifiers and positivists have charged him with importing moralistic value judgements about human behaviour and patterns of social life. The current debate, however, lends support to the view that these two approaches are complementary, since the very language of social evils necessarily includes a moral and immaterial dimension. This conclusion is reinforced by the growing chorus of criticism levied against purely quantitative and 'materialist' accounts of human well-being; a critique to be found in many empirical, historical and theoretical writings on the themes of wealth, welfare and wider human flourishing.

Notes

[1] On Joseph Rowntree's own involvement in social research, see Worstenholme (1986). On Seebohm Rowntree's work, see Briggs (1961).

[2] Rowntree's estimate of a 50% reduction in 'primary poverty' between 1899 and 1936 has been criticised as over-optimistic (Hatton and Bailey, 1998). But the fact that Rowntree in 1936 retrospectively revised his 1899 estimate of primary poverty upwards to take more account of cultural as well as physiological factors, may indicate the opposite.

References

Beveridge, Sir W. (1942) *Social insurance and allied services*, Cmd 6404, London: HMSO.

Briggs, A. (1961) *Social thought and social action: A study of the work of Seebohm Rowntree, 1871-1954*, London: Longmans.

Brown, C.G. (2006) *Religion and society in twentieth-century Britain*, London: Longman.

Central Control Board, Liquor Traffic (1919) *Alcohol as a food, a drug, a poison*, London: National Temperance League.

Cripps, S. et al (1933) *Problems of a socialist government*, London: Gollancz.

Dawson, W.H. (1894) *Germany and the Germans*, London: Chapman and Hall.

Duckershoff, P. (1899) *How the English workman lives*, London: P.S. King.

Flora, P. (1983-87) *State, economy and society in Western Europe, 1815-1975*, 2 vols, Frankfurt and London: Campus Verlag and Macmillan.

Flora, P. (ed) (1986) *Growth to limits: The Western European welfare states since World War II*, Berlin: de Gruyter.

Galbraith, J.K. (1958) *The affluent society*, Boston, MA: Houghton Mifflin.

Harris, J. (2002) 'From Poor Law to welfare state? A European perspective?', in D.Winch and P.K. O'Brien (eds) *The political economy of British economic experience*, Oxford: Oxford University Press.

Harris, J. (2003) 'Transition and transformation: society and civil society in Britain, 1945-2001', in K. Burk (ed) *The British Isles since 1945*, Oxford: Oxford University Press.

Hatton, T.J. and Bailey, R.E. (1998) *Rowntree's life cycle of poverty in inter-war London*, Discussion Paper No 98, Colchester: University of Essex.

Interdepartmental Committee on Physical Deterioration (1904) *Report and appendix*, London: HMSO.

Keynes, J.M (1936) *The general theory of employment, interest and money*, London: Macmillan.

Layard, R. (2003) *Happiness: Has social science a clue?*, London: London School of Economics and Political Science.

Layard, R. (2005) *Happiness: Lessons from a new science*, London: Allen Lane.

Marlier, E., Atkinson, A.B., Cantillon, B. and Nolan, B. (2007) *The EU and social inclusion: Facing the challenges*, Bristol: The Policy Press.

McKibbin, R. (1998) *Classes and cultures: England 1918-1951*, Oxford: Oxford University Press.

Nussbaum, M. and Sen, A. (eds) (1993) *The quality of life*, Oxford: Oxford University Press.

Offer, A. (ed) (1996) *In pursuit of the quality of life*, Oxford: Oxford University Press.

Offer, A. (2006) *The challenge of affluence: Self control and well-being in the United States and Britain since 1950*, Oxford: Oxford University Press.

O'Neill, O. (2002) *A question of trust: The Reith lectures*, Cambridge: Cambridge University Press.

O'Neill, R. (2005) *Fiscal policy and the family: How the family fares in France, Germany and the UK*, London: Civitas.

ONS (Office for National Statistics) (2000-04) *Social trends*, London: The Stationery Office.

OOPEC (Office for Official Publications of the European Communities) (1998) *Living conditions in Europe: Selected social indicators*, Luxembourg: OOPEC.

Peaker, F. (1910) *British citizenship: Its rights and duties*, London: Ralph and Holland.

Pick, D. (1989) *Faces of degeneration: A European disorder, c. 1848-c. 1918*, Cambridge: Cambridge University Press.

Rose, J. (2001) *The intellectual life of the British working classes*, New Haven, CT: Yale University Press.

von Schulze-Gaevernitz, G. (1893) *Social peace: A study of the trade union movement in England*, London: Swann Sonnenschein.

Wallas, G. (1914) *The great society: A psychological analysis*, London: Macmillan.

Webb, S. and Webb, B. (1899) *Industrial democracy*, London: Longmans.

Worstenholme, L. (1986) *Joseph Rowntree (1836-1925): A typescript memoir, and related papers*, York: Joseph Rowntree Charitable Trust.

SECTION 1

Public voices

3

Uneasy and powerless: views from the online consultation

Beth Watts and David Utting

The 3,500 people who took part in the Joseph Rowntree Foundation's online consultation left no doubt that the concept of 'social evil' is one that resonates in modern Britain. It aimed to reach out and get as many diverse views as possible. The richness of the responses, as well as their volume, was impressive. Although, unsurprisingly, this was unlikely to be a representative sample of the British people, it was clear that the vast majority of those who took part in the online exercise had embraced the opportunity to consider the nature of contemporary society with care as well as enthusiasm.

The consultation exercise tapped into issues about which people cared deeply. Participants not only fulfilled the request made for them to prioritise three contemporary social evils each, but also expressed strong views about their causes, their consequences and (more rarely) their potential remedies. The end result was, itself, a web: framed by intertwined and overlapping issues, but also characterised by irreconcilable, conflicting views on a number of key issues.

There was never any expectation that a simple list of social evils would emerge; nor did it. The term 'social evil' was, occasionally, a source of controversy, with fears raised by some respondents that it would prompt and encourage crude, 'black and white' responses to complex social issues. Others, not unreasonably, felt uncomfortable concentrating on problems without acknowledging some positive aspects of contemporary living. There could, nevertheless, be no question about the depth of concern expressed, around a series of recurring themes. Cumulatively, these were seen to reflect an overriding sense of unease at the trends currently shaping society. They also revealed deep feelings of frustration and individual powerlessness to alter their direction.

Dominant themes

A number of themes stood out in the analysis of responses:

- individualism, declining community and greed;
- misuse of drugs and alcohol;
- declining values;
- social virtues;
- family breakdown and poor parenting;
- inequality and poverty;
- apathy, failed institutions and a democratic deficit.

Individualism, declining community and greed

Many respondents revealed a deep loathing of what one described as the "me, me, me society". It was suggested that people today "see themselves only as individuals and not as part of a wider society" and that this individualism has been a root cause of many other social problems. In the words of one participant, it

> "... drives everything from greed and wasteful consumption to eating disorders and a preoccupation with celebrity. It is the darkest force within the modern collective psyche."

Another, engaging in role play, criticised the view that:

> "Nothing is more important than my success, comfort and convenience – and that of my family."

People considered this outlook to be damaging because it was based on a "mistaken belief that humans can exist in isolation and do not need each other" and brought with it an "unconscious sense of fear and hopelessness because individuals know they cannot survive alone in a complex society". Linked to this was concern at a decline in what was variously expressed as 'the community', 'community spirit', 'social solidarity' or 'community cohesion'.

Those who used 'community' in the sense of neighbourhood referred especially to a loss of neighbourliness. For example:

> "People don't care for others, in fact it is safer to walk by on the other side of the street, people don't come into contact with each other, they are isolated by their cars and their televisions."

Detrimental consequences from no longer living in caring communities were said to include "social isolation, depression, loneliness and the fear of personal and community safety". Or, as another participant put it:

"The less people know their neighbours, the less they care about the neighbourhood and the more they feel alienated and scared."

Fear and distrust were common concerns, although there was some disagreement about whether a lack of community cohesion caused fearfulness or the other way round. One person identified a "lack of real, meaningful, open, honest, respectful communication between people" and another described "people not listening, people not talking, and people not giving time". Some also noted that individuals who were increasingly disconnected from one another would suffer "loneliness and disconnection" as a result. Certain groups, including older people, were identified as especially vulnerable:

"Some people who live alone have more regular contact with characters from soap operas than they do with friends and neighbours."

There was also mention under this theme of a lack of public engagement and "withdrawal from public life into private pleasure seeking". This reflected a second, more abstract sense in which respondents mourned a loss of 'community' through attitudes and behaviours that served the individual, not society. Participants identified a "lack of community spirit and involvement" and criticised a "limited desire to take a personal share of responsibility for collective problems".

"It seems that people no longer care about others or the community area they live in."

An overlapping concern was with apathy towards other people or "social lethargy" in relation to those least able to look after themselves:

"The idea that we are all only responsible for ourselves, and that we get what we deserve. Society should be about protecting the weak and vulnerable."

A small number of participants also recognised the growth of new kinds of communities, notably:

- *virtual communities*: perceived as a double-edged sword, with the many perceived advantages created by the internet contrasted with its role as "a Pandora's Box, distributing many evils into the world";
- *global communities*: a 'one world' outlook that was claimed to be responsible for the eclipse of local communities and community responsibilities;
- *gangs*: although most often cited as a social evil linked to violent crime, some respondents acknowledged that they provide "an identity and a social family" for some young people and a place where they could form friendships and "feel safe and supported".

Consumerism and growing greed were, meanwhile, closely associated with perceived trends towards individualism and away from community. For example, one person spoke of a "breakdown of moral commitment to the well-being of community, replaced by selfish acquisition and consumption". Greed for money and consumer goods were portrayed as evils that had blinded society to the needs of other people:

> *"Nothing is enough for the person for whom enough is too little."*

> *"It makes people ruthless [and leads to] a general lack of compassion and community spirit because everyone is 'out for themselves'."*

> *"Too many people want too much and they want it all now."*

Greed and consumerism were variously linked to concerns about the environment, waste, exploitation of the Third World and, not surprisingly, excessive personal debt. Like the authors Zygmunt Bauman and Neal Lawson elsewhere in this book (Chapters 12 and 13), many people felt that 'rampant consumerism' had become ingrained and that there was a "huge cultural pressure to define worth according to consumption":

> *"Everything seems to be based around money and owning things. The more you have, the more successful you are. There's nothing wrong with having enough, but there's pressure on people to go for more and more."*

Responsibility for encouraging consumerist greed was frequently placed on political, financial and media institutions. Government stood accused of promoting its 'inevitability' to promote economic growth, while advertising, media and banks came under attack for lending money to people who could not afford it to buy things they did not really need: "TV is turning our nation into unthinking uncritical consumers whose only satisfaction comes from consumption".

This is an appropriate moment to emphasise that the online consultation took place several months before the banking crisis of 2008 and the economic recession that followed. Since then, it seems probable that a good many contributors to this consultation theme will have either resisted or acceded to the temptation to say "I told you so".

They may also have continued to decry "the spurious cult of self-obsessed celebrity", which was commonly associated in many respondents' minds with the rise of consumerism. Some participants perceived modern celebrities as 'false gods' offering negative role models to young people and promoting "vacuous ambitions", "unrealistic expectations" and "shallow aspirations". Several contributors highlighted a paradoxical connection between shameless over-consumption, obesity and an obsession with body image. Consumerism, it was suggested, places people under pressures that they cannot healthily and happily reconcile.

A combination of greed and celebrity culture was blamed for undermining our relationships with each other:

> *"Money, beauty and youth are prized over love, respect and happiness. People are valued for superficial reasons."*

Another participant said:

> *"We are in danger of losing sight of what is important in life, like kindness, playfulness, generosity and friendship. The immaterial things that can't be bought and sold."*

Another wistfully added:

> *"We can quantify money better than we can quantify happiness and contentment. So we chase it, rather like a rainbow, deceiving ourselves that it will deliver that elusive happiness and contentment."*

Misuse of drugs and alcohol

Alcohol and illegal drugs both figured on Joseph Rowntree's list of major social evils a century ago. In the online consultation they were often cited jointly as a social evil and identified, in the words of one respondent, as "a predominant factor in the social decline of today". Their relationship to other social problems was also widely acknowledged. But while some participants blamed the damaging consequences of misuse on choices made by individuals, many more regarded drug and alcohol problems as a symptom of wider social malaise. People were thought particularly likely to turn to drugs and alcohol as "a means of escape from social, economic, and other personal problems". They were thus characterised as "Reality blockers [which] help people to forget the other social evils". Family breakdown, child abuse, domestic violence, poverty, stress, unemployment and lack of opportunities or education were all identified as risk factors.

People also felt that using and misusing illegal drugs as well as legal alcohol had become increasingly acceptable. This was seen as leaving children and young people particularly vulnerable to being "lured into a world of drugs before they are mature enough to understand the effects their addiction will have on themselves and their families". Some specifically accused celebrities for glamorising drug and alcohol use.

A common view on alcohol was that its dangers are not taken seriously enough, permitting a popular culture in which "mindless drinking is accepted and encouraged". The media was often accused of being complicit: "It is in your face.... There are no role models saying ... 'I don't drink'".

The impact of illegal drugs (especially 'Class A' drugs like heroin and cocaine) was often judged more serious than that of alcohol. One participant described tragic personal circumstances in which her "step-daughter ... died from heroin use aged 30 and my step-son also died from heroin use aged 31". A retired headteacher wrote: "I witness many of my ex-pupils who have succumbed to drug addiction. The consequences for them and their families are heartbreaking".

A number of respondents maintained that, unlike some illegal drugs, alcohol was not an absolute evil because 'sensible drinking' was possible. However, others added despondently that: "We don't seem able to drink in moderation". Binge drinking among young people was especially strongly decried for creating "the perception in this country that ... you don't have a good time unless you are plastered".

Some participants, meanwhile, focused on the damage that drugs and alcohol cause to physical and mental health, and in creating debt and homelessness. Drug addiction was also identified as a key reason for people turning to crime and prostitution to fund their habit. Other impacts identified included a feeling that drugs and alcohol undermine personal autonomy, aspirations and values. More tangibly, misuse was commonly seen as a catalyst for family breakdown, and a cause of bad parenting, neglect and domestic violence. Alcohol was seen to cause antisocial behaviour and violence in towns and cities; illegal drugs were also seen to disrupt local communities and promote crime:

"People today live in fear of leaving their own homes, of opening their purses/wallets in the local shops, of walking alone on their own."

Several participants also highlighted the pressures and costs placed on the National Health Service (NHS), police and courts. One participant looked further afield, blaming the illicit drug industry for "exploitation and abuse, misery, poverty, death and addiction all along the chain, both in the UK and abroad".

While participants offered several suggestions for dealing with illegal drug use, ideas about tackling alcohol misuse were less forthcoming. Some felt that harsher penalties for dealers and users were necessary and berated an "apparent lack of willingness on the part of the authorities to mete out appropriate consequences". Others focused on the need for better support and rehabilitation services. A third group, adopting an argument advanced by the philosopher A.C. Grayling later in this book (Chapter 8), contended that the most effective response to drug-related problems would be legalisation. In their view, this would cut related crime, save police time and undermine the appeal of drug taking as an act of rebellion or subversion:

"If all drugs were legalised then many youngsters would not try them since very often it is the fact that they are illegal that makes them attractive."

Addiction to gambling – another concern highlighted by Joseph Rowntree in 1904 – was also mentioned in the consultation, albeit less often. Online gambling was identified as particularly insidious, with the capacity to foster highly addictive behaviour in private. Others saw gambling as a manifestation of greed that encouraged "an attitude of effortlessly achieving what ought to be hard-worked for".

Smoking was also referred to by some as a social evil, with an emphasis on its impact on health and health services. Some praised the ban on smoking in public places – although others dismissed it as "paternalistic government intervention".

Declining values

Many participants condemned what they saw as a blurring or loss of basic moral boundaries. According to one typical response:

> *"In the world we've created, there's no such thing as 'right and wrong' any more."*

Others variously referred to a lost "moral compass", a "moral vacuum" and a "disintegration of morals". The idea that 'anything goes' was expressed again and again, coupled to a sense that modern behaviour was determined by individual wants rather than social obligations. One person contended that ethical behaviour and supportive relationships had been broken down "by promoting individual well-being, greed, competition, 'win and lose' mentalities and material wealth, at the expense of collaboration and community well-being".

Some avowed atheists as well as those from faith backgrounds were inclined to attribute a weakened sense of morality to a decline in religious influence without adherence to any comparable ethical code. For example: "Although an atheist myself I agree ... that decline in belief in Christianity has unhinged people's moral compass....We need other bases for morality that do not require such beliefs".

A few also insisted that churches should accept some blame for failing "to provide strong moral leadership". Although a decline in the number of traditional 'nuclear' families was also cited as a consequence as well as a cause of changing morality, some felt it was responsible for undermining a shared value system. Without families, people felt there was "no one to guide youngsters in basic morals and requirements of civilised society". Others held poor parenting responsible. One person felt, for example, that "many parents don't have a clue how to raise their children as decent human beings".

Social virtues

There were, in addition, a number of social virtues that participants referred to that they considered to have fallen into regrettable decline, including:

- *Tolerance*, where bigotry and social stereotyping were considered to be on the increase, especially "towards people who are different". This could lead to heightened discrimination, with homophobia and racial intolerance most often cited.[1]

- *Honesty*, with a loss of integrity most often attributed to institutions like the media and government, but also sometimes to individuals.
- *Empathy and compassion*, described as a fundamental attribute of a civilised society, but felt by some to be increasingly absent. Greed, inequality and social division, antisocial behaviour, neglect and intolerance were all identified as consequences of a lack of empathy and compassion.
- *Respect*, identified in a variety contexts ranging from "a general lack of respect on all sides" to disrespectful treatment of particular groups. These included public servants in the police and the NHS as well as women, religions, races and "the vulnerable in society". Young people were frequently criticised as lacking respect for others, although several participants felt that adults were also ill-mannered and disrespectful in their treatment of teenagers.
- *Reciprocity*, reflecting a view that too many people believe they have rights and entitlements, without acknowledging any balancing responsibilities. Most people who discussed this issue felt that responsibilities to family and society were being shirked, although some also argued that it was unfair to expect individuals to fulfil their responsibilities, if their own needs or rights were not being met. This was felt especially strongly in the case of vulnerable groups, such as those with disabilities or health problems.

Family breakdown and poor parenting

Young people emerged as a frequent source of concern to those who responded to the consultation, although participants differed in the ways they placed them in the debate. One fundamental distinction was between those who plainly regarded young people as perpetrators of social evil, and others who viewed them as its victims, not least because of problems within their families. This latter group not infrequently made a connection between the "appalling way we treat so many of our children" and the "irresponsible and uncontrollable behaviour of youths".

Those who were highly critical about "the youth of today" referred to young people having "no manners, no self-control, no respect for anything" or being "switched off from the common goals of our society". Gangs were often mentioned, with many contributors regarding them, with associated gun and knife crime, as a youth problem. The responses revealed considerable fears of gang culture. For example: "It terrifies me. Kids egging each other on to do something daring or brave, otherwise they will seem uncool in front of their mates ... [it] can lead to dangerous consequences".

However, it was not just adults who identified their concerns over gangs. A young contributor wrote:

"I'm a teenager, and adults seem to think we don't suffer just because we're the same age as them [teenage gangs] so they'll leave us alone."

Another group of participants were no less vociferous in their condemnation of the way they felt that children and young people were treated by the adult world. One participant insisted that: "There is a wealth of potential in young people yet they tend to be stigmatised rather than encouraged". Another declared the problem to be "negative, pessimistic, cynical, critical adults not appreciating young people for their qualities and abilities and the contributions they can and do make to society".

Some felt that the self-respect of young people who behaved antisocially had been critically undermined. As one put it:

"How can we wring our hands at the state of the youth of today, when they are criminalised, abused, neglected and ignored at every turn? How can we expect their generation to make the state of society better, when we provide such a poor role model?"

Schools were criticised for failing to provide the right opportunities for young people. The media was also seen to have a negative, consumerist influence on young people, while fuelling what one participant described as the "madness of blaming our young people for society's problems". But by far the most frequent charges of letting children and young people down were levelled at family breakdown and inadequate parenting. For example:

"Families are crucial to a healthy society, yet we're collectively undermining their value."

"Family breakdown ... is probably the biggest cross-cutting issue society faces because it impacts on so many other things."

"Irresponsible, uninformed, ill-educated, unprincipled parenting ... which sadly leads inescapably and directly to many of the problems seen, heard, smelt, felt and experienced in almost every city, town (and

many villages) across the length and breadth of the country involving 'young people' ... all of which are merely the symptoms of this real social evil."

But while numerous participants saw family breakdown as a major social evil, they disagreed profoundly about the importance of traditional family structure. On the one hand, it was argued that social evil lay in "breakdown of the family structure, whether single-parent or not, the lack of a cohesive family unit and the support of the wider family and the values that brings"; on the other hand, that it related to "loss of the family structure, women being wives, mothers, home-makers. Men being bread-winners, head of the home".

Participants generally agreed that the negative consequences of poor parenting included making some children "impossible to teach" and involvement in antisocial behaviour. But while some held parents wholly responsible, other pointed to a "lack of support for parents and parenting". Meeting this latter need was seen as particularly important for young, inexperienced parents.

As well as the problems young people faced within families, there was some concern expressed about their economic circumstances. This related especially to "low skills-based school leavers". The difficulties young people faced in finding affordable housing was another source of comment, as were problems of debt, ascribed to easy access to credit and also to the need for those in higher education to take out student loans.

A "growing gulf between the old and the young" was also identified by some as a latter-day social evil. One respondent felt that that there had been a "reduction in inter-generational communication, learning and respect", while another considered that negative attitudes towards young people were "fostering a climate of mistrust and dislike, if not hatred, between generations".

Inequality and poverty

Inequality and poverty not only emerged as major themes, but were also frequently characterised as fundamental issues underpinning other social evils. To quote two typical responses:

"Poverty – this can take many forms but is at its most extreme as debilitating as a life-shortening illness. It exacerbates many other forms of discrimination and disadvantage that exist within our society and

is one of the hardest barriers to overcome. It cripples whole families, communities and generations of people."

"Inequality.... This is one of the root causes of the increase in crime and in dissatisfaction in modern society. I believe that a more equal society would make everyone happier, both rich and poor."

Participants expressed particular frustration at a perceived lack of action or commitment to tackling poverty. One considered poverty to be a social evil partly "because it can be overcome", while another identified the "worst social evil today" as "the government's failure to prioritise helping the poor, the homeless and those whose lives are ruined by poverty". Another declared that:

"Until this issue is resolved we condemn too many people to bleak futures where their only 'choice' is a cycle of unemployment, benefit, (possibly crime), a feeling of worthlessness, disenfranchisement and lack of opportunity. By continuing to 'keep' people locked in to a life of poverty ... things like anti-social behaviour will continue to be a problem ... drinking and taking drugs will continue to be an issue ... and inevitably people will turn to crime (you need money to buy the things we are told we need!)."

Poor health and educational disadvantage were associated with poverty by respondents often as an issue extending far wider than low income. For example, poor housing, a lack of affordable homes and homelessness were often highlighted.

Inequality is, as the discussion in later chapters of this book will confirm, a more contentious and politically disputed concept than poverty. However, participants in the consultation pointed to an "enormous and growing gap between the rich and the poor" as a social evil in itself and as something that "nurtures the other evils". There was also a feeling among some that inequality had too easily been accepted as inevitable and acceptable:

"In the UK we all seem to be brainwashed into thinking it has to be this way – the 'haves' really should mobilise, or be mobilised to reverse this process."

"We should not have a society where footballers are paid hundreds and thousands of pounds whilst a family is expected to exist on a pittance."

There were references to the "astronomical wealth" or "obscene pay rises/bonuses" of high-earning individuals, which were contrasted with the experiences of those who "do not have fair access to the wealth of western society". One participant felt that it was unacceptable that some people working a 40-hour week were living below the poverty threshold, and others agreed that efforts in the workplace did not necessarily translate into a fair income. Ranging more widely, some participants focused on the role of the economic system in underpinning an unfair distribution, concentrating wealth and power in the hands of a few. Echoing the concerns of others, one went further, labelling "global capitalism" as a social evil, and linking it to other social ills including inequality, environmental degradation and consumerism.

Several people highlighted the role of the housing market in fuelling inequalities that were likely to be perpetuated as those fortunate enough to own valuable properties bequeathed them to the next generation. Another perspective on inequality was that it created divisions within communities and an increasingly fractured society enabling:

> *"the rich to buy themselves out of the society we are creating, the less rich to aspire to buy themselves out of that society and the poor to feel dispossessed and powerless. So whole swathes of society have no investment in making it a success."*

Apathy, failed institutions and a democratic deficit

Government, schools, businesses and the media were criticised for causing or perpetuating many social evils. For example, dissatisfaction with the political system was variously expressed by portraying "the Government", "politicians", "national leaders" or "the state" as social evils. People were especially critical of perceived political dishonesty at both national and local level. One participant maintained that deception is now "seen as a legitimate way to either retain power or to promote a certain ideology". Another agreed that "Politicians lie to get themselves elected, but face no accountability for promises not kept". However, not everyone took the same view. For example, this scathing attack was made on public cynicism:

> *"People behave as though politicians are 'other' and are all corrupt, and yet are happy to benefit from the fact that others are prepared to step up to the task and take the difficult decisions that deliver us a*

functioning society; similarly, those most willing to criticise seem least willing to participate in any way."

As previously noted, central government was criticised by many for failing to act on certain social evils, including poverty and drug and alcohol misuse. However, a number of participants made the opposite accusation: that government was doing too much, rather than too little. Some felt that the state was altogether too active in providing welfare and services, undermining personal responsibility and individual initiative. The "nanny state", "big government", "authoritarianism" and "welfare dependency" were all cited as social evils in this connection.

Other respondents focused their concern on legislative reforms they considered were "telling people how to live their lives" and "restricting personal freedoms". A more common concern was that Britain is being turned into a "surveillance society". The possible introduction of identity cards and increased use of CCTV were frequently cited as examples of a "Big Brother attitude". Participants disagreed about whether the heightened risks of terrorist attack offered a valid justification for these measures. Several thought that terrorism was "being used as a catch-all excuse for further government encroachment upon citizens' lives and restricting freedoms".

Some critics focused less on the perceived failings of government than on the relationship between political institutions and the public. A lack of control over what government does was identified alongside a "lack of connection between policy-makers and those who have to implement the policies or are subject to them". The consultation suggested that feelings of apathy and powerlessness were two main reasons for this disconnection, summed up by a respondent who stated: "We either don't care enough to put ourselves out, or we don't think we can do anything about the things that we think are concerning or unjust".

Low turnout in elections was often cited as evidence of apathy, combined with the view that "my vote won't make any difference". However, others blamed the democratic deficit more squarely on alienation from political institutions and processes:

"Voters are not apathetic, they just don't have a choice any more."

A number of participants cited Britain's involvement in the Iraq war as a reflection of a "lack of real democracy". There were also complaints that non-democratic institutions, notably big business and the media, exerted an unjustified influence on political decisions. It should also be recorded that one group of participants focused very specifically on alleged unfairness and bias in the Local Government Ombudsmen system. These participants had been directed to the social evils website by a campaigning 'blog' site, but their concerns echoed the broader view expressed that public institutions are unaccountable.

A good education system was, meanwhile, widely acknowledged as a necessary foundation for a good society. However, several respondents argued that it was failing to live up to its potential. Criticisms ranged from the system's apparent inability to promote greater social mobility to the privileges of parents able to afford private schooling.

> *"There is no guarantee that a child can get a decent education unless it is paid for and this is a scary situation that is not set to get any better in the near future. Some state schools are fantastic but it seems to be pot luck as to whether there is a good school in a particular catchment area."*

Another key concern was a perceived overemphasis on academic over practical skills and failure to "develop the full potential of those who are not academically talented". Alternative vocational support commanded wide support and there were objections to the existing education system as too target-driven and focused on examinations. One respondent, for example, felt that "the current system is too formal too soon and creates a sense of failure and disillusionment for many young children".

When describing their objections to 'the media', respondents appeared to be employing a broad definition encompassing newspapers, magazines, television, films, computer games and advertisements. Although one person described the media collectively as "a tool that ... could be a tremendous way of improving the lives of so many by educating/informing/discussing the issues that matter", there was an overwhelming view that this was far from being its current role. Instead of informing, the media was charged with undermining the ability to accurately perceive social problems, and creating barriers to their effective resolution. It was accused of fuelling intolerance, promoting unhealthy lifestyles (including unhealthy eating and drug and alcohol use) and encouraging materialism and greed. More specific complaints brought against media institutions were a tendency to:

- *sensationalise and trivialise*: leaving genuine issues ignored and propagating "simplistic impressions of social conditions, relationships and people";

- *misrepresent the facts*: people felt the media conveys an overly negative view of the world and feeds the "belief that bad news is all the news". One person objected to the media hyping-up "activities that have been happening for time immemorial, problematic youths, binge drinking etc." and another felt that this means the media promotes "moral panic rather than workable solutions".

"Big companies", "multi-national corporations" and "big business" also attracted considerable opprobrium. Concerns focused on perceived inconsistency between the profit motive and broader social needs. For example:

> *"Big companies ... aim solely to make a profit, ignoring the needs of people, exploiting the planet, and pressuring governments to make policies which support their financial aims. These make the few rich richer, and widen the gap globally between rich and poor both within countries and between countries."*

Some singled out supermarkets for promoting "unhealthy lifestyles". One respondent accused food companies of putting "profit before health" and blamed them for the "epidemic of obesity". Another participant focused on the impact of supermarkets "forcing out small local shops and homogenising our retail experience".

Further themes

The key themes so far discussed stood out from the consultation. However, six further themes deserve particular mention since, despite being less dominant, they were clearly important issues that participants in the consultation felt especially strongly about. These are:

- violence and crime;
- gender inequality;
- religion;
- social diversity, immigration and intolerance;
- health and social care;
- the environment.

Violence and crime

As already noted, the consultation identified common concerns about violent crime, illegal drug use and crime fuelled by drug abuse and alcohol. People were specially worried by crime and antisocial behaviour among young people. Many also indicated a fear of 'rising' violence and crime that was seemingly disproportionate to anything suggested by objective trend data from representative national surveys, notably the British Crime Survey (Kershaw et al, 2008; Roe and Ashe, 2008). Those who spoke about violence and crime often thought that these were bigger problems than in the past, including one claim that "the UK has turned into a violent society". Another maintained that crime now affects everyone: "It affects how we live our lives on a day-to-day basis – where we go, how we get there, what type of car we have and where we park it".

Some people did, however, suggest that fear of crime was a social evil as opposed to crime itself: "People should feel free and relaxed to get on with their lives. But far too many live in fear of someone committing a crime against them".

Gun and knife crime, as already noted, were sometimes prioritised as social evils in connection with gang culture, especially in urban areas. But others focused on aggressive and antisocial behaviour more generally. For example a view that: "People of all genders, classes and ages seem more angry and likely to react aggressively against someone, whether verbally or through violence". Another respondent stated that "even a walk to the shop to get some milk is a trip fraught with aggression, hostility and apprehension".

Several participants maintained that the criminal justice and penal systems were ill-equipped to prevent crime. These were divided between those who felt that the system was "too soft" and lacking in effective deterrents and those who argued that there was a "misperception that crime can be 'cured' by incarcerating increasing numbers of people". For the latter group, the "growing use of prison as a response to social problems" was destined to fail, not least where offenders "would benefit more from psychiatric help or advice".

Although the consultation took place before the highly publicised 2008 court cases concerning 'Baby P' in Haringey and the abduction of Shannon Matthews in Dewsbury, a number of respondents highlighted child abuse and neglect as social evils. As one wrote: "I am constantly reminded of the fact that children are not safe". Some expressed a view that seems most likely to reflect media coverage that abuse "seems to be on the increase". Others described it as a "hidden social evil" or "a widely unrecognised problem". Conversely, however, there were participants who highlighted the detrimental impact that heightened fears over child safety can have on children. As one put it:

> *"Children's lives are being stunted by parental fears keeping many of them out of the public realm. This means children do not learn the skills of social interaction, empathy, consideration and understanding of others in the way older generations have done."*

Gender inequality

Some participants identified gender discrimination and women's continuing disadvantage in society as a key social evil. This ranged from an all-embracing accusation of bias – "society's entire attitude to women is evil" – to more specific concerns, including domestic abuse and sexual exploitation – "abuse is wide-ranging with combinations of physical, emotional, psychological, sexual and financial abuse as well as social isolation. It is a huge problem".

A number of respondents cited figures and statistics on domestic violence, pointing to its pervasiveness as a largely 'hidden' social evil. One person described the effects of violence in the home:

> *"Home should be a safe and nurturing place and instead is a prison – terrifying and unsafe with no escape. The psychological effects on women and children last for ever."*

The trafficking of women into the sex industry, prostitution and pornography were also condemned. One contributor wrote that these things "reduce women to the status of a piece of meat by objectifying, degrading and isolating them, therefore making them easy to dismiss and dispose of". Other participants lamented the "promotion and normalisation of pornography" on the internet and in computer games. Representations of women in the media were also blamed for perpetuating a view of women as "sexualised commodities". Some participants also worried about the impact on young women and their aspirations:

> *"It is becoming ever harder for young women to establish an identity which is not built on a male idea of who they should be. So much for emancipation."*

Less commonly, it was recognised that "both men and women are limited by narrow cultural constructions of gender". Respondents also highlighted the continuing unequal pay gap between men and women as well as workplace problems, including bullying, harassment and inflexibility shown to employees with caring responsibilities.

However, not everyone agreed. There was a small group of participants who identified feminism as a social evil, blaming it for undermining the role of men in the family and society. One participant thought that when "taken to extremes [feminism] is breaking up the family values that have served us well for generations". Another perceived "real and sometimes blatant favouritism of women over men". There were also several participants who claimed that the family courts unfairly discriminated against fathers.

Religion

One predictable aspect of the consultation was a lack of consensus over the role of religion. Some considered its overall decline and an increasingly "godless" society as a social evil: "There is no one to be accountable to and ultimately how you feel determines your actions". As previously noted, there were some avowed atheists who took the view that growing secularism had failed to produce a sense of moral purpose to counter growing individualism, self-centredness and greed.

Even so, a more dominant group of respondents took the view that religion itself was a divisive social evil, spreading intolerance and conflict. As one put it:

> "Faith in supernatural phenomena inspires hatred and prejudice throughout the world, and is commonly used as justification for continued persecution of women, gays and people who do not have faith."

Other participants condemned religions for undermining rational behaviour by promoting beliefs for which there was no objective evidence:

> "The idea that a person can believe a proposition to be true in spite of no supporting evidence, and even in spite of evidence to the contrary, is something that should not be automatically granted respect, but treated with contempt."

Some participants argued, more specifically, that no political or educational decisions should be based on religion and that state funding for faith schools should be ended. According to one participant, "children should be taught to derive their conclusions from evidence and logic, not the ravings of deluded idiots".

A third group of participants were concerned only with "religious extremism", which they often linked to violence and terrorism. As one put it:

> "Religion itself is not a social evil: quite the opposite. Real religion (such as true Christianity or true Islam) should be about worship, faith and following a set of ideals that promote a harmonious and just way of living, not a vehicle for those who want to fuel or incite suspicion, intolerance, hate and violence."

Social diversity, immigration and intolerance

Perspectives on growing social diversity also varied widely. Some emphasised negative impacts of immigration or increasing multiculturalism, while others maintained that public and government attitudes to immigrants, asylum seekers and other 'outsiders' were the real social evil.

A number of participants referred to immigration as "unrestricted", "unchecked" or "out of control". One stated that "There is so much diversity, that we do not have common values any more". Another accused multiculturalism of causing "friction and loss of common goals". It was also suggested that immigration was causing overpopulation and was damaging to community cohesion and that "Indigenous inhabitants are becoming increasingly resentful and intolerant". Reasons given for this intolerance included a belief that immigrants were unfairly benefiting from social security and other services funded by taxpayers. One person commented that they had "no problem with those with genuine problems entering the country as long as they are working and making a contribution". Another, who expressed sympathy for migrants, nevertheless insisted that we "need to sort out ourselves before we let others in!".

However, other participants were concerned by a lack of compassion or goodwill towards immigrants "coming here to earn a living and contribute to society". Several implored the public to overcome their fears and embrace a more positive attitude, emphasising the diversity and economic advantages that immigration can bring:

"I wish people had a more rounded view of immigration, based on facts, and could see it as being part of the UK's rich tapestry rather than focusing on the scaremongering coverage of a minority's bad behaviour."

Some also criticised "the way immigration, and immigrants, are seen and treated as evil by the media and government (with the undercurrent of racism that goes with it) rather than a welcome, necessary and positive aspect of our society". Asylum seekers and refugees were perceived to be particularly vulnerable: "It is appalling that many vulnerable people are forced into destitution when their claims fail and that so many, including children, are held in detention". A more general view was that attitudes towards immigrants were symptomatic of a socially evil intolerance of outsiders and "the right to be different".

"I think safe communities can only exist when everyone believes that other people are not so different from themselves."

Discrimination and prejudice clearly emerged as social evils and several groups were identified as victims, in particular women, minority ethnic groups, disabled people and Muslims. 'Islamophobia' was specifically cited by several people as a social evil.

Health and social care

Health and social care issues that emerged in the consultation included 'lifestyle' factors such as diet and obesity, as well as concerns about the standards of care available. Some people connected ill-health, 'junk' and 'fast' food, stressing a need to "educate people" to lead healthier lives. As one put it:

"I think obesity is a huge part of today's society and it's not only schools that need to educate the children, but the parents need educating too!"

Allegedly low standards of hygiene and patient care in the NHS also featured in the responses, as did lack of support for particular groups (people with mental health problems, disabled people, drug users and victims of rape or trauma) and a lack of particular services (NHS dentists and maternity services).

However, by far the most frequent concern raised was the care for older people. In most cases this focused on issues of cost and funding.

> *"Elderly people having saved hard all their life, being forced to sell their property for care fees and also their hard-earned life savings. Absolutely deplorable."*

Other participants emphasised a lack of support and recognition for informal carers:

> *"The way UK carers are kept in poverty through no fault of their own, we carers save the government £87 billion a year and get under £50 per week for a reward."*

Concern was also expressed for paid carers whom some participants felt were "underpaid, overworked and undervalued". Responsibility for this social evil was firmly placed at the door of government, which was variously criticised for the "privatisation", "mismanagement" and "lack of funding" of the NHS.

The environment

Although environmental concerns were recognised as "some of the great social challenges of our era", some of the participants who referred to them were not sure whether they amounted to social evils. Others, however, observed that "we cause them" and felt that the implied "lack of consideration for future generations" was a good reason to regard them as evils.

People focused on several issues, including the wastefulness of consumer culture and the "ecological excesses created by large companies". Others emphasised animal welfare issues in farming and science as well as a wider "disconnect between society and environment" and "alienation" from nature. The dominant environmental theme was climate change: "We face unprecedented levels of human displacement, an enormous and irreversible loss of biodiversity and environmental consequences that we simply can't predict".

Strong feelings were expressed that too little was being done to remedy this evil. For example, one respondent criticised a "reluctance of the governments of rich countries to lead by example and take a radical stance on climate change". Others focused on the failure of individuals to accept responsibility:

"Despite all this talk about 'green issues' an awful lot of people still create ridiculously large unnecessary amounts of waste (especially rubbish and carbon dioxide) ... I'm really encouraged by the way that a few small places in the UK have made a concerted and joint effort to abolish plastic bags or save energy and this spirit should be replicated much more widely: we're in this together!"

Some conclusions

Cutting across all the responses to the online consultation was an overarching sense of unease about rapid social change. While often recognising that change had brought a mixture of good and bad effects, people were worried about a decline of things they value – not least morality, community and social responsibility. At the same time, many were plainly dismayed by a perceived growth in individualism, consumerism and greed, inequality and the misuse of drugs and alcohol.

This unease about the past translated into fears for the future, with respondents indicating that they felt like hostages to change, rather than its controllers. While some blamed the social evils they prioritised on government, the media, big business or religion, others recognised that some evils were broadly cultural and entrenched in ways of living and thinking.

Clearly, many of the evils identified by Joseph Rowntree in 1904 remain a concern today, including poverty, drugs, alcohol and gambling. But the consultation also suggests a sense of powerlessness that contrasts sharply with Rowntree's own optimistic determination to commit his resources to explaining the underlying causes of 'evil in society'.

What has most evidently changed in a century is people's sense of complexity and the magnitude of issues. Many of these, as we are constantly made aware by our 24-hour news media, are driven by global rather than national forces. There is, nevertheless, some hope – as well as a concluding irony – to be found in the realisation that the discussion concerning supposed powerlessness arose in the context of a lively and well-supported consultation. Evidently, there is an active and enthusiastic commitment to debating the relevant issues – if not to clarifying how they might be resolved.

Note
[1] A very small number of participants identified homosexuality as a 'social evil', while a similarly small number of responses were incontrovertibly racist.

References

Kershaw, C., Nicholas, S. and Walker, A. (eds) (2008) *Crime in England and Wales 2007/08*, London: Home Office.

Roe, S. and Ashe, J. (2008) Young people and crime: Findings from the 2006 Offending, Crime and Justice Survey, London: Home Office.

4

Truncated opportunities: eliciting unheard voices on social evils

Alice Mowlam and Chris Creegan

The public online consultation described in the previous chapter was successful in eliciting a range of challenging opinions about contemporary 'social evils'. Even so, it was acknowledged from the outset that individuals without ready access to the internet could be excluded from such a dialogue. These, by definition, were likely to include many people from low-income and disadvantaged groups whose voices are often neglected in debates about the condition and direction of society. To address this, the Qualitative Research Unit at the independent research organisation, NatCen (National Centre for Social Research), was commissioned to organise a series of discussion events so that a range of these potentially 'unheard voices' could be elicited.

The priority was to include those people least likely to have heard about the initiative and those least likely to take part without a specific attempt to reach them. With this in mind, the following groups were identified:

- people with learning disabilities;
- ex-offenders;
- carers;
- unemployed people;
- vulnerable young people;
- care leavers;
- people with experience of homelessness.

The choice was also informed by an analysis of the types of people who were participating in the online consultation. This revealed low numbers of young people and people from black and minority ethnic (BME) groups. Although the project did not start with the notions of 'social exclusion' or 'vulnerability', most of those who took part could have been placed in either or both categories. The participants were often, consequently, people with direct experience of many of the social evils that respondents to the online consultation had identified.

Altogether, eight discussion groups involving 60 people were held in locations across England and Scotland during the autumn of 2007, with participants recruited through a range of charitable organisations.[1] (Further information about the sample and the way it was recruited is given in the Appendix.) After an open discussion about the main social evils in Britain today, people were invited to consider some of the online consultation responses and the continuing relevance of the social evils that Joseph Rowntree specified 100 years ago.

Views of 'social evil'

The discussion of what was meant by 'social evil' was always lively although some participants considered that 'social ill' or 'social problem' would be a more appropriate and less emotive terms. Much of the debate concerned problems where it was felt that no obvious 'right' or 'wrong' existed, including teenage pregnancy and drug use. Other issues, such as violence against women, sexual abuse of children and prostitution of young girls were so clearly regarded as morally wrong that there was little or no discussion.

It became apparent that participants were considering the issues from a number of different (but related) angles. Four ways of talking about social evil were especially noticeable, which can be described as:

- *behaviours*: what people do;
- *impact* on different spheres of life;
- *barriers* to personal fulfilment;
- *blame*: responsible bodies.

Not surprisingly, participants tended to begin with issues of particular relevance to their own lives. Prompt cards using findings from the online survey served to broaden the perspective. But when people were asked towards the end of the sessions to prioritise their 'top social evils', it was apparent that they chose to return to issues that mattered most to them personally. It was also noticeable that young people generally were less inclined to dwell on issues beyond their immediate spheres of experience. This tendency was most striking in the group of participants with learning difficulties.

Stereotyping and labelling emerged as a major theme. Participants talked about how they had been personally affected by people making assumptions about them. This was reflected in a striking reluctance to classify particular groups of people as socially 'evil'. For example, participants were quick to point out the complex social issues that lay behind adolescent girls getting pregnant and were not willing to blame the girls. It was also noticeable that, although drug misuse was a prominent theme, drug takers were not generally condemned. Participants tended to focus more on dealers as 'evil', or the wider drug trade.

In terms of topics, the dominant themes raised in the discussion groups were:

- excessive use of drugs and alcohol;
- family disruption;
- decline of community;
- fear of crime and prejudice;
- poverty;
- immigration and unfairness.

Excessive use of drugs and alcohol

Drugs and alcohol were raised at an early stage of discussion in all of the groups. However, as with the online consultation, it was generally considered that alcohol was not, of itself, a social evil. As a young man living in a hostel put it: "Alcohol is not bad as long as you limit yourself". Binge drinking and the link with antisocial behaviour were commonly discussed, for example: "It can cause a problem if people start kicking off and that in the streets" (young man with experience of homelessness).

Personal experiences of the misuse of drugs also featured heavily in some of the discussion groups, particularly those made up of younger age groups and ex-offenders. This was not surprising since two of the groups included people who were on a substance misuse recovery programme, one for crack cocaine addiction. This was a notable example of people talking about a social problem that had played a big part in their own lives. Drug use was not universally dismissed as a bad thing in itself. The positive medicinal properties of drugs were highlighted by some participants, while others made distinctions between different types of drug and the extent of use.

However, one issue that participants were clear in condemning was the link between drug use and gangs, guns and violence. Rap artists were singled out for particular criticism for glamorising drugs and crime. The breakdown of family and community also loomed large in discussion:

> *"[I]f that kid's come from a broken home, there might be drugs or alcohol, the local community is involved in drugs ... it doesn't matter how good the education system is at that school, these people that live around this school affect how these children grow up." (man attending drug recovery programme)*

Young participants, many of whom had grown up in care, described a sense of desolation about the barriers they saw as preventing them from getting ahead in their lives. Money problems, the way society perceived them and a lack of family support were interlinked with a sense of opportunities being curtailed. They suggested that taking drugs could be a welcome, if temporary, relief from these issues, as voiced by this young man with experience of unemployment: *"shall I continue feeling crap about myself or shall I take this drug and feel better for a while?"*.

The role of personal choice was also recognised: *"If I wanted to change my life I could've changed my life, but I didn't, right? I wanted to go down that path, right? I took drugs 'cos I liked drugs"* (man attending a drug recovery programme). However, some older participants highlighted the devastating effects that drugs could have on people's lives, including criminal involvement, prison, unemployment, homelessness and family disruption.

Family disruption

Personal experience of family breakdown was widespread. In particular, many of the young people taking part had grown up in care, an experience that was unanimously described as negative:

> *"[T]hey'd just rather shove you in a kids' home and then keep shoving you round in every single kids' home they can find ... and it don't matter where you come from, if you're from Manchester, Blackpool, Scotland, wherever, they'll put you anywhere in the country." (young woman)*

> *"So they don't care about your needs, it's just about filling a place.... With me they put in me in a hostel and that was the last I heard of them." (young man)*

Participants talked about having been beaten up by parents, or feeling unloved and uncared for. Young people also described periods of family disruption or violent family backgrounds as having been catalysts for 'going off the rails'.

Broader societal changes were raised, including concerns about family breakdown, growing numbers of lone parents, absent fathers and unsupervised young people getting into trouble. In discussions about teenage parents, a link was often made between having a baby and obtaining council accommodation, but with a view expressed that pregnancy could often be a way of escaping a bad situation. Parenting difficulties were not necessarily condemned and there was some sympathy for those labelled as 'bad' parents. Participants acknowledged that people were often doing their best in difficult circumstances:

> *"Some people raising children have no way of gauging how to raise a child. I mean they do the best they can, I wouldn't say that was a 'social evil'." (older unemployed woman)*

Decline of community

Community decline was closely linked with disrupted families. An overwhelming sense of the chaotic nature of the outside world emerged from participants' accounts. This was sometimes articulated in terms of physical isolation and fear, for example a lack of safety walking around neighbourhoods after dark or on weekend evenings. 'Ghettoisation' of inner-city areas, young people having nowhere to go and associated social problems were also widely described. Participants spoke of a lack of neighbourly care, with people living next to each other not looking out for each other. As one unemployed woman commented: "We live in a culture of 'just look after yourself and sod everybody else'".

Middle-aged and older people, in particular, talked about how different life had been in the past:

> *"The community spirit is broken down terribly over the last 20 or 30 years.... Society has changed, it is a lot more selfish and 'me, myself and I'. The emphasis is on success and making money whatever ... it all changed in the eighties, I think." (unemployed man)*

In addition to a perceived increase in selfishness, the widening gap between rich and poor and the issue of poverty (see below) were often raised.

A lack of positive role models for children and young people also featured. One mother (a carer) suggested that rappers and other figures who held young people's respect were a strongly negative influence:

> *"My son aspires to this stuff and that worries me, he's 15 and he watches all these gangster rappers and he's got the earrings and he goes, 'Oh they've got this crib and that and the next thing', and I'm like: 'That's not real life — get a grip!'"* (woman carer)

Participants also referred to the physical decline of communities, for example, a lack of facilities because youth clubs, adventure playgrounds and community centres had closed down.

Fear of crime and prejudice

A very strong link was made between drugs and crime. Participants talked about this from personal experience, with many ex-offenders having become involved in crime as a result of drug misuse. People who lived in inner-city areas also talked about gangs of youths selling drugs in local communities, a proliferation of guns and a violent and intimidating atmosphere on the streets. Parents, in this context, voiced particular fears for their children's futures:

> *"They want to be somebody when they grow up. The only thing they can see around them who's got any money, who's probably doing anything is the drug dealers, you know, it escalates from there. . . . They don't see when a drug dealer's in jail and 10 years down the line he's going to do it again."* (man, ex-offender)

Participants spoke about girls getting hooked on drugs and then being drawn into a world of sexual exploitation and prostitution. Violence against women, once it was introduced to the discussions with prompt cards, was another issue that was universally perceived as morally 'wrong'. Child sexual abuse and exploitation were viewed in the same way.

Experiences and perceptions of crime were frequently expressed as fears of what lay 'out there' on the streets. In some cases, this included a declared unwillingness to go out at night, but there was a much more widely shared sense of unease. Young people's behaviour was a prominent issue, as with the online consultation, but the discussions captured more than one side of the story. Young people themselves talked about feeling uncomfortable with the way they were viewed and felt they were unfairly stereotyped as a problem: "they're stereotyping young kids now as all being little yobs.... There are a lot of yobs out there, but not everyone who just wears tracksuit bottoms and stuff like that" (man attending a drug recovery programme).

The story told by one mother suggested that young people's concerns about stereotyping by adults were not without foundation:

> *"I noticed there was a bunch of youths standing around and my immediate reaction was to stop and think 'Oh my goodness, shall I go the other way?'. Until two seconds later I realised it was my own son and his friends. But that reaction was in me already." (older woman carer)*

A young woman also described how she had tried to help an older woman at a bus stop with her shopping, only for the older person to exclaim: "Get your hands off my bag!".

Prejudice and discrimination were roundly condemned. People saw racism as a social evil, and did not think that individuals should be discriminated against because of religion or race. It nevertheless appeared that there was some difference between what participants believed to be wrong (such as discriminating against young people), and what they actually felt when faced with a particular situation (fear of a group of young people in hoods).

Poverty

Poverty was repeatedly discussed, but not in specific items of income or particular household items that people could not afford. Instead, it was characterised as a constraining force that prevented people from achieving their aspirations of living a good life: "if you're poor, you're struggling all the time – you have no choices in life. That's what poverty does to you, it gives you no choice" (older woman, carer). There was also a strong sense of poverty as a trap from which it was hard to escape. Young people spoke of a struggle to achieve their goals of education, training and employment in the face of financial constraints.

The polarisation of society into 'haves' and 'have-nots' and the gap between rich and poor, was another prominent theme. It was recognised that some people making money might welcome widening inequality, but there was a whole swathe of people not benefiting:

> *"[Y]ou have to get the job and be a success. That may work for a lot of people but not for all, some people become disenfranchised and*

*become marginalised and just fall through the gap. That happens to a
lot of people." (unemployed man)*

Yet while some participants expressed a sense of disillusionment and
hopelessness, others referred to a need for ambition and individual
responsibility: "Why, why are people rich? They obviously did
something to get rich, so ... when people say they're poor, well, why
are you poor? Obviously they haven't got a higher ambition" (man
with experience of homelessness).

Poverty was also seen as closely related to the other themes discussed
above, including drug taking (as a temporary escape), drug dealing (as
a way of making money) and family breakdown.

Immigration and unfairness

Immigration was not usually voiced as a social evil in itself, but there
were criticisms of perceived mismanagement by government and
alleged unfairness. Some took the view that refugees and asylum seekers
were treated too favourably compared with people born in the UK,
with regard to housing or jobs: "They're taking [it] off the people that
need it here" (young woman, ex-offender); "Why bring over more and
more people when you can't sort the problems you got?" (young man
with experience of homelessness).

Concerns, at least in discussion, were attached to the systems in place
for dealing with migrants in social need, rather than asylum seekers or
refugees as individuals. However, there was also a view that help from
public services was taken for granted by migrants:

> *"I have been through really bad states as well. What I get, I really
> appreciate it. But then I see people just come over here and they get
> it just handed to them on a plate and they don't appreciate it, I don't
> understand." (young unemployed black woman)*

More generally, participants felt that the government was failing to
stop criminals and even terrorists entering the UK. Some sought to
distinguish this objection from opposition to particular immigrants:
"I'm not racist, it's not their fault; it's just the government".

However, the benefits to the wider economy were also acknowledged.
People talked about immigrant workers coming to the UK who were
prepared to work for less money and to do unpopular jobs. It was also
acknowledged that immigration had long been a feature of British

society, going back to the days when people from former colonies were invited to Britain to work.

Who is to blame?

Participants often turned their attention to the issue of whether someone or something could be blamed for the social evils being discussed. Most commonly cited were the media and the government, although big business and religious institutions were also mentioned. For example:

- perceived manipulation of public opinion (the media);
- inadequate or inappropriate help to address the problems (the government, religious institutions);
- perpetration of a capitalist society resulting in selfishness and breakdown of community (the government and big business).

The media

Like respondents in the online consultation, participants thought that the media could be alarmist in its approach to news, with a tendency to sensationalise and manipulate issues. Certain newspapers were deemed especially worthy of blame. Specific issues that were highlighted included the portrayal of Muslims. More generally, there was a view that violence was glamorised in popular culture. The promotion of unhealthy or undesirable behaviours was also discussed, including the use of 'size-zero' fashion models. The widespread use of swearing was criticised, especially where it appeared to be condoned (as with TV chef Gordon Ramsay). Participants were concerned about the way that these social evils were portrayed as things to aspire to, especially for young people.

The government

The government was often the prime target for participants who wanted to blame someone or something for social problems. However, it was more the relationship between the government and the social evils under discussion that prompted specific criticism. For example, some felt that the government was out of touch with issues facing 'ordinary people': "They're proposing solutions to problems they haven't got a clue about" (man, ex-offender).

Another view was that state mechanisms for tackling social problems were not working properly. For example, it was suggested that the prison system was failing. A lack of effective rehabilitation and the prevalence of drugs in many jails meant that offenders were being released with the same or worse problems than they went in with. The perceived lack of control over immigration was another area of criticism.

In addition, the government was blamed for the financial hardships experienced by young people who were trying to get an education, meet their travel costs to college and support themselves at the same time: "We're trying to get something out of what we're going to do, in either work or education, and we're just basically spending our money on getting there" (young man living in a hostel).

Religious institutions

Although religious faith was not viewed as a social evil in itself, the ways in which religion was organised and practised were considered problematic. As in the online consultation, religious extremism was seen as a major problem facing the modern world. The link between religion and terrorism was perceived as a new and particularly deadly threat. Some participants also perceived a lack of religious guidance concerning the challenges faced by contemporary society. It was felt that religious leaders across faiths should provide more moral leadership.

Big business

Large corporate businesses were often discussed in relation to the widening gap between rich and poor. They were repeatedly linked to an increasingly selfish society, leaving behind an underclass of dispossessed and disenfranchised people.

Truncated opportunities

As must, by now, be apparent, the social evils given priority in the discussion groups were interconnected to a striking degree. For example, misuse of drugs and alcohol was debated in the context of crime and the limited opportunities for young people, which were, in turn, linked to a breakdown of family and community. Threading through these interwoven social evils was a powerful sense of 'truncated opportunities': a shared story of chances curtailed, lost and wasted. Put another way, participants were confronting such challenging social problems that they felt unable to fulfil their potential because of limited choices and opportunities. This view was expressed in relation to the past, the present and a future where many implied that positive change was an unlikely, probably unattainable goal.

Education was, however, seen as a possible escape route from the social ills under discussion. For example, older participants talked about how they had missed out on the educational opportunities offered to them and were keen to persuade the younger generation of the importance of getting a good education:

> *"I've got three kids, going to school is more important than anything else. The other parents, there are kids hanging out on the streets, I don't allow my kids to do that, they're in by six o'clock, you know, I'm trying to show them the right way." (unemployed man)*

But barriers to education were also identified. For instance, young participants who were still studying talked about difficulties trying to support themselves financially without any help from family. One young man with experience of homelessness and considering the option of going to college reflected that "they ask us for an amount of money that we can't afford to pay. And then because of that maybe, it can stop our future".

The availability of some help and support was recognised, but persuading young people of the benefits of education versus the attractions of other lifestyles (including drugs, crime and gangs) was seen as a challenge.

While young people articulated a sense of truncated opportunities in the future, older participants catalogued their lost opportunities and choices with hindsight. Individuals were rarely mentioned in these discussions, but Margaret Thatcher was a notable exception. Her 11 years as Prime Minister were perceived as marking a shift towards greater individualism and contributing to a growth of selfishness, the fragmentation of family and the loss of community. This was seen by some as an era when loss of opportunity for themselves and others had become entrenched.

Given the involvement of carers in the discussion groups, it was not surprising that the impact on opportunities of having to look after a sick or disabled relative was raised. But a further limiting factor cited was a sense of multiple demands and the accelerating pace of modern life: "The amount of things you have to pack in, you're like a hamster in a wheel and it's really hard to get off and keep things going".

The relationship between the key themes identified by the discussion groups and the notion of truncated opportunities is illustrated in Figure 4.1.

Figure 4.1: Summary diagram of social evils, truncated opportunities and influential bodies

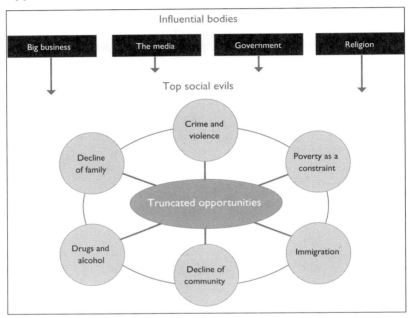

Contemporary social evils (and the influential bodies that people associate with them) exert a profound effect on people's lives and this is more than evident in the stories told by participants in the discussion groups about their own lives. What they had to say about lost opportunities and the entrenched exclusion they had experienced themselves demonstrates the importance and value of listening to people whose disadvantage has been compounded by often having their voices and opinions ignored. Blame (mostly directed at institutions) was by no means absent from their accounts of contemporary social evil; but there was also a pronounced sense of personal responsibility, for what has happened and what might happen in the future.

The next chapter moves on to explore people's day-to-day experiences of living and coping with the social evils that have been identified and discussed. It also reports on what people from disadvantaged groups see as some of the solutions.

Note

[1] The charities that assisted were NACRO (National Association for the Care and Resettlement of Offenders); HFT (the Home Farm Trust), supporting people with learning disabilities and their families; the Depaul Trust, working with homeless and disadvantaged young people; Tomorrow's People, providing support and mentoring for unemployed people; Centrepoint, working with socially excluded, homeless young people; Elect, a social enterprise in Liverpool; Citizens Advice Bureau (CAB); and Vocal, supporting carers in Edinburgh and the Lothians.

5

Living with social evils: further views from people in disadvantaged groups

Chris Creegan, Martha Warrener and Rachel Kinsella

The Joseph Rowntree Foundation's online public consultation and the specially commissioned discussions with socially excluded and disadvantaged groups – described in the two previous chapters – yielded a diverse range of views about contemporary social evils. Although people's perspectives ranged widely, a number of themes emerged repeatedly that related to moral concepts, such as individualism, declining communal values and greed, as well as more tangible problems like poverty, family breakdown and drug and alcohol misuse. Most – although not all – of these were given renewed emphasis during a subsequent phase of the consultation project, which investigated people's direct experiences of living with the social evils that had been identified and sought people's views on potential solutions.

Experiences of social evils

In this second phase of the research conducted by NatCen (National Centre for Social Research), 60 people from socially disadvantaged groups took part in three workshops and two discussion groups held across England, Scotland and Wales.[1] The sample profile of participants captured a broad spread of characteristics (see Mowlam and Creegan, 2008). The aim was to avoid further detail on what constitute 'social evils', in favour of finding out how people were coping with these issues from day to day, and obtaining their views on possible solutions for dealing with them.

Social evils were clearly interconnected in participant's day-to-day lives. For example, among the young people who were living in a hostel, violence was cited as one of the main causes for their own family breakdown and they described how it had often stemmed from their parents' drug and alcohol misuse. Age also played an important role in shaping views and experiences. This was particularly evident in relation to young people and a decline in values. Older people tended to associate crime and violence with young people with a strong sense of fear and anxiety. Young people did not always make the same link, instead describing how they felt discriminated against and stereotyped by older people. Another striking finding was the extent to which participants spoke about the constraining forces of poverty – including a view that people resorted to crime as a means of 'getting by' and making their way in the world. This reflected the notion of 'truncated opportunities' explored in the preceding chapter, where people felt limited and constrained by their situation. More specifically:

- Discussion of *decline of community* tended to revolve around how well people felt they knew their neighbours. Some insisted that there was still a strong sense of community where they lived, but others said that this was far from their own experience. The three factors that most appeared to influence views were location, how long they had lived in their neighbourhood and broader, societal changes. For example, one suggestion was that close-knit communities were more likely to be found in rural areas than in cities. Older participants were especially likely to consider that the level of care people showed for each other had diminished over time. Participants also felt that there were not enough activities or facilities for young people anymore.
- *Individualism* was less explicitly discussed than some of the other social evils given prominence in the previous consultations. However, it arose in relation to other themes, for example an increase in selfishness, which was – in turn – associated with a decline in community. There was a view that too many people were 'out for what they can get' in terms of financial or material gain. *Consumerism* was discussed mainly in relation to young people. Older participants considered celebrity culture and peer pressure to have made young people more materialistic. Young people also spoke about the pressure they felt to have the latest things in order to 'fit in'. However, some young people – including those living in a hostel – made it clear that they cared much less about designer clothes than having a roof over their heads, warmth and food.
- Personal experience of *family breakdown* was common among participants, not least among ex-offenders and young people with experience of homelessness. Some also talked about how a family member's drug and alcohol addictions had led to violence, homelessness and prison sentences. Other young people described how they had reacted to unwelcome changes in the family, such as

the arrival of a disliked step-parent, by running away, spending time sleeping on the streets or getting 'mashed' with friends to try to forget problems at home. A common experience among participants who had been in care as children was feelings of being unloved, insecure, alone and angry. Strong views about fathers who were largely absent during their children's upbringing also emerged, although some men insisted they had turned out 'alright' despite not knowing their fathers.

- Personal experiences of *drug and alcohol misuse* featured heavily in the lives of participants, notably the young people, unemployed people and ex-offenders. Wide-ranging reasons advanced for involvement in misuse included boredom, escapism, being in care, bereavement, peer pressure and stress. However, there was general agreement that alcohol was a problem when used to excess. Young people also talked about the negative effects drugs had on their personal and family relationships, including friends and relatives involved in crime and violence, homelessness, divorce or unemployment.

- Drugs and alcohol had also been a catalyst for *crime and violence* in people's experiences as both victims and perpetrators. Some participants talked about committing crime to support drug habits, or becoming involved in criminal activity and violence while under the influence of alcohol. They also described being the victims of violent attacks from people using drugs and alcohol, including family members. Other crime was also widely discussed, with some of the offenders and ex-offenders maintaining that their involvement in robbery, stealing, car crime and vandalism had been motivated by boredom, lack of money or a desire to 'look cool' with friends. Some older people ascribed crime to high levels of youth unemployment and a lack of respect for parents. There was also a common view that crime was linked to poverty and even an insistence that if people had to steal to survive it was not their fault.

- Experiences of low income and *poverty* spanned all groups and ages, although the greatest discussion of the material and social impact of these took place among young people. For example, those living in a hostel spoke about the difficulties of surviving on benefits. Yet participants also believed they would be worse off with paid work. They found it 'boring' and 'depressing' not having anything to do and got annoyed when people assumed that they were lazy. However, some people who were unemployed gave graphic accounts of how their inability to provide for their families through work had left them feeling ashamed and powerless, including one woman whose caring responsibilities had obliged her to stop working.

- Although some positive aspects of *immigration* were acknowledged, including wider economic benefits and the willingness of migrants to do unpopular low-paid jobs, accounts of immigration were predominantly negative. For example, some young people living in a hostel believed that immigrants were given greater priority than they were for rehousing. Some participants also believed that they received fewer benefits than migrant workers and expressed concerns that their social security payments would be lowered as more immigrants entered Britain. One unemployed woman asylum seeker shared these concerns, stating that she had left Somalia fearing persecution, but criticised others who moved to Britain and "milk[ed] the system".

- More generally, *declining values* were defined by older participants in terms of a loss of respect for parents and authority figures. It was suggested that stronger discipline and moral education should come from parents and be reinforced at school. Another recurring view was that 'political correctness' had gone too far, allowing young people to think they could get away with antisocial behaviour without adults or the police intervening. Discussions with young people, meanwhile, revealed a strong feeling that respect should be mutual. They described a sense of despair in relation to the way older people perceived them, feeling that they were stereotyped and discriminated against. The young people living in a hostel suggested that young people were forced to grow up a lot quicker than their parents and grandparents had been.

Coping with social evils

Contrasting and competing definitions emerged from the discussions of what 'coping' with particular social problems meant in practice. However, among the most prominent coping mechanisms described by participants were the stories people told themselves about what was happening to them.

Trying to stay positive

This included positive attempts to look forward to a different place and time and more negative efforts to block out the reality of a harsh situation.

> *"Just stay positive no matter what. No matter how much you get run down just stay happy, that's what I say." (young man living in a hostel)*

A belief that the situation would change for the better was recurrent among young people living in hostels. Commonly, education was seen as the key to this. However, participants argued that they faced barriers to further education, such as lack of money and no family support. Some also talked about changing their situation through work, moving away, getting married and starting a family of their own.

> *"Me personally, I'm not gonna be poor my whole life, you get me? The way I see it, if you can't beat 'em, join 'em, so I'm going to be rich. I'm getting a career and a job.... If you have it in your head and aim high you'll get there." (young man living in a hostel)*

A recurrent claim was that religious faith could help put things in perspective and avoid a narrow focus on their personal problems. This viewpoint was particularly evident among carers.

> *"If you are thinking of the man up there or the God in charge you are relating in a way to something bigger than yourself, and not necessarily your immediate problem." (female carer)*

Both young and older participants also mentioned valuing the things they did have, such as basic necessities like food and water, and comparing this with starving people in the third world. Some lone parents said they also said this to their children when they complained about being unable to afford things they wanted.

A different approach to 'coping' involved ignoring the situation rather than dealing with it. Some people said they would "just get on with it" or put problems to the back of their minds.

> *"[L]ike I said, there's no coping method ... you've gotta get on with it ... you just don't think about ... you just think fuck it and carry on." (young woman living in a hostel)*

Participants discussed using housework and college courses as a way of distracting themselves from their problems. Turning to family and friends or statutory and third sector organisations for practical help and support was another way of coping (see below). One key theme to emerge, however, was about not getting upset. Suppressing emotions was a strategy commonly discussed by women across the discussion groups:

> *"Sometimes you don't [cope] though, sometimes you do just break down and have a cry and you think, 'Oh I can't deal with everything', but you've gotta carry on. But then you think, what's crying gonna change? You're sat here crying wasting a few extra minutes of your life." (young woman living in a hostel)*

This resonated with responses from other women who talked about crying being pointless and having to "pull yourself together".

Perhaps not surprisingly, older participants appeared less inclined to look to their future as a way of coping. For them, a more typical coping story was the need to "take one day at a time" and not planning too far ahead.

> *"I can cope with breaking it down into dealing with my life in days, rather than planning for the week or the month or the year. I don't do that because I just find it creates far too much stress for me to have to cope with that." (unemployed woman)*

Distractions

Attempts to 'escape' from day-to-day difficulties might also include hobbies such as listening to music, watching films or reading. This tended especially to be a technique employed by the carers and lone parents who took part in the research.

> *"I can get lost in a good book, in a good song, in a really fantastic piece of theatre or a good film. I suppose it's just finding your release. I mean people find their release in ... drugs and alcohol. I find it in theatre and dance so I'm a bit cheesy, but I really don't care." (female carer)*

The more negative forms of escapism that were frequently discussed were drinking alcohol and taking drugs. Thus, in order to cope with one social evil, such as poverty, family breakdown or homelessness, people had not infrequently turned to another. This was especially true of young people who talked about going out with friends to get "wrecked" to forget financial worries. Ex-offenders and unemployed people also discussed becoming inebriated to "forget the burden of poverty". One previously unemployed male carer discussed using cannabis as a way of relaxing when he "thought life was falling apart": "you are so mellow you didn't give a monkeys about anything".

However, there was also acceptance, among older participants at least, that drugs and alcohol could make a bad situation worse:

> *"I suppose, in a way the drugs and alcohol is a way of coping perhaps with your situation to begin with and then it becomes a problem in itself." (male ex-offender)*

Young people, meanwhile, identified a lack of family support, feeling unloved and being in local authority care among the reasons they had turned to alcohol and drugs. Yet while they see this as enabling them to forget about problems at home or the fact they did not live with their family, it was evident that substance abuse was ultimately a consequence of *not* coping.

Venting frustration was also discussed. Emotions were said to be expressed through crying, writing poetry or talking to people about problems and physical exercise.

> *"When I get angry I get really angry and I let the little things build up ... I'll save it and I'll go to a nightclub and I will dance my butt off and just, I mean even a case of go to a gym, go on the treadmill, find a punch bag, beat the hell out of that, beat the feeling like you want to do it to someone else." (female carer)*

A more negative way of venting frustration was through violence. This could include physical or verbal abuse directed at self as well as others. Those who had resorted to violence against other people talked about just "losing your head". Young people referred to violence as a reaction to family breakdown, feeling unloved and having no money. In contrast, one older unemployed man said that his resorts to violence arose from the aggression and disrespect shown to his family by other people.

Self-harm was also mentioned. By causing themselves physical pain, some participants said they were able to deal with the emotional pain of family problems. For example, two women described how self-harming had enabled them to vent the anger and frustration that arose through feeling unloved and living in care.

Turning to crime was another way that people said they 'coped' with social problems. Personal robbery, stealing, shoplifting, prostitution and drug dealing were all discussed as ways of making 'easy money'. For example, those who had at some point been homeless identified obtaining food as a reason for turning to crime. Another reason could be a desire to obtain consumer goods that were otherwise unaffordable. In one group, the young women discussed shoplifting as a way of getting hold of hair and beauty products. Ex-offenders also discussed crime as a way of paying for their drug habits.

Seeking external help

External coping strategies involved looking either to family and friends or to formal support services for emotional or practical help and support. Self-evidently, given the way they were recruited, all the workshop and discussion participants had received some form of help and support from a statutory or third sector service. But in addition to those organisations directly involved in the research, participants had frequently received help from other agencies and organisations, including probation, counselling services, drop-in centres and hostels.

A common coping theme was the importance of having someone to talk to. Talking to family and friends was said to help "get it off your chest" and deal with stress. Women, in particular, emphasised the importance of having family and friends to talk to when going through difficult times. For example, one unemployed woman described her mother as her 'rock' for constantly talking to her about her problems and reassuring her that she was loved.

Service providers were a further source of emotional support, especially for those without family or friends to talk to. Staff working for the organisations that helped recruit participants were said to provide this when needed. But there were also participants who had decided they needed professional help in order to deal with certain issues. For example, one unemployed man with alcohol problems had sought counselling to help him stop drinking. However, views about the value of counselling varied. Some younger as well as older participants felt it had helped them to come to terms with personal issues, such as family breakdown. Other young people said they would rather talk to friends or other people in similar situations than a counsellor.

Emotional support was also gained from talking to other service users. Meeting people in similar situations had meant that participants were able to discuss their problems with people who could empathise with them and offer advice based on experience. The resulting social networks were not only an important coping mechanism but were also felt to provide a lost sense of community. As described by two lone parents:

Female 1:   *"It's just a bit of socialisation isn't it, a couple of times a month?"*

[*Others agree*]

Female 2:   *"Getting together and having a brew and...."*

Female 1:   *"By being in the group; you're getting like a sense of that community...."*

Young people living in a hostel also referred to a sense of everyone being in the 'same boat'. However, although they were prepared to socialise with each other, there was a marked reluctance to 'open up' to others. One reason given for this was a feeling that others had their own problems and would not want to hear about anyone else's. Another was the insistence that they were trying to move on and not wanting to dwell on the past.

Practical support

Family and friends

Family and friends were mentioned as a source of help with both money difficulties and childcare. Young people discussed receiving financial help from their parents. But in some cases the tables had turned and older, unemployed participants mentioned being offered money by their children. Two unemployed men, one of whom was homeless, discussed the embarrassment of having their teenage children offer to buy them new shoes. Although grateful for the support, they felt embarrassed.

Family and friends also offered assistance with childcare, something that was especially important for lone parents as it meant "time to yourself to escape". However, one lone parent described what it felt like to be without such support:

> *"A lot of people had this sort of [help from family] every other weekend. I've never had that ... that sort of isolates you further ... if you've got a free weekend, it gives you a chance to start a new life ... and meet other people."*

Support through services

Support services were said to offer practical help with housing and arranging activities. Some of the organisations that were used to recruit participants (see the Appendix) also specifically helped unemployed people to find work and apply for jobs. It also emerged that accommodation had been provided for most of those who needed it through different charities and voluntary organisations. This included young people, unemployed people and ex-offenders who were living in hostels or supported and sheltered housing or had done at some point. Other types of drop-in centre and hostel for homeless people and drug addicts were mentioned as offering accommodation, food, showers and help with alcohol problems or giving up drugs. The importance of having a 'stable environment' was underlined as a way of helping people to cope with poverty, crime and violence, and drugs and alcohol.

Organisations also arranged activities, such as trips to museums or theme parks, or pottery classes. Lone parents discussed these pursuits as an opportunity to get out of the house and mix with other adults. Children might join in with the activities, or alternative childcare might be arranged. Some activities could be seen as an indirect attempt to change behaviour. For example, people with alcohol and drug addictions viewed them as a way of keeping them busy.

> *"If I were at home now, I'd be on my second and third pint ... so it gets me out, getting me doing things, meeting other people, instead of just sat at home." (male ex-offender)*

Other activities, such as anger management and relaxation courses arranged by the Youth Offending Team, were more direct attempts to modify antisocial behaviour.

Coping in different ways at different times

The general consensus was that different people have different ways of coping at different points in their lives. Participants also discussed their individual choices, and a sense of pride at not resorting to negative forms of coping. Turning to music, films, books and physical exercise to 'escape' and deal with pent-up frustration was often mentioned:

"You couldn't get more stressed out than me, panic attacks and everything, but I still haven't reduced myself to drugs and alcohol yet." (female carer)

"[Dancing is] a good way to let off steam instead of going out and committing a crime or being violent against someone that you don't know for no reason whatsoever." (female carer)

How people cope was summed up more generally by the following comment from a young man living in a hostel:

"Everyone's gone through different things in their life. Everyone has their own way of coping. You have family around you; you write it down on a notepad; you sit and talk to someone. Like people have therapy. You drink, you smoke. Everyone has their own way. It depends, with the person, it depends how strong you are, mentally and physically. Some people can go through the maddest things you could ever think of and they still cope with it, without having to talk to anyone, without having to go to another country, without having to want to kill themself, you know what I mean? Everyone is like different, I think."

Finding solutions to social evils

When asked what could or should be done to address social evils, participants primarily saw the task as one for government and politicians: "The government need to stop, listen and take action" (unemployed woman). A desire for the media, business and financial institutions and faith groups to play a more constructive part was also identified. However, in contrast it was also generally accepted that individuals had an integral part to play in tackling today's social evils.

Government and politicians

Discussions about the perceived failures of government suggested that it – and politicians – could help to solve social problems in three main roles. These can be usefully characterised as 'enforcer', 'educator' and 'distributor'.

The *enforcement* role identified for government arose out of concerns about a lack of discipline in society, linked to the decline of values and community. For example, it was argued that more should be done to tackle antisocial behaviour, particularly among young people. However, it was also suggested that government sometimes wanted it 'both ways'; for example through its ban on public smoking while continuing to raise revenue from tobacco duty.

> *"If the government don't want us smoking in certain areas why would you sell us the product in the first place? You're selling us a product that says smoking kills. You're still selling it." (young man living in a hostel)*

The *educative* role identified for government related to the perceived decline of values and family. It was argued, for instance, that more should be done to promote 'traditional' family values and ensure that children and young people learned about them:

> *"... educating families, parents, children about values and you know, where they can go, give them a direction in life...." (lone mother)*

> *"Maybe ... to make it compulsory ... to have parenting classes ... children and maybe family classes." (lone mother)*

The *distributive* role of government arose from concerns about achieving greater fairness. For example, participants underlined the importance of government playing a role in altering priorities and ensuring a more equal distribution of wealth.

> *"[The government has] obviously got funding for housing, how much they can allocate to each person per year, whatever the budget is. And they must have money for NHS and things like that. Maybe they should equal it out better." (young woman living in a hostel)*

A related concern was that cutbacks would disproportionately affect the poorest in society. Concerns about immigration also led to calls for British citizen's needs and interest to be prioritised, as the following conversation by young people living in a hostel demonstrates:

> *Male:*   *"There's a housing shortage basically and all these houses are been took up by immigrants,..."*

> *Female:*   *"... by people from other countries, why? It's our country, we should have priority."*

Participants also felt strongly that politicians were too remote from ordinary people's lives. This was related to a view that politicians should take responsibility for 'practising what they preached'.

> *"Politicians [are] at the top of the ladder, I mean ... they do get some stick and I think rightly so, because if you're setting yourself up that high and to take a job with that amount of responsibility, they deserve the flack that they get. I mean, how can you have two sets of standards?" (lone father)*

There was also discussion of ways of making politicians understand what it was like to live on state benefits, illustrated by the following conversation between a group of carers:

Male: *"Who was the guy that went and lived on state benefit for a week?"*

Interviewer: *"Michael Portillo."*

Male: *"Michael Portillo, now he did it for a week ... he wants to try it for a year, not a week because at the end of that week he is like I'm going home to my big mansion with my big driveway."*

Female: *"And he's got something to look forward to ... and he knows that he is not going to be hungry and cold at the end of that week.... Whereas if he had to do it for longer then he wouldn't have that thing to look forward to."*

There was widespread concern that politicians did not listen enough and that they should do more to ensure that people knew that they cared about the problems they experienced in their day-to-day lives.

The media

After government, the perceived power and role of the media tended to provoke the liveliest discussion. There was a common view that the media was 'selective' and tended to focus on bad news, including violence, sleaze and scandal, as the following carers insisted:

Male: "[If] there is something good being done the media doesn't want to know, do you know what I mean?"

Female: "They only want to know the bad things."

A second area of concern related to the glamorisation of celebrity status, even when celebrities were involved in social evils themselves such as drug taking and violence:

"You go in the Big [Brother] house and you come out a celebrity. These people are nothing ... they're not a positive role model.... The press follow them and glamorise them, and then you see young people are looking at them thinking ... is this good?" (lone mother)

"It's the same with some of these football stars ending up in trouble.... So the kids are saying, 'He's a great football player. He's making all this money.... He can get away with that'. You know?" (lone father)

Participants felt that the solution lay in a more responsible media with a more balanced coverage of news, which would include stories about the successes of ordinary people:

"There are so many negatives in the press. I think it's bad for everybody's morale." (female carer)

"Promote success stories every week of some people, you know, not the children that have necessarily gone off the rails but the ones that have done some good in the community." (lone mother)

It was suggested that local media had an important role to play in this.

"Your local paper, I think you should ... advertise more community groups and let you know where you can go to find things out and things like that ... so you know where to go for stuff." (lone mother)

Business and financial institutions

Discussion of the role and responsibility of business tended to focus on banks and credit companies. The need for having banks at all was questioned by some participants. Particular concern was expressed about the part played by financial institutions in promoting consumerism and in excluding the poorest people in society.

> *"Poor areas ... renowned for low income, unemployment and all the rest of it, and that is where all these credit card people hit. They go there because they know these are low-income families, they are unemployed families, single mums, single dads, whatever, you know, we'll get them a credit card." (male carer)*

> *"You haven't got a job, you can't get a bank account, you can't set up a direct debit and that way you are penalised ... you've not set up a direct debit, they're going to charge an extra £3 to pay that bill ... and the government in my opinion, you know and all these big credit companies are doing nothing, nothing to get people out of it." (male carer)*

Another issue that emerged was the negative effect of big supermarkets on small local traders. Participants' views about supermarkets were not wholly negative, however, and it was accepted that they 'did their bit' for the community in some instances. More generally, business was seen as having an important role to play by investing in local infrastructure and initiatives and in creating sustainable employment.

> *"Big businesses should be investing in the local community more because they don't do, much of that." (lone mother)*

> *"There should be [an] incentive scheme for [big businesses] taking on children, straight out of school, with the promise of an apprenticeship or some sort of trade in hand...." (lone mother)*

Religious institutions and faith groups

Although some participants questioned the relevance of faith groups, there was an implicit acceptance that religion had a role to play and that faith might have greater significance in some communities than others. It was also suggested by some that Christian churches, especially, could do more to create a more 'moral' society.

> *"The church should do a lot more.... Put the moral fibre back into Britain because its gone. As far as I'm concerned, Britain's 'kaput'. It hasn't been great for about 40 years." (unemployed woman)*

Both secular education and faith groups were seen as having a role and were not seen as mutually exclusive.

Individuals

The role of individuals in addressing social evils also stimulated much discussion. Although clearly related to the way in which individuals coped (see above), this was approached from a less personal viewpoint – as though participants were considering how others, rather than they themselves, should respond. Implicit in their accounts was a sense that personal resilience was important, and that this involved personal responsibility and personal aspiration. For example:

> *"I think that every citizen should realise that they have rights, but they also have responsibilities … and it should be impressed on everybody that they might have the right to do something, but they also have a responsibility to everybody else to do it in a civilised way."* (female carer)

> *"It's up to us to change our lives. That's the way I see it, yeah? I don't care how hard your life has been, whatever you've been [through] … everyone can turn around their life."* (young man living in a hostel)

There was a commonly shared belief that rights needed to be seen in the context of responsibilities and also shaped by them. Parents and other individuals were seen as having a particular responsibility to set boundaries for children and young people and to act as positive role models.

Personal aspiration, however, was often mentioned as a quality that should be tempered by tolerance (including learning from and respecting different cultures) and altruism. A recurrent view was that greater personal satisfaction could be successfully combined with less materialism. The importance of individuals working collectively to influence big institutions such as government was also noted.

There were, nevertheless, perceived limits to the efficacy of individual agency. A possible lack of willpower was referred to, but also limits and constraining forces, including social class, which could restrict whose voices were heard in society:

> *"None of us are posh. If you can hear the way we're speaking, we've got a bit of a south-east accent…. So if we went to the Houses of*

Parliament, they would not listen to us at all." (young woman living in a hostel)

There were also deemed to be limits on what individuals could achieve collectively, as the following conversation between two carers highlights:

> Female: *"It's very difficult because individual people feel incapable of [making a difference], but I think nowadays people power is becoming more evident. You get marches. You don't think it is?"*

> Male: *"I mean, they highlight a cause, but I don't think they solve it. I mean, you've got the stuff going on here with Tibet at the moment, I mean, you'd think China would sit up and listen but they don't.... It's like the war in Iraq, they do marches, but you highlight a cause but what's done about it? At the end of the day, nothing, they are still fighting Iraq. They are still occupying Tibet."*

As can be seen, finding ways to cope with social evils was a real day-to-day survival issue for many participants in this phase of the 'unheard voices' consultations. The relationship between the truncated opportunities identified in the first-phase discussions, and the sense of power or lack of control that people felt, was complicated and dynamic. It could lead to forms of 'coping' that were either constructive or destructive. People's perspectives on how far individuals could be held responsible for their changing personal situations and for influencing societal change varied both across and within subgroups; as did views about the extent to which it would ever be possible for change to be achieved.

What emerged strongly, however, was a feeling that individual aspiration ought to be balanced and tempered by a sense of collective responsibility and altruism on the part of individuals who 'succeed'. To put it another way, there was a view that – far from being mutually exclusive – individual and collective responsibilities needed to be rediscovered and realigned if social evils were ever to be overcome (see also Chapter 15). Despite all the contradictions and complexities that emerge from the accounts of those who took part in this research, this sentiment emerged both implicitly and explicitly in their accounts. People whose life opportunities had been limited and even wasted, and whose day-to-day lives were profoundly affected by social evils, nevertheless wanted a better life for themselves and recognised that, in order for that to happen, a better world is needed too.

Note
[1] The organisations were the National Association for the Care and Resettlement of Offenders (NACRO); Red Kite Learning, a social enterprise helping disadvantaged people into employment; Supporting Others through Volunteer Action (SOVA), a volunteer mentoring organisation; One Parent Families Scotland (OPFS); One Parent Families/Gingerbread (Manchester); Powys Youth Offending Service (YOS); and Voice of Carers Across Lothian (Vocal).

Reference

Mowlam, A. and Creegan, C. (2008) *Modern-day social evils: The voices of unheard groups*, York: JRF.

SECTION 2

Viewpoints

6

Preface

David Utting

As will be evident from the previous section, the Joseph Rowntree Foundation's online consultation and its series of workshops and discussion groups with people from disadvantaged groups produced a rich variety of views on the nature of contemporary 'social evils' and their consequences. There were inevitable conflicts in many of the views expressed. But there were a number of concrete issues in contemporary Britain that participants identified with relative frequency as well as considerable passion. These included:

- family breakdown and poor parenting;
- misuse of drugs and alcohol;
- violence and crime (especially youth crime);
- inequality and poverty;
- social diversity, immigration and intolerance;
- gender inequality;
- health and social care;
- religion;
- the environment;
- apathy, failed institutions and a democratic deficit.

It was also common for people to discuss these issues in terms of social values, morals and individual or collective traits whose existence (or absence) was also commonly considered 'evil'. They included:

- greed;
- consumerism;
- individualism;
- a weakened sense of community;
- loss of shared values, such as tolerance, compassion and respect.

These public concerns are abstract in ways that not only distinguish them from the associated, but more concrete, issues listed above, but also from the tangible social evils that Joseph Rowntree referred to a hundred years earlier when establishing his trusts. With this in mind, it was decided that one useful way to take forward the debate about contemporary social evils would be to invite a number of prominent political thinkers, practitioners and social commentators to contribute viewpoints, exploring issues raised by the consultation and suggesting solutions.

The authors, whose contributions appear as 11 separate chapters in this section, come from a range of social, cultural, philosophical and ideological backgrounds. While concentrating on particular themes, they were not under any injunction preventing them from ranging across other topics raised in the consultations. Their viewpoints are, therefore, more diverse and overlapping than the titles used to subdivide this section might imply. It should also be noted that while the chosen categories refer to abstract concepts, the author's arguments are often made in concrete terms, and with reference to practical 'real-world' examples.

A decline of values

Under this heading, *Anthony Browne* (former Director of the Policy Exchange think-tank) contends that there have been many moral improvements since the 1950s, but also distinct areas of decline. He argues that the latter include family breakdown, drug and alcohol misuse, welfare dependency and violent crime; all linked to a loss of binding 'social capital'. While clear that state intervention can make matters worse, he calls for politicians to use legislation, where necessary, to put more emphasis on individual responsibilities rather than on rights.

The philosopher *A. C. Grayling* is similarly convinced of the 'liberating power' of self-discipline, but is sceptical about many claims about declining values, disintegrating communities and family breakdown. He also sees nothing inherently wrong in people enjoying their increased power as consumers. Inequality kept within certain bounds is, he argues, a 'norm' in society, whereas poverty (whether 'absolute' or 'relative') is unacceptable.

Julia Neuberger, a rabbi, Liberal Democrat peer and government 'Champion on Volunteering', is more convinced that society has become less caring, especially for older people, and that the sense of mutual obligation that once existed in communities has "taken a battering". She sees part of the problem as an increasingly 'risk-averse' culture among professionals in the caring services, and an obsessive fear of strangers that has encouraged a focus on personal rather than group welfare.

Distrust

Shaun Bailey, writing from the perspective of a black man working with young people in inner London as well as a prospective Conservative parliamentary candidate, describes a loss of trust between different groups, including residents and migrants and adults and young people. While determined that young people should be made aware of their responsibilities and that social excuses for bad behaviour will not wash, he criticises the demonisation of young people in the media. He also decries the 'walk past and don't get involved' culture that leaves people doubting the very nature of humanity.

The writer and journalist *Anna Minton* also condemns a pervasive and disproportionate fear of crime in society, evident in the spread of private 'gated communities' and intensive security in shopping centres as well as restrictive policing on 'problem' estates. Noting the connection that research has exposed between higher levels of trust, greater equality and better mental health, she highlights the role of the media and politicians in creating a damaging climate of fear and mistrust.

The absence of society

For philosopher and sociologist *Zygmunt Bauman*, the most disturbing aspect of contemporary social problems is that they stem from an absence or withdrawal of society, rather than its pressures. Concern with the way the world is managed is, he maintains, giving way to an individualistic concern with self-management and self-promotion. The 'social state' that recognised people's dependence on each other and provided collective insurance against misfortune has been supplanted by a doctrine of individualism stoked by heavily marketed dreams of wealth and celebrity.

Individualism

Neal Lawson, Chair of Compass, the democratic left-wing pressure group, embraces Bauman's notion of excluded 'failed consumers', but adds the concept of 'social recession' where individuals may enjoy greater choice as consumers, but are increasingly disempowered as citizens. Global competition and economic recession have not only left people feeling insecure, but also undermined the cohesion of communities. While he attributes loss of the post-war consensus supporting collective welfare to the 1980s triumph of the New Right, he accuses New Labour of going further in embracing market forces than Margaret Thatcher would ever have dared.

A stronger civil society is also identified by the urban policy specialist *Stephen Thake* as an essential part of any attempt to counter a current loss of social solidarity and retreat into protective individualism. He maintains that new practices are already being established by ordinary people in their communities, ranging from individual decisions to reduce carbon emissions or recycle more waste, to the spread of non-profit community organisations and enterprises. Government's role, he suggests, should be to invest in grassroots activity and foster an expanding role for social enterprises in delivering public services.

Inequality

Chris Creegan, Deputy Director in the Qualitative Research Unit at NatCen (National Centre for Social Research) carried out the consultation exercises described in the previous section of this book that were designed to capture often 'unheard voices' of disadvantaged groups. Inspired by those experiences, he makes an impassioned case against pigeonholing people into categories like 'hard to reach', and in favour of ensuring that their views are communicated to policy makers. Beyond that, he develops the concept of 'truncated opportunities' to describe the way that people's experiences of inequality, poverty and restricted life chances are threaded with stories of loss and waste at different stages of their lives.

Ferdinand Mount, author, political commentator and former advisor to Margaret Thatcher, caused a stir with his 2004 book *Mind the gap*, acknowledging widening social inequalities. He progresses his argument, here, by suggesting that although strides were made towards more equal opportunities in the first three quarters of the 20th century, it came to a halt through failure to address other inequalities that cause estrangement and resentment in society. He discusses income inequalities and unequal access to opportunities for social advancement, but especially emphasises 'inequality of treatment', including the means-testing of benefits.

By contrast, the author and journalist *Jeremy Seabrook* dismisses the political pursuit of 'equality of opportunity' as a 'shallow and meretricious' approach to social, educational and cultural disadvantage. He equates it with support for a 'meritocracy' that conveniently ignores the concentration of supposed 'merit' among those already favoured by birth or wealth. The huge increase in wealth and income standards since the Second World War has contributed, he suggests, to the dissolution of collective action among the minority who are poor. However, with 'heroic age of consumption' now seemingly over, he believes that there may be greater scope to question conventions that equate wealth with progress and regard money as a source of hope.

These synopses can give only a flavour of the viewpoints, and the contrasting styles and enthusiasms of their authors. Collectively, they can be seen to contribute additional layers and depths of meaning to the perspectives identified by the consultations described in the previous section.[1] Readers can look forward to honing their own views by investigating the authors' detailed arguments and discovering for themselves the undoubted areas of consensus as well as disagreement on contemporary social evils.[2]

Notes

[1] Longer versions of the 'Viewpoints' can be found on the Joseph Rowntree Foundation's social evils website www.socialevils.org.uk. These essays were mostly written in the first six months of 2008. The authors have had an opportunity to update their contributions for this book in the light of the deepening economic recession at the turn of the year.

[2] In addition to the published essays, a number of 'live' debates between the authors were organised in the autumn of 2008. These can be downloaded as podcasts from the website.

Reference

Mount, F. (2004) *Mind the gap: Class in Britain now*, London: Short Books.

A decline of values

—
7

Has there been a decline in values in British society?

Anthony Browne

Is there really a problem?

It was once said that a Victorian who fell asleep in 1848 would not have recognised his country if he awoke in 1851. So it is not unreasonable to assume that Victorians waking up in early 21st-century Britain would not only find their country unrecognisable, but also be profoundly shocked by it. They would no doubt be astonished by the technical wizardry and stunned by social changes such as the universal franchise (even of young un-propertied women!), the demise of the peerage and the multiracial society. But changes in values would surely perturb them the most. Among the most striking would be:

- the demise of marriage between heterosexual couples;
- the existence of marriage between homosexual and mixed-race couples;
- the quarter of dependent children living with only one parent;
- the millions of non-disabled people paid by the state to be idle;

- the disappearance of deference (even to the monarch); and
- the empty pews on Sundays (and the full mosques on Fridays).

Everything the Victorians held most dear – the Christian, God-fearing ethos, the family, marriage, the monarch and the value of hard work – would appear to them to have been decimated.

Values change dramatically over a century, but also over decades. This is highlighted by the fact that when 10 mainly Eastern European countries joined the European Union (EU) in 2004, European Commission officials said that admission would have been unacceptable on human rights grounds if they had not legalised homosexuality. Yet when Ireland joined the EU in 1971, homosexuality was illegal in that country, and remained so until 1993. What changed in the intervening years were shared values, the prism through which we interpret our laws. Our values have, indeed, altered beyond recognition within the course of a single lifespan. Attitudes to sexuality, lone parenthood, marriage, race, welfare benefits, alcohol, drugs and violent crime have all been transformed.

People are bound to be confused if the fundamental values they grew up with have been ditched by society by the time they hit middle age. They invariably tend to see any change as threatening. It is part of the psychology of problem-solving humans to quickly take for granted any positive changes, but to dwell angrily and at length over negative ones. An inevitable consequence is that quickly changing values – unless the changes are overwhelmingly positive – lead to a widespread sense of decline. Thus, a poll conducted in 2007 for the BBC by ComRes found that 83% of people believed that Britain was in moral decline, with only 9% disagreeing. This sense of moral decline was felt overwhelmingly across all social classes and in all regions of the country.

But while values change, panic about their decline is also one of the constants of history. The 16th- and 17th-century Puritans despaired of drama, dancing and games of chance. Aldous Huxley wrote *Brave new world* out of fear of the lack of morals in the roaring 1920s (Huxley, 1932). Since then, we have had moral panics about Teddy Boys, Mods and Rockers, Hells Angels, skinheads and hippies. And each moral panic turned out to be ill-founded: at least in the long run.

The study of cyclical moral panics has produced a whole genre of academic literature. In *Moral panics: The social construction of deviance*, Erich Goode and Nachman Ben-Yehuda anatomise three moral crusades to hit the US – the prohibition movement from 1900 to 1920, the anti-marijuana movement in the 1930s and the sexual psychopath laws of the 1930s to 1950s (Goode and Nachman, 1994). The classic text *Folk devils and moral panics* was written by Stan Cohen in 1972 and its 30th anniversary edition was updated with the 1993 case of the murder of Jamie Bulger by two 10-year-old boys (Cohen, 2003). This triggered a prolonged wave of national moral panic, about a new breed of feral children, absent fathers and violent videos. *The Sun* newspaper called for 'a crusade to rescue a sick society', while *The Independent* declared that 'Britain is a worried country, and it has a lot to be worried about'.

Yet in the grand scheme of things, it is difficult to make a case for long-term decline. It is one of our open secrets, rarely admitted in public discourse, that in almost all measurable ways life is better now for Britons than it has ever been. We are healthier, wealthier, wiser (or at least better educated) and freer. Compared to 100 years ago, it is not just our lives, but also our values that are also almost incomparably better; defined in the functional sense that widely held abstract beliefs inflict less unnecessary misery on individuals. Catholics have been emancipated, women liberated and the poor enfranchised. Children of unmarried parents and single mothers are no longer shunned, homosexuals are no longer imprisoned, girls are no longer left uneducated, black people are no longer banned from shops and poor people are no longer routinely left to die because of lack of basic care. The historical increase in tolerance and fairness is an unequivocal improvement in our values.

But people are not comparing 'now' to the 19th century. Their point of comparison is, rather, with their own childhoods. Many clearly remember the 1950s, a comparatively crime-free era of strong communities and solid families (albeit with endemic homophobia, sexism, poverty and racism). It is the sense of decline in their own lifetimes that causes such concern. Thus, while moral panics may be one of the constants of history, it would be too simplistic to dismiss the concerns of 83% of the population as paranoia fuelled by a scare-mongering media. Family breakdown, drug use, alcohol abuse and welfare dependency have all unequivocally increased in the last 20 years, as has violent crime by some measures. A mere glance at the 2008 edition of *Social trends*, published by the Office for National Statistics, will satisfy the most ghoulish of appetites. For example, the number of people identifying drug dealing as a local problem doubled between 1992 and 2006, while the number of people worried about teenagers hanging around on the streets was up by half. Death rates from alcohol abuse had almost doubled since 1991. There were 32,000 children on the child protection register, and spending on social security had almost doubled since 1978. Britain also had a record number of people in prison (ONS, 2008).

The growth of violent crime

While society has persistently been worried about yobbish male youths, we are now also worried about criminal girl gangs. Figures from the Youth Justice Board (*The Times*, 16 May 2008) show that the number of crimes committed by girls aged 10 to 17 climbed from 47,000 in 2003/04 to 59,000 in 2006/07. But it is not just the media that regards the stories behind these statistics as alarming. The judiciary, teachers and the police all bemoan the state of our national morals. Judge Anthony Russell, in sentencing two youths who drunkenly kicked a gap-year student to death because she was a Goth, said:

> *This was feral thuggery of a kind that is quite unacceptable. It raises serious questions about the state of the society which exists in this country at the beginning of the new millennium, which was heralded with such optimism. (The Times, 29 April 2008)*

The Labour government has trumpeted a decline in property crimes – largely a result of the decreasing resale value of electronic goods – but statistics show that violent crimes have been rising sharply in recent years, with those using guns and knives rising the fastest. Home Office figures show that the number of people injured in firearm incidents rose from 864 in 1998/89 to 3,821 in 2005/06 (Home Office, 2007). Assaults and injuries from knives and sharp implements led to 12,340 people going to hospital in England and Wales in 2007, a 19% rise on five years ago. The number of children suffering stab wounds nearly doubled from 95 in 2002/03 to 179 in 2006/07. In the first seven months of 2008, 31 teenagers were shot or stabbed to death in Britain. Children openly tell newspapers that everyone they know carries knives for protection.

Parents of the victims frequently blame the decline in values for their tragedy. In a BBC radio interview, Richard Taylor, whose son Damilola was stabbed to death in a Peckham housing estate, said:

> *"There is a breakdown of moral values in Peckham and some other areas of London. We are living in a world which requires discipline. If there is no discipline in society, things like this will become so rampant in society." (BBC News, 18 June 2001)*

Barry Mizen, whose 16-year-old son Jimmy was killed with a shard of glass in a London bakery in 2008, said:

People are saying something must be done. I just wonder how futile it is with more and more legislation and laws. Perhaps we all need to look to ourselves and look to the values we would like. (The Independent, 18 May 2008)

The breakdown of the family

Most notably, there has been a collapse of the traditional nuclear family. This is true across Europe, but is most acute in the UK. Fewer people get married in the UK than in most other EU countries, and those who do are the most likely to get divorced. The UK also has the highest proportion of single-parent families in Europe, at 24%. Our children are more likely to engage in under-age sex, and they are more likely to get pregnant. A report for the United Nations agency UNICEF found that young people in the UK were suffering greater deprivation, worse relationships with their parents and were exposed to more risks from alcohol, drugs and unsafe sex than children in any other developed country (UNICEF, 2007). A study by the children's charity NCH noted a doubling of emotional problems and conduct disorders among young people since the 1930s. One in 10 children now have a mental health disorder to a 'clinically significant' level. Nearly a quarter of children live in official poverty, and they are more obese than before (*The Times*, 20 June 2007).

Mr Justice Coleridge, a senior family division judge in England and Wales, has voiced the view that Britain is being gripped by an epidemic of family failure:

In some of the more heavily-populated urban areas of this country, family life is, quite frankly, in meltdown or completely unrecognisable. In some areas of the country, family life in the old sense no longer exists. (Daily Mail, 4 April 2008)

The decline of social capital

What statistics do not measure is the unease in people's lives: a pervasive sense that society is fracturing, that there are no longer any shared values and that no one can trust anyone anymore. 'Social capital', the glue that binds society together, is a vague concept. But however measured, there seems little doubt that there has, in recent years, been a decline. Francis Fukuyama, author of *The great disruption*, which charts the breakdown of social norms in the 1960s and 1970s, defines social capital as the 'set of informal values or norms shared among members of a group that permits co-operation among them' (Fukuyama, 1999). Its decline, he argues, has led to family breakdown, rising crime and the demise of shared values and trust.

Across Left and Right, few dispute that social capital has been receding. Robert Putnam, the liberal American sociologist, plotted the demise of social capital in the US in his totemic book *Bowling alone* (Putnam, 2000). Dr John Sentamu, the Ugandan-born Archbishop of York, declared that Britain had lost its way, warning that 'the loss of purpose has led to a crisis in Britain and a crisis in Christianity. Britain is in a very, very uncomfortable place' (*Daily Telegraph*, 2 March 2008). The Pakistan-born Bishop of Rochester, Michael Nazir-Ali, blamed the social and sexual revolution of the 1960s and 1970s for a moral vacuum being filled by self-indulgence and radical Islam (*Daily Telegraph*, 29 May 2008). The Conservative peeress and crime author P.D. James declared in a speech on 21st-century policing that there is now little that binds us to our fellow humans: 'Our society is now more fractured than I in my long life have ever known it,' she said (*Daily Telegraph*, 2 May 2008). Increasingly there is a risk that we live with a strong commitment to our local community, but little contact with those outside it. Mutual respect and understanding and recognition of our common humanity cannot be nurtured in isolation.

Why have our values changed?

The two big remaining questions are: why have our values changed, and what should be done about it? Changes in values often trail social changes, which are themselves driven by technological and economic changes. Sometimes they reflect a decline in traditional elites that used values to uphold their status. Sometimes values change as a result of increased knowledge. To quote John Maynard Keynes: 'When the facts change, I change my mind' (Malabre, 1995). Sometimes, social and economic changes collide to reinforce a trend. The taboo of divorce has withered partly as a result of the growing financial independence of women, partly of growing societal affluence and partly of the increase in life expectancy. Financial independence means that women can now afford to leave their husbands, while growing affluence means that women no longer routinely marry men much older than themselves to achieve financial security. Changing divorce laws both reflected the change in attitudes and accelerated them. Mass education and literacy has, meanwhile, led to the passing of the age of deference. People from ordinary backgrounds are now willing to question and dispute with those to whom in earlier times they would have just listened.

This might be uncomfortable for elites, but this empowerment of the masses is an enormous strengthening of society as a whole. No longer can 'donkeys' lead 'lions' into battle, as they did in the First World War. The problem is that the age of deference has swung to the other extreme of an age of cynicism, where large sections of society hold all authority in contempt.

There is no single underlying and overwhelming cause to the decline in social capital over recent decades. Rather, there has been a whole barrage of smaller causes, each chipping away at our former moral confidence. Each cause in itself is relatively insignificant, and each could on its own terms be welcomed. But combined they have so weakened our values and beliefs that we are now left with pervasive anxiety. Whether you look on the 1960s as a good or bad decade, there is no doubt that it was preceded by a commonly assumed set of values that simply does not exist now. The received moral orthodoxies of 1950s society were undermined by countercultural revolutionaries who set out to destroy the suffocating conventions and hierarchies by making 'love not war' and by 'turning on, tuning in and dropping out'. Their path was smoothed by the decline of mainstream religion in our sceptical, know-it-all, believe-nothing scientific age. Even atheists like myself have to accept that organised religion helps provide a common set of beliefs that can tie society together. In highly religious societies, such as Middle-East Islamic ones, there can be such strong, shared values that social capital can be very high.

The decline of a unifying religious belief system has been fuelled not just by the astonishing success of science at giving God-like powers to men, but also by the rise of the television and the jumbo jet. While television marketed the attractions of Western life to other parts of the planet, the growing ease of international transport made it possible for more people to migrate. The dramatic rise in immigration to Britain from the developing world has turned a largely monocultural society into a multicultural one in the space of a generation. Instead of a single religion unifying the country, a supermarket of different religions are competing cheek by jowl; each with its own value system.

Instinctive classical and social liberals like myself find it astonishing that debate is being reopened on such varied issues as forced marriages, gay rights, violence against women and the rights and wrongs of sending Christmas cards. The profusion of beliefs has been complicated by an unthinking moral relativism that has taken the anti-establishment message of the 1960s to intellectually unsustainable extremes. In the wake of the terrorist attacks of September 11th 2001 in New York and Washington (and subsequently those in Bali, Madrid and London), the discrepancies between moral relativism, multiculturalism and liberalism has sent shockwaves through the intellectual Left. We have seen Britain's most prominent race campaigner Trevor Phillips using almost blood-curdling language about the need to ditch multiculturalism (Asthana and Hinsliff, 2004). These are complex, confusing times for any well-meaning citizen who just wants to get on with their life. Robert Putnam (2000) has used the term 'hunkering down' to describe the defensive behaviour of people living in multicultural societies they do not understand where they cut themselves off from what is going on around them.

Believing little, Britons have been engorging themselves with an anti-intellectual obsession with celebrity and consumption. The psychologist Oliver James has pronounced that Anglo-Saxon countries are particularly prone to what he dubbed 'the Affluenza virus' – a set of values that increase our vulnerability to psychological distress by placing a high value on acquiring money, looking good in the eyes of others and wanting to be famous. He argues that these increase our susceptibility to depression, anxiety, substance abuse and personality disorder, and prevent us from fulfilling such basic human needs as a sense of security, competence and connectedness to others. When a society prefers to relate to itself through the 'Big Brother' household, it is not surprising that it has profound problems (James, 2007).

However, multiculturalism and moral relativism have little to do with another major factor in our present social decline – the demise of the family. Causes range from the decline of religion to a very welcome rise in financial independence for women. The consequences – in terms of poverty, educational underachievement and antisocial behaviour – are well known. The lack of father figures, of a stable home environment and of an inculcated sense of right and wrong has set a large section of our youth adrift with nothing to hold on to except the feeling of belonging that gang membership gives them and the short-lived high of fear-induced respect achieved by waving a knife or gun.

Beyond moral relativism and the decline of the family, lies a lost sense of individual responsibility towards other members of society. This has arisen from the growth of the rights-based culture and the inexorable growth of the state into every aspect of our life. The rights culture originally had a lot to commend it. Enshrined in various international post-war treaties (the United Nations Convention on Human Rights, the European Convention on Human Rights), it was designed to stop dictatorships re-emerging by protecting individuals from the abuse of governments. 'Human rights' has progressed inexorably into an almost overwhelming legal doctrine, and has permeated almost every aspect of our culture. But the conventions are largely fighting yesterday's battles, not today's. The main threat to society is no longer from the actions of dictatorial governments, but from the actions of law-breaking individuals, whether violent criminals or terrorists. As recent Home Secretaries have found, human rights legislation makes it more difficult to fight these problems because it gives rights to the perpetrators while limiting the capacity of government to tackle them. More importantly, human rights laws place no emphasis at all on the responsibilities of individuals. A generation has grown up believing that they have rights their predecessors could only dream of, such as freedom from physical punishment, the right not to be discriminated against, free universal healthcare, or the right to receive benefits without having to work. At the same time, they do not think they have the responsibilities to others that their predecessors would have taken for granted – such as caring for elderly relatives, raising children in a stable environment or working when able. People, consequently, only think about their own concerns without thinking about the impact of their actions on society around them. This mass solipsism is corrosive for society and is the antithesis of social capital.

The effect of the rights culture has been reinforced by the growth of the state and other changes that have withered away a sense of duty. Children no longer feel that they have to make sacrifices looking after their parents because they know the state will do it. People do not feel it a duty to help vulnerable people because their taxes pay for public workers to do the job for them. Perhaps most corrosive of all is the welfare culture. Introduced for a very good reason – to fight destitution – it has ceased to be seen as a last-resort safety net and has led to mass dependency. Social housing, although very necessary, all too often becomes a trap discouraging social mobility. Incapacity Benefit gives a financial reward to people for persuading others that they are 'unwell', rather than encouraging them to do their best. There can, indeed, be few things more indicative of a retreat from the Protestant work ethic than the state paying people not to work because they are addicted to drugs or alcohol. However, the number of people on Incapacity Benefit as a result of such addictions has doubled from 48,700 in 1997 to over 101,300 in 2007. The British government pays more people not to work because they are chemically addicted than it employs in the army.

Technology, too, has played its part in promoting individualism, eroding conversation and shared experiences. We no longer have to make music together in social gatherings because we have electronically canned it. We do not have to interact with others because we can play with computers. We no longer have to watch the same film in the cinema as our whole community because we have televisions at home; we no longer watch with our family because we all have televisions in our bedrooms; and we no longer watch the same programmes as others because of multi-channel television. The rise of text messages and emails has eroded the most fundamental communication of all – talking face to face. We order online from our solitude at home and no longer have to talk to a cashier in the shops.

What can be done?

Policy makers are left wondering what can be done about all this. The first challenge is to be clear about which changes have been for the good and which for the bad. For example, the legalisation of homosexuality was an undoubted improvement, as was the decline of the taboo in premarital sex. There are many other things we would not want to change because the benefits they bring are so large. We do not want to un-invent female emancipation, even if the earlier lack of freedom of women meant fewer families broke up. We cannot un-invent television.

Even where there is widespread agreement that we should tackle aspects of our moral and social decline, government has been notably ineffective. In Britain in 2008, we have tried a decade of ever-more draconian laws to curb behaviour, such as binge drinking; but it has simply got worse. Behaviour can be powerfully affected by a change in culture, but a change in culture is notoriously difficult to achieve. For half a century we have had a value system that declared that the state knows best, and had the right to intervene in the most private part of people's lives. That, hopefully, is now on the wane.

There are many other things we can do, too; not least to start talking about the problems. Politicians can use their pulpit to bring to national attention some of the issues that we face as a nation. We can shift legislation, so it puts more emphasis on responsibilities than on rights (such as a responsibility to do community work in return for unemployment benefit). But there is no magic bullet. We should be concerned, but not despair. We have an open society that talks about and confronts its problems in a generally honest manner, which is the first step to making things better. Each age has been concerned about moral decline. Ours is no exception – although a lot of what is happening to society now is exceptional.

References

Asthana, A. and Hinsliff, G. (2004) 'Equality chief branded as "right wing"', *The Observer*, 4 April, www.guardian.co.uk/uk/2004/apr/04/race.britishidentity

Cohen, S. (2003) *Folk devils and moral panics* (3rd edition), London: Routledge.

Fukuyama, F. (1999) *The great disruption*, New York, NY: Simon & Schuster.

Goode, E. and Nachman, B.-Y. (1994) *Moral panics: The social construction of deviance*, Cambridge, MA: Wiley-Blackwell.

Home Office (2007) *Statistical Bulletin 2005/06*, London: Home Office.

Huxley, A. (1932) *Brave new world*, London: Chatto and Windus.

James, O. (2007) *Affluenza: How to be successful and stay sane*, London: Vermillion.

Malabre, A.L. (1995) *Lost prophets: An insider's history of the modern economists*, Cambridge, MA: Harvard Business School Press.

ONS (Office for National Statistics) (2008) *Social trends*, Basingstoke: Palgrave Macmillan.

Putnam, R.D. (2000) *Bowling alone: The collapse and revival of American community*, New York, NY: Simon & Schuster.

UNICEF (2007) *An overview of child well-being in rich countries*, Innocenti Report Card 7, Florence: UNICEF Innocenti Research Centre.

8

Social evils and social good

A.C. Grayling

For a student of ethics and history, the Joseph Rowntree Foundation's (JRF) consultations on social evils confirm the observation that every generation thinks that the past was a better place, and that its own time is one of crisis. Yet by almost any standard one cares to mention, contemporary Western liberal democratic societies offer greatly better lives for the great majority of people than was the case 50 or 100 years ago. In late Victorian London — whose streets swarmed with child prostitutes, where it was too dangerous to walk at night and abject poverty and suffering were a norm — life was much less pleasant, safe, civilised and well provided than it is now. I would not myself wish to be a woman in any other period of history or part of today's world, than in contemporary Western democracies. This fact alone, concerning half of humanity, should be evidence that the great majority in today's UK arguably live in some of the best times and places, from the point of view of individual human experience and opportunity.

This does not mean that there are no problems in contemporary society — far from it — but it does mean that they need to be put into perspective. There is always a risk that debate on these issues will be biased towards the opinions of those who feel exercised by their perceptions of what is wrong in society. This makes it a matter of the first importance that such perceptions should be put into context and examined. If public policy is determined by the attitudes of the more conservative and fretful members of society, who see bogeymen under the bed when none are there, the resulting distortions will be harmful. The social evils first expressed by a self-selected, concerned minority, are then inflated by the media, and finally acted on by governments wishing to placate manufactured 'public opinion'. The skewed results, not infrequently, make matters worse rather than better.

Four debateable social evils

For that reason, I want to question and challenge some of the attitudes and views expressed in the JRF consultation, beginning with the four main evils identified.

'A decline of community'

It is true that communities of a more traditional kind, such as existed in villages or working–class suburbs two generations ago, are much less common because of increased mobility and population diversity. That is the neutral fact, which some see as regrettable and others as a marker of social, economic and demographic change, bringing considerable advantages with it. Many of the functions traditionally performed by neighbourliness, such as help in times of trouble, mutual support and sharing of information, have been taken over by public institutions such as schools, the health service, the media, the police and other civil society organisations. All of these arose because traditional community life was insufficiently regular, reliable, organised and resourced to be a sure basis of support. That society has shouldered these responsibilities in place of the uncertain abilities and inclinations of neighbours is assuredly a gain.

Lament over the demise of traditional forms of community overlooks the new forms of community, especially among the young, made possible by the internet. The internet gives wider, even international, reach to acquaintanceship and friendship with opportunities for sharing experience and learning about others. This can only be a good thing. True, the internet allows for various kinds of abuses too, but that has also been a risk with more traditional community relations. Whereas community tended once to be highly local and, therefore, exclusive of other communities (even the village down the road), public media have created a far wider range of shared experience and knowledge. 'Community' has become a larger concept as a result. With the institutionalisation of community activity through pooled resources (such as the National Health Service) a much better framework for individual life is assured.

'Individualism'

It is true that individualism can lead to selfishness and insularity, but both these characteristics were present in the past. One need only think of the narrow-minded, lace-curtain-twitching village community of continual observation and nosiness, which could blight lives. Greater scope for individual expression of life possibilities is a positive thing; autonomy in the moral and social spheres is as much an opportunity as a demand for responsible self-determination and self-reliance. The scope afforded by individualism is not inconsistent with community and cooperation, which becomes voluntary and selective rather than being imposed. Historically, church and state sought to impose uniformities of belief and behaviour, and punished divergence, including death for heresy. A key to the Enlightenment of the 18th century was the concept of individual autonomy, the responsibility to think for oneself and to take responsibility for choices and values. It provided the freedom to pursue personal goals and interests: subject always to the principle of not harming others or interfering with others' freedom.

'Individualism' is thus the opposite of any view enjoining conformity and uniformity, and the limitations required to ensure them. But it is not the opposite of appropriate altruism and concern for others. Its pejorative use to denote selfishness and lack of concern for others is a misuse. The right terms are the words 'selfishness' and 'lack of concern for others' themselves. In all ages and all moral systems these are rightly regarded as lamentable characteristics. Today, as throughout history, there is a perception that selfishness and lack of concern for others is increasing. The explanation for this is straightforward: as children in the great majority of homes, we experience courtesies of social intercourse in relation to our parents' friends and relations that exist far less in the bustling public arena when we grow into adults. This creates the illusion of a breakdown in civil intercourse, for which individualism is blamed. But it is much more the function of a contrast between the worlds we occupy as children and as adults.

Personal autonomy and responsibility, self-determination and independence are, in fact, far more likely to promote than degrade concern for others. Any reflective individual recognises that humans are social animals, that individuals benefit from cooperation and mutuality, and that the fullest growth of individual potential lies in a social setting. To stress the point: 'cooperation and mutuality' are not 'conformity and uniformity'; individualism is the rejection of the latter, not the former.

'Consumerism and greed'

The enjoyment of quality goods and services was once the province of the rich and privileged alone. One thinks of Venice in history as the trading post for luxury goods – silks, spices, glassware, art and the like

– which relatively few could afford. Now that Western societies are richer and freer, such enjoyment is a far more widespread phenomenon; the opportunities to beautify one's home, dress well, enjoy travel and leisure and take pleasure in rewarding one's labours with choosing, buying and owning constitute a legitimate activity. The idea that people are manipulated into consumerism by advertisers is at best a very partial truth; witness the canniness of shoppers, their eye for a bargain and the way that economic downturn has immediately affected retail sales in the high street. This is proof that people are generally autonomous in decisions about what they buy. By the same token their consumption, when they have the cash for it, is equally considered.

Everything is subject at the margins to abuse and addiction, and there are people for whom consumption is an end in itself. But most consumption is instrumental. It acts as a means to enjoyment and the satisfactions that possession offers. It is an added value that the process itself is often pleasurable – as the humorous reference to 'retail therapy' implies. It is an austere view indeed that says we should not reward ourselves in this way with the money we earn by our own labours. It misses the point that the good and well-lived life must be satisfying for the one living it, as well as fruitful in good towards others.

'A decline of values: lack of a sense of right and wrong'

As an example of a conviction that 'the grass was greener when we were young', this is a classic. The vast majority of people live responsible lives, and there is wide agreement about what is right and wrong in society. All the focus of public discussion in the media tends to be about the areas where, as in any period of its history, there is negotiation about changing attitudes. Think, for example, of the legalisation of homosexual sex between consenting adults, and the greater social acceptance of gay people. Some fiercely opposed (some still oppose) acceptance of homosexuality, believing that the country was in steep moral decline because it was admitting the sin of Sodom. Others thought we were achieving a moral advance by being more understanding, inclusive, generous and humane in our attitudes.

People look back to Victorian times as more moral and restrained. But while middle-class Victorians were undoubtedly more moralistic, this was surely because so many people were less morally restrained in practice. A profoundly inequitable society saw tens of thousands struggle and sometimes starve in abject poverty, not infrequently being forced into crime to survive. The better off were largely indifferent to their plight – itself a moral outrage of a kind that throws our own age into a favourable light by comparison. Our own time is emphatically more moral, equitable, just and caring. We have a welfare safety net for those in difficulty. We have a National Health Service open to all and free at the point of need. We try to provide everyone with an education to give them a platform for making something of themselves in life. And our legal system is independent and technically everyone is equal before it.

Of course, disparities in wealth continue to play their role in making society unequal. Those with money can get medical and legal services of a quality barred to those without the same level of wealth. Disparities in wealth are not inequitable, but they are a cost of having the kind of society we have, rather than Victorian arrangements where the haphazard and uneven application of charity or community was the only protection people had against the abyss.

Six concrete social evils

Taking issue with participants in the JRF consultation over the four most salient social evils does not, however, entail disagreement with six other social evils that were frequently identified. Here too, though, there is a need for qualification and care.

'The decline of the family'

There have always been dysfunctional families, especially among communities suffering from poverty and low educational aspirations on the part of the parents. Population growth has increased this sector in absolute terms, although one would confidently predict that in proportional terms the number of dysfunctional families in contemporary society is far less than a century ago. One would further surmise that the proportions vary between the native British community and some immigrant communities with different traditions of family life. Generally, however, fewer people marry, more people divorce and one-parent families are commonplace. Yet one-parent families were also common in the 20th century during two world wars because of soldiering duties and military fatalities. There is no evidence to suggest that this fact was, by itself, socially destructive.

Rather, there continue to be certain negative consequences of a family having only one parent in it, such as poverty and lack of a (usually male) role model, which can cause problems for children. Adequate resources and the presence of helpful others in a family's circle of acquaintance go a long way to address these problems, as does the quality of parenting provided by the single parent. There is no inevitability that one-parent families will produce dysfunctional children, and it is unhelpful to people who valiantly parent single-handedly, whether through widowhood or divorce, to be told that their children are doomed to difficulties because of mere arithmetic. It is not the arithmetic of one-parent families that is the problem so much as what it can mean if the result of lone parenthood is poverty and lack of support.

None of this implies that it is not better for children to have as many loving and caring adults in their lives as possible. I express this in terms that allow for gay couples to be as good parents as heterosexual couples, and that acknowledge that children are best off with a variety of adults to be loved by, including grandparents and uncles and aunts. All can make a contribution to the confidence and good socialisation of children. This is what should best be meant by 'family'. But there are good and happy families with only one parent in them, and achieving the best for children is the desideratum that society should work towards without preconceptions about traditional family models.

'The behaviour and treatment of young people'

In 2008, the Youth Justice Board announced a 'further drop' in crimes committed by youths, and issued the information that the great majority of youth crime consists of theft (such as shoplifting) and 'minor assaults'. No crime is acceptable, but the perception that a significant sector of the youth population is engaged in crime is misleading; even more so the belief that youths often engage in serious crime. This can confidently be said even in the light of knife crime, which mainly involves youths and young adults. As a proportion of crimes committed by these age groups, knife crimes are, fortunately, a tiny fraction of 1% – although even that is too much. Again, the media focus on youth crime and knife crime greatly inflates the problem. This is not to say that there is no problem, but that its scale and nature require a proper perspective.

Another cause for concern about some young people is the fact that discourtesy and inconsiderate behaviour goes unchecked, or when challenged by adults is sometimes met with violence. A major part of the reason is, indeed, likely to be a breakdown of discipline in some homes, or its uneven and ill-considered over-application. There are also questions about the assertion of discipline in schools, given that sanctions employed in the past are no longer legal or acceptable. There are, likewise, questions about the withdrawal of certain kinds of policing that gave bobbies on the beat an extension of the parental role in checking misbehaviour. The presence of rowdiness in some areas of towns and cities, notably at certain times of the week, is probably far greater in appearance and volume than actual numbers. Most young people in most of the country are not involved.

A contributory factor is something that is, in itself, either neutral or good: the greater freedom, mobility, spending power and communication capacity (with mobile telephones and internet resources) of young people. Trying to solve the problem of antisocial behaviour by limiting these things would be counterproductive. The use of antisocial behaviour orders (ASBOs) has likewise been counterproductive: for a certain sort of young male these are regarded as badges of honour; for those with civil liberties concerns, they seem an inappropriate response to subcriminal behaviour. The problem results partly from the factors mentioned above and partly from the lengthened time that young people are kept in the relatively disempowered status of minors. Given the paradoxical mobility and spending power considerations, this creates ambiguities and tensions. In times past, the period between the onset of adolescence and full adult status often coincided with apprenticeship or military service for males, and apprenticeship or early marriage for females. Responsibility and status are powerful incentives for young people to behave more sensibly, but in our present arrangement of society they have capacity (mobility, money) without status and responsibility. This is an unhelpful combination for some, especially those for whom school is irksome and unsatisfying.

This is not the place to set out a full menu of options for dealing with the problem, but it must include finding ways of giving young people responsibility, recognition, self-respect and a chance to acquire and internalise self-discipline. Self-discipline is, I would suggest, the greatest boon anyone can have. It is the liberating power par excellence and transforms life for the better in almost every case. This implies changes of structure and practice in education from puberty onwards. Ideally, education would be mixed with paid work and involve older youths in educating younger youths and inculcating responsibility towards others. Responsibility advances maturity and personal growth because it is educative, provides insights and satisfies the need for a means to self-respect and self-worth. Hooligan behaviour is seen by some youths as a means to the same ends simply because better ways of achieving them are absent.

'Drugs and alcohol'

Conjoining 'drugs' and 'alcohol' illustrates a problem that society has created for itself: criminalising certain drugs and their use, yet accepting and tolerating alcohol – a drug that is every bit as harmful and dangerous as most proscribed drugs. Why is the way one dangerous drug – alcohol – is handled so different from the treatment of others such as cocaine, heroin and marijuana? The failed experiment of Prohibition in the US in the 1920s teaches two valuable lessons that a mature and sensible society ought to take on board. The first is that outlawing alcohol and its consumption is not socially practicable and creates a huge criminal industry. The second is that the use and abuse of alcohol are separable questions. Age limits, licensing restrictions, penalties for driving or using machinery while intoxicated (the word, remember, means 'poisoned') by alcohol, work to keep alcohol use and abuse within acceptable bounds. Replace the word 'alcohol' with the words 'cocaine', 'heroin' or 'marijuana' in the two previous sentences and similar considerations would seem to apply. Yet society has burdened itself with massive policing costs, and has outlawed and marginalised sections of the community, in its effort to apply temperance principles to drugs. It has thereby created a drug crime industry with gang warfare and murder among the consequences.

Drugs (including alcohol) are harmful, especially when abused, but criminalising them makes a not very good situation vastly worse. To decriminalise drugs and their use, and to place them into the same framework as alcohol, would not result in a mass epidemic of drug taking any more than the legality of alcohol results in permanent population-wide drunkenness. It would reduce the allure of drugs, free police time and wipe out the criminal drug industry at a stroke.

'Poverty and inequality'

Putting 'poverty' and 'inequality' together muddles the question from the outset. Inequality is a norm in societies where, quite justly, greater effort, attainment and talent are valued over laziness, lack of ambition or having less to offer. Inequality is not the same thing as inequity (injustice), which is, of course, unacceptable. If inequalities exist because some are deliberately excluded from opportunity, education or healthcare, then those inequalities are unjust. But overall our society endeavours to level the playing field somewhat, through such institutions as nationally provided education and healthcare and a fair legal system. 'Somewhat' is the right word here because private education and health, and the unequal distribution of wealth at the starting point, skew the system unequally and therefore sometimes inequitably. This itself is the result of the 'equitable inequality' that begins with differences in effort and talent, but causes imbalance later: typically with advantages conferred on the children of successful people. So it is right that there should be constant efforts to redistribute in favour of the less advantaged – again, through education, health and the legal framework. That inequalities persist is a cost of the other benefits that accrue from the arrangements of contemporary Western liberal democracies. So long as continual efforts at rebalancing are maintained, it is a cost worth paying.

Poverty is an entirely different matter. In any society it is corrosive and disabling for those who suffer it. A society might be unequal, but its bottom layers might still have a decent sufficiency of the necessities of life, plus opportunities to enjoy other goods that ameliorate life and add to the value of lived experience. The ideal is, consequently, a society without poverty, even if there are inequalities of wealth. Poverty is either relative or absolute. Having to subsist on a dollar a day or less, and having to walk for miles to get clean water, is the experience of absolute poverty in third-world countries. People suffering relative poverty in today's Britain might have a television set, a car and somewhere to live and yet be poor relative to the average.

It can be argued that relative poverty is worse than the absolute poverty experienced in developing countries, because at the same time as fostering resentment, it prevents people from participation in society on a fair basis with fellow citizens – thus resulting in exclusion. While some enjoy very high standards of living and others suffer deprivation and immiseration, a society cannot be regarded as decent. The effort to redress this imbalance through welfare and employment schemes is right, although few societies have yet found the magic mix of incentives and requirements to help people help themselves out of poverty. No society in which the poverty of some is necessary for the wealth and well-being of others is acceptable. This is not, and need not be, the case in liberal Western democracies.

'Immigration, unfairness and intolerance'

Immigration is far too large a question to be dealt with here, except to say that the JRF consultation correctly emphasised the point that social problems are prompted from two directions: from those who feel hostile or intolerant towards immigrants and fear that their presence will cause social division; and from those who suffer from the discrimination engendered by the foregoing attitudes, and who occasionally exacerbate the difficulty by their own reaction. Those who object to immigration all too often do so on grounds that are uncomfortably close to racism and xenophobia. At the same time, the impact of immigration can be negative, giving rise to criticism of the way that government has handled the question. Muslim communities in Britain have assimilated less well and are perceived to be more divisive than (to cite the prime examples of uncomplicated 'fitting in' while retaining distinctive cultural elements) the Jewish and Chinese communities. This is the chief reason why 'multiculturalism' is now perceived as a failure, with a demand for different and better solutions to the genuine problems that immigration poses.

'Crime and violence'

Crime and violence are endemic in human societies and always have been. They are a perennial problem caused by relatively few, but placing a great strain on society as a whole in costs of policing, criminal justice, penal institutions, and loss and harm to citizens. Continuing with efforts to prevent crime and to minimise its impact when it happens is the rent we pay for the benefits we enjoy in the kind of society we have; namely, a society where there are private property and differentials in income and wealth and where ordinary management of life is a complex matter. Because of these facts there will always be a small proportion of people who will not or cannot live legitimately, and who will therefore prey on the majority to get what they want by the shortcut of crime. This is not new, and people (aided by the media) tend to over-inflate its seriousness. It is serious enough without being made disproportionate.

Who or what is to blame?

Respondents in the social evils consultation blamed the government for being out of touch and ineffective, the media for fuelling anxieties, religion as a cause of conflict and division, and big business for promoting consumerism and inequalities. There is a measure of truth in all these judgements, especially the second and third. The first illustrates the fact that people have far too high an expectation of government, whose capacity to address some problems (those caused by immigration, for example) is not matched by its capacity to deal with others (the alleged problems of individualism and consumerism). If it sought to address these last two by legislation, it would make itself a tyranny, and the objections would be vastly greater than complaints that it does not do enough.

All societies have problems at all phases of their history, and the task is to understand and cope with them. The complexity, diversity and benefits of social living carry costs that we do our best to minimise and – where possible – change, as part of our responsibility as joint curators of society. How many respondents nominated themselves as the sources of some of the problems – "*my* racist feelings … *my* greed … *my* selfishness"? One would guess very few. Yet it is the responsibility of each member of society to play a part in confronting difficulties. The first step is getting them in proportion, working out whether they really are difficulties and, if so, what each of us individually, and all of us collectively, can do about them.

9

Unkind, risk averse and untrusting: if this is today's society, can we change it?

Baroness Julia Neuberger

There is a rabbinic saying that sums it all up:

> *If I am not for myself, who will be for me? And if I am only for myself, what am I? And if not now, when? (Mishnah, Ethics of the Fathers, 1: 14)*

Broadly interpreted, the rabbis were saying:

> *"I have to look after myself, for I have to stand proud and know who and what I am. But if that's all I do, what kind of a human being am I? Selfish, uncaring and unkind. The world needs to be made into a better place and though I may not be able to do much, I can do a bit, and it's no good saying someone else can do it. The responsibility lies with me, and I cannot leave it till tomorrow."*

Selfish society

I have watched bemused as we seem to have become less and less caring for, or even aware of the suffering of, the most vulnerable in our society. This is not to say that there are not hundreds of thousands of people who carry out acts of kindness for those in trouble, day by day. Nor is it to say that we are bad people, or uncaring – although we may be insensitive to the needs of others, incompetent or somehow unaware in other ways. Nor is it to argue, as religious leaders have often done, that we have become selfish – although that may be partially true. I believe that something else is going on: a complex pattern of interactions of ideas, events, zeitgeist and personal human attitudes that has somehow allowed us to reach this position.

The idea that we have an obligation to society beyond the demands we wish to make of it ourselves is becoming unfashionable. Utilitarianism – the greatest happiness (or welfare or benefit) for the greatest number – is a philosophy now held in disrepute. Individual endeavour is adulated, as is personal autonomy. The old sense of mutual obligation, somewhat fostered by wartime, has taken a battering. We are into understanding ourselves and into self-improvement: improving our homes, our looks and our minds. Our view of faith is also increasingly individualistic. Individual salvation is part of the appeal of the evangelicals with the carrot of personal salvation held out to us. But the requirements our various faiths put on us to care for others may get less than their fair attention. We look at ourselves, not beyond.

Yet we also know that more than half of all adults in England and Wales volunteer at least once a month (Low et al, 2007). People clearly do get out of bed to help others. They want to make a difference. Opinion surveys show that people want 'to improve things or help people', or that they feel that 'the cause (is) important'. Nor, despite the stereotypes of volunteers being old ladies who sort clothes in charity shops, is it simply older people who volunteer.

So why does the accusation of selfishness in society stick? First, without denying the value of volunteering, it is easy to see that one of the motivations for many volunteers is having a reason to get up in the morning. They may be doing it more for themselves than for the people who need help. Second, those who are genuinely altruistic, or who want to make a difference because they cannot bear looking at their community as it is, often find it extremely hard to lend a hand. And that is because we have become seriously risk averse. We are fearful as a nation, scared of terrorists, child molesters and violence on the street. As a result, we make it harder and harder to help those who need our aid, and so we become more and more withdrawn into ourselves.

The clearest example of this is our obsession, not wholly misplaced, with sexual predators on young people. That has made it necessary for anyone who works with children or vulnerable adults to be checked by the Criminal Records Bureau (CRB). Until recently, this meant that a child in the care of foster parents could not spend a night at a friend's house unless the friend's parents were themselves prepared to undergo CRB checks too. Yet what children in care need more than anything else is to have ordinary friends and to live ordinary lives. The need for teachers in schools or volunteer helpers with reading to be CRB checked is no bad thing, in itself. But the fact that we have become so stringent in our requirements about checks on those who work or have any relationship with children has perverse consequences. First, children are encouraged to be suspicious of adults in a way that may be quite unhealthy, both for themselves and for society as a whole. Second, those who are inclined to look after a child or young person who is distressed will be nervous of getting involved. An example of this is the tragic case of Abigail Rae, a two-year-old child who drowned in a pond after she escaped from her nursery school in Warwickshire. The inquest into her death heard how a man had passed the toddler as she wandered down a road alone, but failed to stop and help because he was afraid people would think he was trying to abduct her (BBC News, 23 March 2006). The anticipated suspicions of others has, thus, forced some people, particularly men, to restrain themselves from showing ordinary common decency.

As if this were not enough, we also have the growing public worry that some apparently stable men may be interested in sexualised pictures of children downloaded from the internet. While such men undoubtedly exist and may pose a real threat to the young, well-publicised cases increase the tendency to view all kinds of men through nervous eyes. In this way, the picture begins to emerge of a society that wants to protect children from potential attack, but risks scuppering valuable relationships between young people and older male role models because the fear of sexual attack takes precedence over a belief in ordinary common humanity. When pictures of children at nursery school cannot be taken without parental consent for fear of pornographic use, we have a problem. When we are so suspicious of adults' motives that one cannot help in a school without a police check, we will deter all but the most determined volunteers however legitimate our concern may be. The question arises, as Professor Frank Furedi puts it, as to whether the fears of attacks on children are themselves being stoked by a stealthily expanding growth in child protection measures (Furedi and Bristow, 2008).

Our parental fears of sexual predators are by no means unfounded. In recent years we have lived through the Soham murders, a series of scandals surrounding children's homes and special schools, the disappearance of Madeleine McCann and the bizarre story of Shannon Matthews. Yet the level of protection we have instituted will make children unable to trust anyone. It is as if we are trying to create a risk-free society, which we know in our heads and hearts is impossible. We restrict and regulate, hoping to make abuse impossible. And, in that way, we deter the willing and the kind.

Community breakdown

Contemporary attitudes to older people epitomise our less caring society in a different way. In this case, we are quite prepared to tolerate a level of neglect and abuse of older people that we would consider wholly unacceptable for young people. We have tolerated older people suffering from preventable infection and malnutrition in hospitals (BBC News, 11 October, 2007; Revill, 2007); a lack of pain control in care homes; and inadequate payments for residential homes which leads to poor-quality food and insufficient care. We talk about hospital 'bed blockers' as if it is older people's fault that they have nowhere to go, and we discuss euthanasia rather than improvements in the quality of care. We allow our frailest and oldest to be cared for by people with no qualifications and poor pay and prospects, yet we seem surprised if the care provided is not always first rate. And we fail to learn from other countries that living arrangements for older people, including those with dementia, can be infinitely better, kinder and more satisfying. Worst of all, we tolerate a dramatic increase in reported loneliness among older people: up from 5% of older people surveyed by Help the Aged in 2005/06 to 13% in 2006/07. Nearly one in three of the older people questioned said their life had got generally worse over the previous year (Help the Aged, 2007). But still we fail to see what we are doing to our communities by not including older people within them.

We are also increasingly unclear as to who our 'neighbours' are. Our attitudes to community have shifted. We still have a certain amount of suspicion of 'outsiders', although many people relish the diversity of our cities. There is also a growing body of opinion that feels that our policies towards asylum seekers are plain cruel. While cynics might argue that many immigrants are here to exploit our welfare systems, the presumption should surely be that people have come to Britain for the right reasons. There should be a fast, firm, fair and compassionate system that sieves out those who have not. If we cannot sort that out, or set up a sensible system for doing so, it is hardly appropriate to make people looking for a safe haven suffer for our incompetence. Indeed, it might be argued that our incompetence should lead us to treat them better, rather than worse.

These principles have to be set against increasing xenophobia, which ranges from a general distrust of asylum seekers and refugees to a more particular and frightening hostility towards Muslims. In the wake of 9/11 and 7/7, such hostility has embodied the fear that all young Muslims are the extremists so often portrayed in the media. There are many who have sympathy with Muslim communities over this, but their opponents are many and various. Hostility emerges from the mouths of people who would otherwise think of themselves as tolerant. This seems to be, in part, because many Muslims do not share many Western liberal values. Some politicians, shamefully, play to this xenophobia, and allow genuine asylum seekers to be treated with outrageous hostility.

We are also frequently intolerant of those who have mental health problems or learning disabilities. While attitudes have improved in some ways since the old habit of locking people away in long-stay hospitals, there is still an extremely high incidence of mental ill-health in prisons. In 2002, 72% of male and 70% of female sentenced prisoners suffered from two or more diagnosable mental disorders (Social Exclusion Unit, 2002). In 2004, 20% of prisoners had four of the five major mental health disorders (Paul Goggins MP, *Hansard*, 17 March 2004). This suggests that people with mental illness are all too likely to drift into what is our last 'closed' institution, now the old mental hospitals have gone. By and large, little heed is given to, and inadequate treatment provided for, people with mental illness in prisons. Far less is spent on each patient within the prison system than on a comparable patient outside (Durcan, 2008).

We are also surprisingly unmoved by the fate of children who have been in care. For example, we often choose to ignore the disproportionate number of prisoners who have been in care, or experienced severe mental health problems or educational difficulties. Although we continue to have high expectations and hopes for our own children, it appears that many of us have given up any hope or sense of responsibility for the children placed in society's care. Yet they are undoubtedly part of our community – or should be. Most of us will know something of what happens to children when they leave care. And we will also have met them: the sad children asking for spare change; the young boys going from door to door with trays or kitbags of dusters, candles and CD cleaners. The children on drugs, alcohol or glue, sitting in the park staring vacantly into space; or the girls hustled and bullied into the sex trade.

Not all young care leavers have these experiences, but enough do for us to notice, observe and pass by on the other side of the street. Yet we blame family breakdown for their predicament, rather than our own lack of attention to what is going on around us. While we agonise over the risk of sexual predators who might attack our own children, we ignore the sexual exploitation of those children who leave our care system. What kind of society are we that locks up young people with mental illness in prisons, rather than placing them where they can get proper help and care? What kind of society are we that allows young care leavers to get into the criminal fraternity so easily, without making sure they have the support of sensible adults as mentors and befrienders for their late teenage years and early twenties? And, returning to an earlier theme, what kind of society are we that makes it so unattractive for young men, particularly, to act as volunteer mentors? According to one NCH survey, 13% of male volunteers who had not put themselves forward to work with young people said this was due to their fear of being perceived as paedophiles (BBC News, 27 June 2008).

Values beyond community

Our inability to address some of these issues in our local communities has led to two conflicting developments. One is the concern felt by many people, largely younger, about the environment and scarce resources. It is this movement that has drawn our attention to climate change, water shortages, the damaging effects of air travel and the potential waste of 'food miles'. Many of the same young people will volunteer abroad, raise money for aid charities and support children to ensure they receive proper healthcare. But their conscientiously held environmental views may themselves be part of a problem. Slogans are surely less helpful here than a considered view on how best to help and support marginal farming. The view that 'globalisation' is intrinsically bad leads to a moralising position that may well harm the world's poorest, making it another luxury that only the developed world can afford.

Risk aversion

Meanwhile, risk aversion all too often takes precedence over kindness and militates against communities supporting themselves. One consequence is that it is often ordinary people who display the greatest caring and kindness to those who are most vulnerable because they have not had it professionally frightened out of them by the system. The kindness one encounters in hospitals often comes from porters and care assistants rather than from senior staff. More kindness is often shown to people with severe mental health problems by the owners of cafés where they sit for much of the day, or the staff in public libraries, than from trained professionals. Many nurses and outreach workers are wonderful, dedicated human beings, but the system they work for is increasingly loath to allow them to take on any risk. An arm around the shoulders might be deemed common assault. An invitation to a meal might be seen as some of kind of sexually predatory lure.

Risk aversion has increased a natural human reluctance to get involved. That reluctance will grow unless we look carefully at why we have deliberately grown such a culture and the regulation to go with it, why we are so suspicious of sexual motives and why we no longer trust the 'stranger'. To counter these tendencies, we need to examine our own personal experiences. If we fall in the street, it is the stranger who picks us up and dusts us down. If we have a car crash, it is the stranger who calls the police and stays with us to give comfort. If we are mugged, it is the stranger who, all too often, gives us the wherewithal to get home. If we are suddenly distressed, or feel ill or overcome with fatigue, it is often the stranger who carries our bags, who asks if we are all right or who offers to take us to the Accident and Emergency department of the hospital. Yet we are making it more difficult for caring strangers to intervene. Why, as evidence grows that crime is down, are we ever-more fearful and frightened of each other? And why do politicians foster that fear, encouraging us to be ever-more watchful, and surrounding us with CCTV so that 'Big Brother' apparently has his eye on us?

Fear of others has turned us inwards. We have never been so internally reflective, so obsessed with ourselves and our feelings or so enveloped in understanding ourselves. As we look deeper into ourselves, we lose the inclination to help, serve or work for others. We also fail to look into the middle or near distance and deal with what we find within our communities. Part of this desire to look inside ourselves is precisely what leads to that lack of a longer, more measured view. Psychotherapy has brought great gains, allowing those with unusual behaviours to understand themselves and behave differently. But it does encourage an emphasis on the personal over the group. Its rightful place is in the clinical setting and not in the everyday encounter with self-examination that, at worst, leads to an inability to act.

One could argue that all this emerges from an unfortunate confluence of events, or of intellectual and emotional pressures. For at the same time as individualism became paramount, the-then Prime Minister Margaret Thatcher stated her belief that there was 'no such thing as society' (*Woman's Own* interview, 31 October 1987); and consumerism hit new heights. This was the very period when the obsession with looking inwards grew in intensity, combined with a political and philosophical view that the individual should control what happened to them. All these factors led to a distaste for looking at the welfare of society as a whole.

For we are individuals now. We understand our own needs. We look inside ourselves. We know what we want and we demand it. We have become demanders, not citizens – people who look to ourselves rather than to the whole society. The tendency is not new; but it has acquired far greater weight. The words so often uttered by older people in years gone by that 'I have had my turn, it's someone else's now' are becoming rare. We see no need to moderate our demands; it is no longer about what we regard as our fair share. Instead, it is about when we feel, as individuals with autonomy, that we have had enough.

Trust

Trust is both political and ethical. In a society where participation in elections is declining and where trust in politicians is at an all-time low, reassessing what we provide for the most disadvantaged is difficult to do. Combined with an aversion to risk, we have a failure of trust. Those who work in our services do not trust the politicians not to blame them when things go wrong. What we have is a society that thinks politicians lie when they promise things for all of us, including the most disadvantaged. Yet trust is essential if we are to value our services. And risk aversion makes for poor services, where no one will do what seems natural and kind in case they are accused of behaving improperly. They do not feel they are trusted to do the right thing.

Trust is 'blowing in the wind', and a trusting society will be hard to claw back. Politicians are, often unfairly, regarded as only out for their own ends, not ours. But if we want a society where people feel that fairness is part of the ethos, we need to be seen to be involved with our politicians and thinking about our society. We cannot just let it go, and then complain. If we are too individualistic, then we will suffer. Our happiness, as Richard Layard (2006) has argued so cogently, will suffer, and so will our sense of belonging. In his campaign for the Conservative leadership, David Cameron argued that: "We know we have a shared responsibility; that we're all in this together, that there is such a thing as society – it's just not the same as the state" (speech, September 2005). He was reflecting back on his predecessor Lady Thatcher's comment about society consisting only of individuals. But he was also making an important point by acknowledging that while we are all interrelated, the state may not be able to put all the ills of our society right. The suggestion is that everyone will have to make more of a contribution to righting the wrongs of society. Altruism will need to be fashionable again, and helping others, for whatever reason, will need to be a part of our daily lives.

But that is not so simple. It begs the question of who we accept as 'belonging' to our society and how we regard them. It is about 'insiders' and 'outsiders', 'trusted' and 'distrusted'. If we recognise mutual obligations, how far does that mutuality extend? Who is 'us', and who can we legitimately say we do not count as being part of 'our' society, to whom we therefore have no obligation? If we only look to ourselves, we narrow the view, and in the end become automata, selfish, self-obsessed and shirking responsibility. If we are only interested in long-distance travel and adventures miles away, we miss what is under our noses. Both the furthest and the nearest gaze negate the need for trust. It is in the middle distance, from one's fellow citizens to one's politicians, where trust, debate and discussion, and making the world a better place, truly sit. Unless we rethink our obligations and the trust we accord to those in charge, we will become even more cynical, atomistic and individualistic. Then there really will be no such thing as society.

Reinventing altruism

We must rebuild trust. That means politicians being less frightened of the voters and closer to them. It means doctors and other professionals talking frankly about risks and benefits. It means the media applying self-denying ordinances to stories of blame, day after day. It means all of us heeding W.H. Auden's famous line in the lead-up to the Second World War: "We must trust one another, or we die" (1 September 1939).

Acting with appropriate care, we must open out our institutions so that ordinary people can see what happens in our care homes and children's homes. These are institutions within *our* communities and ordinary people need to go into them on our behalf. We must challenge the insurers and the writers of policies in care homes and other institutions. Fear of fault-finding has led to masterly inactivity. That must cease. We need to stop blaming people and stop seeking their dismissal, unless in extreme circumstances. We need to recognise that getting most things right most of the time is an impressive record in human interactions.

We must also reassess family breakdown and put more emphasis – in settlements, counselling and relationship support – on those who suffer as a consequence but never choose to part the ways, notably children and other dependants. We must also reassess the prevailing emphasis on ourselves; on our own contentment and inner feelings. Sometimes those selfish things need to be addressed. But all too often a focus on self leads to an inability to do things for others. We must work out how to focus on the glorious sense of purpose that comes out of doing things for others rather than ourselves.

We need, in short, to reinvent altruism, and take up the challenge which argues that the state cannot do everything for everybody. It probably cannot do everything, but it can undoubtedly set out the circumstances in which more of us can – and would wish to – do things for each other as part of normal behaviour without being threatened with burdensome regulation and an atmosphere of mistrust.

References

Durcan, G. (2008) *From the inside*, London: Sainsbury Centre for Mental Health.

Furedi, F. and Bristow, J. (2008) *Licensed to hug*, London: Civitas.

Help the Aged (2007) *Spotlight survey*, London: Help the Aged.

Layard, R. (2006) *Happiness: Lessons from a new science*, London: Penguin.

Low, N., Butt, S., Ellis Paine, A. and Davis Smith, J. (2007) *Helping out: A national survey of volunteering and charitable giving*, London: Office of the Third Sector, Cabinet Office.

Revill, J. (2007) 'The dirty truth on the wards', *The Observer*, 14 October.

Social Exclusion Unit (2002) *Reducing reoffending by ex-prisoners*, London: Office of the Deputy Prime Minister.

Distrust

10

What and who is it we don't trust?

Shaun Bailey

My focus is on the lack of trust that increasingly runs through our society. I am going to start with the mistrust between different communities and races, but I also want to look at the mistrust between adults and young people, which was flagged up by many who responded to the Joseph Rowntree Foundation's (JRF) social evils consultation. I will also comment on relationships between individuals, state and community and the effects they have on daily life that may have led us to no longer trust institutions – or one another.

Racism: can you really trust someone you 'tolerate'?

Many white communities up and down the country feel terrified at the changes they see in their local areas due to the influx of foreigners of all shades in recent years. The latest government projections show that the population of England is set to grow by 9.5 million over the next 25 years, and 70% of this increase will be the result of immigration. Figures like these make people worry. The familiar Britain that people grew up in is disappearing and leading to growing mistrust of the people around us, whose cultures and behaviour we no longer recognise.

There is often a disconnection between a person's public and private life. It would nowadays be unacceptable to call someone a 'coon' or post a sign saying 'No Irish, no blacks, no dogs' in a public arena. But in many households up and down the country, racism is alive and kicking. This is indicated by the re-emergence of the British National Party (BNP). It is also evident in the way some respondents to the JRF consultation spoke about *a greater fear of the 'other'* – in other words, fear leading to dislike or even hatred of people of a different race. Although there have been big improvements in 30 years in the way people express their racism, we are starting to lose some of the ground gained in this area. Growing mistrust means we mix less now than ever before. It has led to 'white flight' from some urban areas as the indigenous population move out to more exclusive areas in an attempt to recapture a piece of 'the old Britain' as they see it.

Thus, while many migrant communities mix, the white community is often conspicuous by its absence. Immigrant communities are accused of being insular, but I suspect they would level the same accusation at white indigenous peoples whose frosty reception has left them in no doubt about how unwelcome they are. Overriding suspicion of all that is different leads people to pass judgement based on stereotypes. The media often play on this fear themselves with sensationalist headlines like: 'Too many immigrants: UK tightens immigration rules'.

There has been a profound change in the make-up of British society; in our cities more than anywhere. It seems that ordinary people are left feeling like they have no control or say over the debate. They hear sections of our middle-class, liberal media talking about how good immigration has been for the economy. But for them it just creates fear when 'foreigners', as they see it, take their jobs, jump the queue for welfare, take their housing, scrounge off the benefit system and abuse the National Health Service. It is not even a black–white thing. It is anybody they see as not 'British'. I, as a black man, often get a warmer welcome than someone of Eastern European extraction, in London at least.

British people have begun to believe that these people have deliberately left their country and come to scrounge off Britain as a 'soft touch'. This has led to a great mistrust between many working people and the state. This is where policy makers on the left wing of politics are far removed from the man in the street who believes that only immigrants get social housing. There is a real disconnection between what the liberal intelligentsia maintain and the reality of what people are really feeling. People start to attribute the hardship in their life with what they see as the new competition. This is exacerbated by recent government figures that show that somewhere in the region of 80% of new jobs our economy has generated in recent years have gone to foreign nationals. In ordinary people's eyes, this gives fuel to their fears.

British workers have also had to suffer the claim that they are expensive and lazy. This has bred real anger. One man who used MyGeneration's job club told me that while he has to pay British taxes and living costs, his foreign counterparts do not. Although he was not entirely correct, his sentiment is widely shared. He said he knew of one house were 20 or more migrant workers were sleeping in shifts and splitting the rent. Their living costs were less, enabling them to work for less. "It's not that we don't want to work, it's that we can't afford to," he said.

All of these things are happening in a climate where people continually talk about tolerance. 'Tolerance' in Britain often turns into a quest to make everybody the same, pushing communities apart. What many 'tolerant' people forget is the amount of comfort and direction that immigrant groups and many established communities often draw from their traditions. Examples of this are family structure and religious beliefs. Integration is a key tool in combating mistrust, because people do not distrust things they understand and know. However, attempts to *make* communities change can prevent them from integrating, because they do not trust the changes being forced on them. 'Tolerance' in this context is the lowest form of human togetherness; in fact, it is not togetherness at all. In the words of one young person: "I don't want be tolerated, you only tolerate things you don't like. I want be accepted."

Responsibility: do we trust ourselves?

The issue of trust between the state and individuals is entering our homes like never before. More and more of our private behaviour is dictated by the law and we are now even feeling it in our most intimate and important relationships. You are no longer allowed to smack your kids. People shouldn't have to be told not to beat their children. People who do need to be told do not listen anyway. So this robs parents of some of their authority. What more fundamental relationship is there than the one between a parent and child? It is not a loss to young people that they now have all these new 'rights', but what is missing from the conversation is their responsibilities. Children who grow up without learning responsibility become adults who will not take responsibility.

We do not trust ourselves, or at least other adults. This is a definite change because in the past we would trust other adults to discipline our children, or at least challenge them. It is now very difficult to 'look out for' children at home, in school or on the street. People will no longer challenge children who are not their own for fear of the law. This has robbed parents and adults of their confidence and their rights when dealing with young people. We are quite simply beginning to fear children. How many people do you know who are prepared to ask children on the bus to be quiet? The ultimate expression of this is that we have the largest youth prison population in Europe, a multitude of new laws to criminalise young people at an early stage and a criminal age of responsibility of just 10 years old.

One of the features of youth crime is that there is actually more adult crime, and young people are more likely to be a victim than a perpetrator – although you would not know this from reading the press. Yet the way the press represent children is easier to believe than the official representation, because the official representation includes so many excuses for the bad behaviour of children such as coming from a poor background, or boredom. As with female crime, we seem to take greater offence when children perform a crime. Nowadays we don't trust our children on the issue of crime, they don't trust us and they are increasingly taking the law into their own hands; therefore we trust them even less. The question is, should we fear them or should they fear us?

Many young people are abusive and cocky because they feel they are beyond adult control. And to a point they are right, because if you take action against a child, the adult is automatically seen as in the wrong. We treat all our children as if they are angels and that is definitely not the case. The number of times I have heard the words "I'll sue you" is unbelievable. It is an expression of the new-found power that children enjoy over adults and which they are well prepared to use. Another more alarming example is that of children attacking adults. This has been one of the major changes I have seen during my years in youth work. We have handed power over to children, which means we often cannot act in their best interests, because as parents and adults we unreasonably fear the rights of children.

Many children have been left unprotected by the adults around them and this is why we are now seeing a rise in bullying, because young bullies thrive in an environment without adult control. The rise in the power and size of the industry around children's rights has fundamentally changed the relationship between children, parents and society. Indeed, they are no longer called children; they are called 'young people'. I dislike this term as it suggests they are a separate body of people and that they understand the responsibilities that come with such a title. I have used this term throughout because it is a term most people understand. However, they are not separate, they are our children and the responsibility lies with us for their safety and future, not with them or an agency.

We claim to be doing things for young people's protection but it looks to me as if we are setting up systems in law that allow us *not* to take responsibility for our children. We have a system that is happy to fill the role of parent or at least says it will, but we all know that the authorities are the worst parents. For example, on the issue of health and safety, we wrap our children in cotton wool to the point where schools cannot take pupils off the premises for fear of prosecution. Yet your 14-year-old daughter can have an abortion without your knowledge or consent. This kind of change in our thinking tells children that even those people closest to them cannot be trusted, and if this is the case, why would they think they can trust anyone else? Although I understand the need for rules and guidelines around children, we must trust the parents involved to carry out their jobs.

Many people no longer want to work with children who are not related to them because they feel the law treats all adults as a risk. This has had a profound effect on the voluntary sector, especially when it comes to recruiting men. Is this why we have so few male primary school teachers? Much of the antisocial behaviour carried out by young boys in particular is based on their false ideas about what it is to be a successful man. It could be argued that this stems from a lack of trustworthy male role models. All adult–youth interaction now has to have the seal of approval of the Criminal Records Bureau check. This licensing of adults is the government's response to our fear of other people and can often breed mistrust itself.

Children: friend or foe?

Respondents to the JRF's web consultation seem to be split between a view that young people *are* the problem and a view that young people *suffer* from the problem (in other words, young people are either perpetrators or victims). The first view shows how bad behaviour by a small minority of children has a big effect on the level of trust we have with all children. The latter acknowledges the way that neglect puts children in survival mode. An example of what I mean is that many young people do not feel safe on the streets and so arm themselves for protection. Safety in our public areas should be the concern of adults, not armed children. When asking a 17-year-old boy that I work with if he would report to the police that he had been 'jumped' (attacked), his stunned reply was: "Why? What can they do about it?" He gave a clear indication that he believed that the powers-that-be are useless. The confusion caused by not giving young people clear boundaries has led many to be angry. Once children, or indeed adults, are angry their behaviour becomes unpredictable and extreme.

The kids I work with may not speak to you in these 'big picture' terms but they do understand that they are under pressure. In the words of one 16-year-old, when asked "Do you feel safe on the street?", to my surprise he answered "Yes". When I asked him why, he said with a smile, "I have a borer [knife] and I know everyone in my area". The most telling part of what he says is not the fact that he carries a knife, although this is alarming. It is his certainty that he knows everyone in his area. This means that he views anyone he doesn't know as a threat.

This level of mistrust is far higher than when I was a 17-year-old. It transforms people's behaviour. It is why so many young people swagger about as if they own the place – a front to ward off the threat of others. Another reaction to this is to hide under their hoodies. Their defensive bravado can then evolve into an offensive form of intimidation.

Another problem is the exposure of children to sexual and violent materials. Watch an hour of MTV Base, listen to any rap music or read popular teen magazines and you will see some extreme behaviour portrayed as the norm. Young people then reflect this in their behaviour and we punish them for it. You can also factor in the way that criminal involvement is seen as cool. In the words of one of the world's most famous rappers, Tupac: "Crime pays". If you watch how groups of kids rob and assault an adult, it often starts out as a game, which is pushed further and further until the point of no return when they attack. Then, when the adult reacts defensively, they use that as an excuse for their attack.

Many people nowadays believe that if you give children what they want, it is enough to see them through. The current generation of children are notorious for being spoilt. Anybody who has children will tell you they know a lot about what they want, and little about what they need. That is why many respondents to the JRF consultation spoke in terms of young people 'having a loss of respect for all human life', and spoke of 'undisciplined young people with no manners, no self-control and no respect for anything'. They can see that young people today receive a lot of extra help relative to when they were young themselves, and still seem to misbehave.

The low opinion of young people held by a growing section of society is based on a number of factors. The main thing is the continuing development of a global Western youth culture based on disrespect, money, sex and violence, all of which stem from major aspects of our adult culture. Our youth do not trust adults because we say one thing then do another. An example is our attitude to drinking: we tell young people not to drink, but we drink to excess ourselves. The situation is set to worsen as we raise our children in a climate of mistrust.

There are also conspiracy theories of distrust. These allow us not to make any effort with people outside of our friendship group. We all expect people will change and be like us, and if they don't we treat them as untrustworthy. Young people's mistrust of adults is largely based on their limited experience of not being able to trust their contemporaries. So many young people now grow up surrounded by criminals and criminal activity that create what for them becomes a very normal paranoia. There is no honour among thieves and when you are surrounded by them, it doesn't pay to have honour yourself. One of the lesser-known things about gang membership is the high level of violence and intimidation within the gang itself. This is often an unpleasant surprise to younger children who have been groomed to become members and is hidden from them until it is too late.

An interesting example of this is a young boy I worked with called Jake who met another boy in jail called Tao.[1] Together, they agreed to help rob each other's gang. When they got out of jail, Jake lent his gang's only gun to Tao who then used it to rob Jake's gang. This goes to show a really selfish nature. As Tao said to me: "Get rich, or die trying!" This is a term popularised by the American rap star 50 Cent, and it goes to the heart of a major problem for all our young people – the fact that individualism and greed take precedence over friendship and trust.

Lack of manners: small but important

By manners, I don't just mean people being courteous to one another. I am talking about what the learning and teaching of manners does. This is socialisation at the most basic level, because it teaches our children that sometimes you have to give up your wants for somebody else's needs. The older generation recognise this behaviour and when they don't see it from children, it makes them suspicious. They see younger people as less concerned about the common good. This is not new. Since the 1950s the older generations of the British public have viewed youngsters with a little contempt, but in recent times this has turned to outright hostility and fear. The lack of manners, as adults see it, is one of the driving factors behind this change. It is a primary sign that the two groups don't share a value system and have very different social protocols. One example is the use of language. When was the last time you called someone 'my bitch' as a term of endearment? Do you refer to your best friend as 'big dog'?

Much of the fear of crime is based on the lack of manners, which leads to a barrier of misunderstanding and distrust between young and old. This is shown by the fact that much of what is normal behaviour for young people is seen by adults as antisocial behaviour – for example, the phenomenon of children playing their music on public transport without headphones. This shows a lack of concern about how anybody else may feel about the noise. But if adults fail to teach young people good behaviour such as manners and then punish them for not using them, why should they trust us? Bad manners are not confined to children, but, as in most societies, we are more offended by bad behaviour in children.

We can also see that our children are significantly different from their counterparts outside the Western world, where there is generally a less liberal view on childrearing. A demonstration of this is the amount of time young people spend socialising with their adult guardians, in ways that would develop their soft skills and engender trust and respect. There is not enough of this in Western society – we are always trying to find someone else to look after our children or at least take responsibility for their behaviour. This leads to a society that is not child-friendly because adults outside of a child's family group feel no responsibility for children in general and often see children as a problem. Our lack of trust in our children is entirely of our own making. Lack of trust can also be about lack of control. If you are dependent on others and have no control or say over the most basic parts of your life, you will find it hard to trust anyone.

The price of individualism

Concentration on the rights of the individual has been part of the move towards individualism and selfishness. It has been done at the cost of the community and family. We no longer teach our children that they are part of a wider community, which they should support as a place where they can expect to find trustworthy people. Respondents to the consultation said they felt that individualism has damaging consequences, such as an "unconscious sense of fear and hopelessness" because individuals know they cannot survive alone in a complex society.

Is this the result of mistrust of one another or is it stupidity? I say that because when you are in prison and they want to punish you, they put you into solitary confinement. So why would people want to punish themselves by doing this of their own free will? Or should I say, why would they not fight against it happening to them? This is where the feeling of helplessness starts to affect people's ability to be happy because we feel like we cannot affect our own world. Consequently, we put all our hopes and trust in a liberal ideology that many feel has delivered the opposite to what we all say we want.

We live in what appears to be such a violent world and this has a profound effect on trust. Ask anybody who has been attacked in the street if they feel like they will be able to trust a stranger anytime soon. The answer will definitely be: "No". One of the most horrible things for young people, and black men in particular, is that they are seen as dangerous. It is soul-destroying to see people cross the road or look at you uncomfortably because of who you are. The frustrations of this turn into anger and some start to think "OK, I will be what they think I am". Of course, we distrust others when we are constantly told how dangerous the world and the people in it are. This has led to a rise in the 'walk past and don't get involved' culture, which leaves people doubting the very nature of humans, or at least British people.

Conclusion

I have used the word 'behaviour' again and again, because a lack of trust influences our behaviour in a way other phenomena do not. If a person or community doesn't feel safe, they will take action that is not always predictable. This is happening more and more and because we no longer live in a homogeneous society, individuals no longer know what to expect from other people's behaviour. This has led to a lot of uncertainty and mistrust. When you add this to the big questions of the day, such as globalisation, poverty and war, people live with more uncertainty now than ever before. This is, naturally, worrying to them. The basic problem is we believe in systems, we are raised on them, we are told how great they are and when these systems fail to work, the trust is broken. Ultimately, trust is hard to earn and easy to break!

Note
[1] Not their real names.

11

Fear and distrust in 21st-century Britain

Anna Minton

Monica tells me that when she moved into a gated community after 20 years living on an ordinary terraced street in London, she expected to feel safer. But recently the electronically controlled gates surrounding her development went wrong and had to be propped open. As a result, she spent the whole night lying awake, feeling far more scared than she had ever been in her terraced house, despite more-than-adequate locks on her new front door. Two hundred miles to the north, in a very different part of Britain, higher security is also creating an atmosphere of increased fear. In part of Salford, designated a 'Respect Action Area' by the government, two teenage boys report being stopped and searched by police at least once or twice a week. Curtis, 16, and Scott, 17, explain to me how this routine occurrence makes them feel bullied and belittled. 'Respect' in their experience feels a lot like humiliation....

One of the ironies of contemporary British society is how little our increasingly heavy investments in security have done to make us feel safer. All over the country, people are experiencing a corrosive climate of fear, and the media's commercial needs, rather than any mission to inform, have played a significant role in heightening it. Stories that sell fear, sell newspapers.

The interaction between the media and policy making is critical because more and more policy is made in response to headlines rather than rigorous research. Ill-thought-out, short-term responses can then be 'spun' to generate the headlines the government wants. The real causes of fear and distrust are swept under the carpet, where they multiply rather than go away. Policies that tackle symptoms rather than causes mesh with the spin culture, to sell us control-based solutions that only make things worse. People are, not surprisingly, fed up with the spin that is breaking the ties between citizens and politics, and adding to distrust. The government often accuses the public of apathy and talks of the 'disconnect' between people and politics. But the real problem is not apathy or lack of interest, but a lack of trust – which in turn correlates with the rising levels of fear in society (Layard, 2006).

Inequality and segregation

From the Second World War to the present day, a large body of evidence has demonstrated how levels of inequality in societies are linked to distrust. It is well known that the Second World War was a period of high social cohesion, stereotyped as the 'Blitz spirit'. Less well known is that many important health indicators showed a possibly counterintuitive improvement, including mental health (Titmuss, 1950). For the sociologist Richard Titmuss, one important explanatory factor was the universal availability of policies that actively worked to reduce inequality – from free school milk to pensions. This had led to what he called 'less social disparagement', a term interchangeable with higher self-worth and self-esteem. In other words, a reduction in inequalities had served to promote respect and trust between people.

More recently, a wealth of research has echoed the links between higher levels of trust and better mental health in more equal societies. Most notably, the economist Richard Layard (2006) highlighted the direct correlation between levels of trust, happiness and depression. In his book *Happiness* he cited the World Values Survey, which found that Norway, one of the most equal societies in the world, had the highest levels of trust, while Brazil, with enormous wealth inequalities, had the lowest. Yet there is a feeling among today's political and media elite that, despite the economic downturn, too much discussion of inequality is somehow 'old news', harking back to the divisions of Thatcher's Britain 20 years ago. New Labour seized control of this narrative in the 1990s and claimed that its policies would alleviate poverty, but it failed to meet its targets. Now the need to alleviate poverty has been replaced by an emphasis on punitive zero tolerance approaches in poor areas. Yet however unfashionable the topic may be, we need not look far to see how inequality is still reflected in the physical environment and underpins today's growing culture of fear.

This is clearest of all in Liverpool, a city that was much in the news following the shooting in 2007 of 11-year-old Rhys Jones. His tragic death contributed to a longstanding perception that Merseyside is a high-crime area – a perception that became entrenched in the national consciousness 15 years ago with the murder of two-year-old James Bulger by two 10-year-old boys. Except that Liverpool, with crime figures significantly lower than in Leeds and Manchester, is not a relatively high-crime city.[1] Many people believe that Merseyside is the highest crime spot in the North West, but it is actually the second lowest. It is, in fact, the classic example of a place where fear of crime rather than crime itself is the problem.

But while it is not a particularly high-crime city, Liverpool does rank as the most deprived city in England according to the Index for Multiple Deprivation 2007 (Gaines, 2008). It is also one of the most segregated and security-conscious places in the country. It has one of the largest CCTV networks in Britain, with even black cabs notifying passengers that CCTV is operating inside the taxi. In the city centre, the newly privatised shopping area employs uniformed private guards to police the streets, and enforces restrictive policies. Begging, selling the *Big Issue*, skateboarding and political demonstrations are all banned. Even taking photographs is not allowed outside designated areas. There are also outlying parts of Liverpool, where drones (the unmanned spy planes used in Iraq) are being used to patrol disadvantaged neighbourhoods.

What is happening is a segregation of enclaves that defies the Thatcherite notion of wealth trickling down to those who need it the most. Instead, people from the heavily policed, outlying areas are being shown that the new wealth of the privatised centre is 'not for them' while being targeted by drones, dispersal orders and a heavy CCTV presence. Liverpool is an especially clear example of privatised city centres, where only those with money to spend feel welcome, that are springing up all over the country. In these strangely similar environments not only the homeless but also the young, old and anyone else who just likes to wander around is moved on by security guards. Anyone who looks too different becomes strange and someone to be feared.

Fear of 'the other'

Segregation is damaging to people's psychological well-being because it fuels the human tendency for people to associate with groups similar to themselves, and to perceive those who are different as dangerous. Social scientists and psychoanalysts refer to this duality as fear of 'the other'. When it is politically created and manipulated, it can have horrifying results, including genocide and ethnic cleansing. But its persistence in less extreme contexts is also important. Research in the US has shown how people who are visibly different can be associated with crime even when there is no supporting evidence. A study in Berkeley, California, found that there was a perception that the homeless people who congregated around a park were responsible for crime in the area.

Yet official figures confirmed that crime was no higher there than in the rest of the district (Mitchell, 2003).

As segregation and the homogenisation of places becomes more common, even small differences between people can come to seem threatening. A contemporary fear of 'the other' is the anxiety people feel when confronted by women choosing to wear the burkha, who combine visible difference with an appearance that may seem threatening through its associations with militant Islam. Liberal Britons voice concern for the human rights of veiled women, but the likelihood is that they also feel threatened by such a visible 'other'. Immigration similarly raises fears of 'the other' and has led Richard Layard (2006) to conclude that societies with lower rates of immigration are more cohesive.

These are challenging debates, made superficially simple by the temptation to demonise 'the other'. For example, rather than taking a long-term approach to working with homeless people, new policies simply ban them from large parts of the city centre. Ironically, the people in this environment who really do look visibly different are the security guards who are there to create an atmosphere of safety. Counterintuitively, it is their presence with the high-security paraphernalia that accompanies them that contributes to feelings of sterility and fear. In contrast, the 'light touch' presence of public police has been shown to promote feelings of safety.

It is, in fact, surprising just how important a role small policy changes can play in creating environments that are welcoming or unwelcoming. Unfortunately, rather than trying to tackle this challenge, policy makers have fallen into the trap of demonising 'the other'. Two narratives, one concerned with the 'telling and selling' of news and one about the creation of 'defended space', serve to illustrate how this can happen.

Telling and selling the story

Knife crime in London has been continually in the news. But a proper look at the statistics reveals a complicated picture much closer to the forgettable reality – in news terms – that knife crime has not actually risen. Figures from the Metropolitan Police[2] showed that recorded knife crime in London fell significantly from 12,124 incidents in 2006-07, to 10,222 in 2007-08. Knife crime among young people between the ages of 10 and 19 had also fallen by more than 20% between the end of 2006 and the end of 2007. It was also true that the number of teenage murder victims in London showed a significant jump from 17 in 2006 to 26 in 2007. But a comprehensive review of knife crime published at the end of 2007 by the Centre for Crime and Justice Studies (Eades et al, 2007) found that the number of deaths involving knives nationally was at its lowest level since 1994. The study also found no discernible increase in violence involving knives, although there was some evidence of increased knife carrying among children and young people. Yet for a visitor to London or an older person who relies on newspaper and television news for their information, the notion that kids are killing kids on every London street would be understandable.

The media ought, therefore, to shoulder some responsibility for the widespread perception that crime is rising when it is falling. However, the context within which most news organisations operate ensures that their primary concern, over and above informing the public, is to sell news. The sad truth is that people are also drawn to fear and violence and enjoy this kind of story far more than complex tables of confusing crime statistics. Fear 'sells' and teenage murder is a 'good story' for the media, invoking human interest, tragedy, revenge and calls that 'something must be done'. Moreover, once a story takes off, as knife crime has done, it takes on its own momentum. Stories involving stabbing might not previously have even made it into a newspaper, but now they are almost guaranteed the front page. But although each stabbing incident is a tragedy in itself, we need to remember that the overall number of cases remains low.

Narratives that focus on the horrifying story of a particular individual, rather than placing events in context, were identified by Barry Glassner (2000) in his book *The culture of fear* as the key reason behind the media's promotion of fear in the US. But they are also popular with contemporary politicians eager to appear 'tough on crime'. When Jack Straw was Home Secretary, he anticipated current interest in contemporary social evils by declaring that fear of crime was on a par with the giant evils of want, disease, ignorance, squalor and idleness identified in the 1940s by Beveridge (Straw, 1999). Although he did acknowledge that crime had fallen, Straw put the need to address fear of crime at the centre of a new drive to build a safer society. This, he said, would be based on the biggest ever investment in CCTV and the introduction of antisocial behaviour orders (ASBOs) – two policies that were based on scant research evidence.

Today, despite research calling both CCTV and ASBOs into question, the same interaction between the media and politicians continues. Politicians respond to the headlines on knife crime with calls for curfews and increased stop–and–search powers for police, even though evidence dismisses these approaches. For example, a review of knife crime concluded that the extension of police stop–and–search powers was 'a problematic response', with 'huge potential to create resentment' (Eades et al, 2007, p 28). It was based on the Home Office's own research, but this did not prevent Home Office Minister Tony McNulty from subsequently dismissing criticisms by the Children's Commissioner for England as 'plumb wrong and miles away from where the public are' (Alleyne, 2008). Thus, evidence-based research has been ignored and policy made on the basis of what is deemed likely to please a public misinformed by the media.

Defensible space and security

The segregation and excessive security that increases fear and distrust can be seen as a physical reflection of growing wealth inequalities. But in Britain this is only part of the picture. Far more important is the attitude of policy makers, developers and the insurance and security industries to the concept of 'defensible space', first described by an American town planner called Oscar Newman in the early 1970s. Newman's main principle was based on 'territoriality': the creation of space that defends itself by marking out boundaries and encouraging residents to control a place so that strangers are discouraged from entering (Newman, 1972). This idea of 'designing out crime' overlaps with 'zero tolerance' approaches and has proved very popular with American and British politicians. Although he is little known outside planning and design circles, Newman's principles have determined the design of British housing since the 1970s, with planners and developers favouring cul-de-sacs with only one point of entry rather than a traditional street pattern. Backed by a police initiative called 'Secured by Design', the principles behind 'defensible space' have determined the security-conscious look and feel of most new development today. However, 'defensible space' remains controversial, with debate centring on whether 'natural surveillance' can be better created by the 'eyes on the street' of strangers, as Jane Jacobs, another influential author, has argued in her book *The death and life of great American cities* (Jacobs, 1961).

The widespread use of 'defensible space' ties in with what American commentators describe as the 'FIRE economy' – an acronym for Finance, Insurance and Real Estate (Parenti, 1999). Because developers can fit more houses onto a plot built out as a cul-de-sac or gated complex, it is more profitable than the traditional street pattern. There is no great evidence that these types of houses and places are actively sought out by people; it is more that there is little else on offer. Meanwhile, there is mounting evidence that enhanced private security and CCTV does not reduce fear of crime and might in some situations lead to an increase in actual crime. For example, a study funded by the Scottish Office in Glasgow found no improvement in feelings of safety after CCTV was introduced, accompanied by an increase in crime. The author concluded that the 'electronic eye on the street' threatened to erode natural surveillance and represented a retreat from collective and individual responsibility to self interest and a culture of fear (Ditton, 2000, p 707, citing Reeve, 1998).

Increasing use of satellite navigation systems in cars, means we are less likely to get lost, but also less able to cope when we do. In the same way, growing reliance on technological systems brings a kind of predictability that offers false reassurance. But despite this, people continue to like having them. This makes their introduction politically popular. A perfect illustration of the resulting fusion between populist policy and tabloid television can, thus, be found in Channel Five's *CCTV Cities*, which shows scenes from CCTV control rooms around Britain. As footage of drunken fights, police and paramedics streams in, an erroneous impression is created that the CCTV crime fighters are putting the world to rights. CCTV also happens to be a cheaper solution than putting more police on the beat or more conductors on the buses. Yet research demonstrates that it is 'light-touch' policing and 'natural surveillance' that really makes people feel safer.

Celebrity values

Accompanying the fears exacerbated by segregation and security, is the distrust that arises from having every aspect of our lives treated as something to sell. People, places and institutions have become commodities in a way that is changing the nature of social relationships. Real relationships between people are being supplanted by artificial relationships with celebrities, who reflect a new value system based on fame and status for its own sake. The ongoing preoccupation with celebrity is escapist and arguably fun, with celebrities built up or knocked down by the press for being overweight, drunk or on drugs. Just as soap operas have long provided comforting, mythical places to take the place of long-gone communities of friendly neighbours, so the existence of celebrities, charted in minute detail by scores of magazines, brings daily involvement in their lives. 'Reality' television programmes fill a similar emotional space, creating the impression that the audience really knows the contestants, and allowing them to become emotionally involved with them. However, the harm that can arise when artifice is substituted for real emotional engagement is well illustrated by a helpline, which was advertised in *Heat* magazine, for people suffering from depression following the end of a series of 'Big Brother'.

Celebrity culture brings with it the artificial impression that we know people when we don't, creating an emotional emptiness. It also encourages a misplaced pursuit of perfection, exemplified by the growing popularity of plastic surgery. This drive for perfection is mirrored by the popularity of contemporary approaches to the fear of crime, with people keen to be surrounded by as much security as possible in their attempt to feel perfectly safe. It does not work because it is not possible to create a perfect world. The truth is that, no matter how much people have, they always want more – because feelings of safety and self-esteem are fundamentally emotional issues that cannot be addressed by consumer power.

Respect and happiness

Richard Titmuss (1950) pointed out more than half a century ago that 'less social disparagement' is central to greater cohesion, trust and happiness in society. Today the term 'disrespect' serves equally well for 'social disparagement', indicating how important it is to foster a sense of self-worth and self-respect among people. Ironically, the government's 'Respect' agenda, which is based on zero tolerance policies pioneered in the US, has done exactly the opposite. Zero tolerance, like 'defensible space', aims for increased control over the environment rather than an understanding of social problems. It emerged from the 'broken windows' theory, first outlined by the American criminologists James Q. Wilson and George Kelling in a famous article in *Atlantic Monthly* in 1982 (Wilson and Kelling, 1982). They argued that tolerating routine incivilities, such as window breaking, begging and drunkenness, increased 'respectable fears' and encouraged a spiral of community decline. This strategy, accompanied by a pleasing and easy-to-understand media narrative, has been incorrectly credited with the clean-up of New York City.[3] Despite this, the 'broken windows' approach has been warmly embraced in the UK and is linked to the arrival of 'antisocial behaviour' on the political scene in the mid-1990s as a term for criminalising minor incivilities.

Antisocial behaviour orders are increasingly seen as a failure, with their use dropping by more than a third and nearly two thirds of teenagers breaching them. But despite this, the policy approach has survived and is embodied by the Labour government's Respect agenda and the enthusiasm expressed by both main political parties for police powers to 'stop and search' without reasonable suspicion. Ironically, policy makers remain blind to the rather different issues of respect and disrespect that Titmuss showed to be critical for everyone, and for young people in particular. 'Less social disparagement' is inextricably linked to greater equality, self-esteem and higher levels of trust, which in turn reduces fear between people.

Fear of crime also causes depression, as a study by University College, London found, showing that people with a strong fear of crime were almost twice as likely to suffer from depression (Stafford et al, 2007). The links between fear, trust and unhappiness were further explored by the economist Richard Layard and the psychologist Oliver James in respective works on happiness and well-being. Layard (2006) pointed to far higher levels of trust and happiness in Scandinavian societies where wealth inequalities are lower, while James (2007) cited figures showing that rates of mental illness are twice as high in America, Australia and New Zealand, where wealth inequalities are greater, than in continental Europe.

Despite these clear messages, growing political interest in the concept of well-being has bypassed the question of inequality. Instead, it has concentrated on cognitive behavioural therapies and positive thinking to ease depression. Since there is evidence that this type of therapy does reduce depression in the short term, the government has been persuaded to fund the training of thousands of therapists. However, like zero tolerance approaches to policing and law enforcement, cognitive behaviour therapy focuses on symptoms rather than causes. Arguably, it directs sufferers away from the real causes of their dissatisfaction, which often lie with feelings of 'social disparagement'.

Conclusion

Taking a pessimistic view, it seems likely that the narrative which views inequality as 'yesterday's news' will continue to prevail. There is seemingly little political will from either of the main parties to recalibrate the rising inequality, which all the evidence indicates is behind growing fear, distrust and mental illness. In their conclusions the authors of the recent research review into knife crime said: 'The link between crime and the deeper structural causes of inequality, poverty and social disaffection needs to be acted upon if the solutions are to be more than cosmetic and short term' (Eades et al, 2007, p 31). They also concluded that 'the lack of research and co-ordinated, evidence-based policies to deal with the problem is hard to justify'.

This reflects a political culture where research is too easily dismissed in favour of headlines. As a consequence, the government has continued to focus on zero tolerance policies, which are not backed up by evidence, but which promote 'social disparagement', making the problem worse. With some exceptions, newspapers remain keen to sell newspapers on the back of lurid crime stories, and it is hard to see how a more responsible media, helping to build trust between citizens and institutions, could ever flourish in such a commercially driven environment. A few media outlets, notably the BBC and Channel 4, do provide more rigorous coverage in response to their public service remit. Thus, if there is to be any chance of improving trust between institutions and the public, the public service remit needs to be supported and extended.

Meanwhile, visible segregation continues to grow in our communities, encouraged by policies like defensible space and the creation of privatised parts of the city. As mental health problems increase, quick fixes are pursued instead of dealing with the root causes, which lie in segregation and inequality. It would take a shift away from our American model of capitalism towards a more interventionist model, common in parts of Europe and Scandinavia, to seriously begin to tackle rising inequality. Ironically, the financial collapse, which is highlighting how seriously this needs to be considered, could make it possible for real alternatives to be considered. At the same time, smaller shifts in policy direction can make a difference, and an awareness of the importance of 'social disparagement' might divert politicians away from zero tolerance, defensible space and high security, towards policies that undermine fear and promote trust.

Notes

[1] Home Office research development statistics.

[2] Communication with Press Office.

[3] Figures showed that crime fell by similar amounts during the same period in comparable American cities that did not employ 'broken windows' policing.

References

Alleyne, R. (2008) *The Daily Telegraph*, 27 May.

Ditton, J. (2000) 'Crime and the city: public attitudes towards open-street CCTV in Glasgow', *British Journal of Criminology*, vol 40, no 4, pp 692-709.

Eades, C., Grimshaw, R., Silvestri, A. and Solomon, E. (2007) *'Knife crime': A review of evidence and policy* (2nd edition), London: Centre for Crime and Justice Studies.

Gaines, S. (2008) *The Guardian*, 30 August.

Glassner, B. (2000) *The culture of fear*, New York: Basic Books.

Jacobs, J. (1961) *The death and life of great American cities*, London: Vintage.

James, O. (2007) *Affluenza*, London: Vermillon.

Layard, R. (2006) *Happiness: Lessons from a new science*, London: Penguin.

Mitchell, D. (2003) *The right to the city: Social justice and the fight for public space*, New York, NY: Guilford Press.

Newman, O. (1972) *Defensible space: People and design in the violent city*, New York, NY: Macmillan.

Parenti, C. (1999) *Lockdown America*, London: Verso Books.

Reeve, A. (1998) 'Risk and the new urban space of managed town centres', *International Journal of Risk, Society and Crime Prevention*, vol 31, no 1, pp 43-54.

Stafford, M., Chandola, T. and Marmot, M. (2007) 'Association between fear of crime and mental health and physical functioning', *American Journal of Public Health*, vol 97, no 11, pp 2076-81.

Straw, J. (1999) Speech to the Labour Party Conference.

Titmuss, R. (1950) *Problems of social policy*, London: HMSO.

Wilson, J.Q. and Kelling, G. (1982) 'Broken windows – the police and neighbourhood safety', *The Atlantic Monthly*, March.

The absence of society

12

The absence of society

Zygmunt Bauman

What price the social state?

The most remarkable and insidious feature of the present-day edition of social ills is that they arise mostly from the absence of society, rather than from its pressures. They are products of a gradual, yet relentless, withdrawal of 'society' as an entity that defines individual obligations while guaranteeing individual rights. 'Society' in that sense is now conspicuous mostly by its absence. Margaret Thatcher famously declared: 'There is no such thing as "society". There are only individuals and families.' Peter Drucker (1989), the influential voice of emergent neo-conservatism in America, likewise announced that there was 'no longer salvation from society'.

More than anything else, the 'welfare state' (which I prefer to call the 'social state') is an arrangement of human togetherness that resists the present-day 'privatising' tendency to break down the networks of human bonds and to undermine the social foundations of human solidarity. Where 'privatisation' shifts the task of resolving socially produced problems onto the shoulders of individual men and women (in most cases much too weak for the purpose), so the 'social state' has tended to unite its members in the struggle to protect them from the morally devastating competitive 'war of all against all' and 'one-upmanship'.

A state is 'social' when it promotes the principle of communally endorsed, collective insurance against individual misfortune and its consequences. It is this principle that lifts the abstract 'society' to the level of a tangible, 'felt-and-lived' community. It replaces the mistrust-and-suspicion-generating 'order of egoism' with the confidence and solidarity-inspiring 'order of equality'. And it is this same principle that lifts members of society to the status of citizens. It makes them stakeholders, in addition to being stockholders. They are beneficiaries, but also the actors responsible for the creation and decent allocation of benefits – citizens defined and moved by their acute interest in the common property and responsibility. The application of this principle may protect men and women from the bane of poverty. But, most importantly, it may also become a prolific source of social solidarity that recycles 'society' into a common, communal good. Society is raised to the level of community as long as it protects its members against the twin horrors of misery and indignity; that is, against the terrors of being excluded, of falling from the fast-accelerating vehicle of progress.

Originally, the 'social state' was intended to serve precisely such purposes. Lord Beveridge, to whom we owe the blueprint for the post-war British 'welfare state', believed that his vision of a comprehensive, collectively endorsed insurance for everyone was the inevitable consequence of the liberal idea of individual freedom. Franklin Delano Roosevelt's declaration of 'war on fear' was based on the same assumption. Complete liberty of choice for the individual entails, after all, uncountable risks of failure with which many people would find it beyond their personal ability to cope. For most people, the liberal ideal of freedom of choice needs to be mitigated by the insurance policy issued in the name of community; a policy they can rely on in case of personal defeat or a blow of fate.

No rescue from individual indolence or impotence could be expected from a political state that is not, or refuses to be, a social state. Without social rights for all, a large, and in all probability growing, number of people would find their political rights of little use. If political rights are necessary to set social rights in place, social rights are indispensable to keep political rights in operation. The two need each other for their survival. The social state has been the ultimate modern embodiment of the idea of community: that is, the institutional incarnation of an 'imagined totality' woven of reciprocal dependence, commitment and solidarity. Social rights tie that imagined totality to the daily realities of its members and the solid ground of life experience. They certify the veracity of mutual trust and of trust in the shared network that endorses and validates collective solidarity. 'Belonging' translates as trust in the benefits of human solidarity, and in the institutions that arise from that solidarity. We need each other. We live our lives in the here and now, together with others, caught up in the midst of change. We will be richer if we are all allowed to participate and nobody is left out. We will all be stronger if there is security for everybody and not only for a few.

Social justice and economic efficiency, loyalty to the social state tradition and an ability to modernise swiftly are not, and need not be, at loggerheads. Yet we seem to be moving in an opposite direction: with societies becoming increasingly 'absent'. The range of individual autonomy is expanding, yet the social functions of the state are being ceded ('subsidiarised') to the self-concern of individuals. States no longer endorse the collective insurance policy and leave the task of achieving well-being to individual pursuit.

The outcome of increased individualism

Left increasingly to their own resources and acumen, individuals are expected to devise individual solutions to socially generated problems. Such expectation sets them in mutual competition. This leads to a view of communal solidarity as by and large irrelevant, apart from temporary alliances of convenience. If not mitigated by forceful institutional intervention, it renders differentiation and polarisation of chances inescapable. Indeed, it makes the polarisation of prospects and chances a self-propelling and self-accelerating process.

The effects of this tendency have been easy to predict – and can be now counted. In Britain, for instance, the share of the top 1% of earners has doubled since 1982 from 6.5% to 13% of national income, while Chief Executives of the 100 FTSE companies are earning not 20 times more than the average earners as in 1980, but 133 times. On the other hand, thanks to the new network of 'information highways', every man or woman and child, whether rich or poor, is invited to compare their own lot with the circumstances of all other individuals. Most of all, we are encouraged to compare ourselves with the lavish consumption of public idols; those celebrities constantly in the limelight. The driving force of conduct is no longer the more or less realistic desire to 'keep up with Joneses' next door, but the infuriatingly nebulous idea of catching up with supermodels, premier league footballers and rock and pop stars. As the psychologist Oliver James (2008) recently suggested, a truly toxic mixture is created by stoking up 'unrealistic aspirations and the expectations that they can be fulfilled'. Great swathes of the British populace 'believe that they can become rich and famous' even though the actual likelihood of this occurring has diminished since the 1970s.

Mapping the cause of social evils

Max Scheler, the German ethical philosopher, noted in 1912 that the average person comes to appreciate a value only 'in the course of, and through comparison' with possessions, condition, plight or quality of (an)other person(s) (Scheler, 1955[1]). Personal experience of a value is secondary to social evaluation and social interaction. Quite often, however, the outcome of such comparison is an individual's discovery that they do not possess a value that is socially appreciated and deemed desirable. This arouses resentment: a mixture of rancour, vexation and indignation, caused by feelings of having been harmed, offended, deprived, robbed or left behind and rejected. Resentment breeds two opposite tendencies. On the one hand, the missing value is hotly desired and the failure to appropriate it becomes ever-more difficult to bear. On the other hand, it promotes a tendency to demean, deride and degrade those who are lucky enough to possess the value (in the manner of Aesop's fox concluding that the unreachable grapes were sour).

This ambivalence, termed 'cognitive dissonance' by psychologists, is a response to the need to hold two incompatible opinions simultaneously. Humiliation casts the valued objects as both desired and resented, tokens of prestige and brands of shame. It tends, therefore, to be a source of perpetual anxiety, spiritual discomfort and, often, sizzling hostility. Having no evident rational solution, it feeds irrational responses in the shape of acts that are ineffective in removing the cause, although possibly useful for a temporary release of resulting tension. Just as Scheler anticipated, a growing number of our contemporaries have become afflicted in this way. Indeed, few of the denizens of our liquid-modern society of consumers can claim to be fully immune to the threat of contamination. Our vulnerability, says Scheler, is unavoidable (and perhaps incurable) in a society where relative equality of political and other rights goes hand in hand with enormous differentiation of genuine power, possessions and education (Scheler, 1955[2]). In other words, a society where everyone 'has the right' to consider himself equal to everyone else, while knowing there are those whom we cannot equal.

Cognitive dissonance is inescapable when such a gap exists between the extent of formal rights and the material ability to fulfil them. The detrimental, evil-generating consequences of that gap are sharply aggravated when, as in our liberal democratic society, it is the individual who is instructed, nudged and expected to close that gap through their own efforts. Closing the gap is commended as individual achievement, while its persistence is blamed on individual indolence or sloth, adding offence to injury. United States Senator John McCain, the unsuccessful Republican presidential candidate in 2008, restated what has long been the explicit principle of individualist philosophy, declaring: 'It is not the duty of government to bail out and reward those who act irresponsibly' (*New York Times*, 28 March 2008).

Our society has, thus, come to meet all the conditions for widespread cognitive dissonance and resentment. Their universality reflects the inner contradiction of a society that sets a standard of happiness that most of its members are unable to match, or prevented from matching. Even among the relatively well off, as Jeremy Seabrook points out, the moments of security and spiritual comfort tend to be poisoned by the fear of threats emanating from an explosive mixture of dire inequality and rampant individualism.[3] Although the rich may live in the enclosures of home, car, work and places of leisure, there are still intersections where their lives are crossed by those they fear. We are all products of the same culture of a savage individualism that emanates from the consumer market – the piper we all pay daily for setting the tunes for us to daily intone. To quote Seabrook again: 'In this new social order, there is only one thing worse than domination by the market, and that is exclusion from it, since there is now no other source of knowing who we are.'[4]

In the market society, the phantom of untold happiness is waiting to be discovered in the shopping malls. It hovers over our life pursuits, in tandem with the spectre of untold misery called 'exclusion'. Staying in the game and trying to catch the phantom, while escaping the clutches of the spectre, is the never-ending task of a life otherwise sliced into short-lived episodes. The art and compulsion of playing this addictive game are at the core of a market-guided and market-administered socialisation that extends from 'cradle to coffin'. Those who remain immune to the consumerist pressures are fated to become outcasts.

The meaning of failure in a society of consumers

Exclusionist practices in a society of consumers are much more harsh and unyielding than in a society of producers. In a society of producers, it is males unable to pass the test of producing or soldiering capacity that are cast as 'abnormal' and branded 'invalids'. However, in the society of consumers, the 'invalids' earmarked for exclusion are 'flawed consumers'. Unlike the rejects of industry or of military service, they cannot be conceived of as people deserving of care and assistance because consumer pursuits are presumed to be universally available to everyone who wants them. All investment in 'failed consumers' is condemned as a waste of taxpayers' money because it adds nothing to the profit-making activities by which the 'health of economy' is measured. And since any verdict of 'social invalidity' is assumed to be the outcome of individual faults, it only adds insult to injury; making the sense of resentment more acute and the desire for vengeance more violent.

To shop and to consume means nowadays to invest in one's own social membership. This, the market society translates as 'saleability': obtaining qualities for which there is already a market demand, or recycling existing qualities into commodities for which yet more demand can be created. Most consumer commodities on offer derive their attraction from their genuine or implied investment value. Their promise to increase the attractiveness and, thereby, the 'market price' of their buyers is written, in large or small print, into the prospectuses of all products. Consumption is an investment in everything that matters for an individual's 'market value' and self-esteem. Thus, we increasingly think of ourselves, and either appreciate or demean ourselves, in the manner of market commodities. By such reckoning, the sole road to inclusion is to consume more, whereas the inability to do so is seen as a sure recipe for exclusion.

The supremacy of individualism

When reduced to the consumption of 'made in Marketland' commodities, the pursuit of happiness remains a thoroughly individual activity. This has led two German sociologists, Ulrich Beck and Elisabeth Beck-Gernsheim, to ask how two individuals who want to be equal and free can discover the common ground on which their love can grow. With interpersonal competition and one-upmanship elevated to the rank of a life strategy, how can the other person avoid becoming an additional hindrance, if not a disruptive factor (Beck and

Beck-Gernsheim, 1995)? 'One-upmanship' cannot be easily squared with partnership and love, and particularly the kind of love that shelters us from the turbulent and mercilessly competitive life of markets and marketing.

The newspaper columnist Mariella Frostrup (2008, p 61) has recently stated, as though it were self-evident truth, that 'love is the least reliable of human emotions'. She added that, if you sacrifice yourself to the needs of your partner in the name of love, 'you are left with nothing but a tenuous connection to another human being that time, daily wear and tear, and the pressures of the 21st century will no doubt take their toll on'.

The sociologists Ehrenreich and English, years earlier, argued that in a post-romantic world where the old ties no longer bind, all that matters is 'you': you can be what you want to be and choose your life, your environment and even your appearance and emotions (Ehrenreich and English, 1979, p 276). The old hierarchies of protection and dependency no longer exist and there are only free contracts, freely terminated. The marketplace has expanded to include all relationships. 'Sacrificial culture is dead,' declared Giles Lipovetsky (1993, pp 327-8), the French sociologist, towards the end of the last century. 'We've stopped recognising ourselves in any obligation to live for the sake of something else than ourselves.'

This is not to say that we have turned entirely deaf to the misfortunes of other people, or with the sorry state of our planet. Nor have we stopped declaring our willingness to act in defence of the downtrodden. Superficially, the opposite might seem to be the case. Paradoxically, the spectacular rise of egotistic self-concern runs shoulder to shoulder with rising sensitivity to human misery and abhorrence of pain and suffering visited on even most distant strangers. But, as Lipovetsky observed, such moral impulses and outbursts of magnanimity are instances of 'painless morality' stripped of obligations. When it comes to acting for the sake of others, the well-being of self tends to be both the preliminary and the ultimate consideration. It tends to set the limits to which we are prepared to go in our readiness to help.

As a rule, manifestations of devotion to others, however sincere, stop short of self-sacrifice. For instance, dedication to green causes seldom goes as far as adopting an ascetic lifestyle. We would seldom be willing to accept even a minor personal inconvenience to renounce the lifestyle of consumerist indulgence. The driving force of our indignation does not tend to be renunciation of excess, so much as a desire for superior, safer and better-secured consumption. We don't seem to feel any longer that we have a mission to perform on the planet. Concern with the way the world is managed is giving way to concern with self-management. It is not the state of the world and its inhabitants that tends to worry us, but rather a recycling of its outrages and injustices into spiritual discomforts and an emotional giddiness that impairs the peace of mind of concerned individuals. This may be, as Christopher Lasch (1979, p 43) observed, the result of transforming 'collective grievances into personal problems amenable to therapeutic intervention'. 'The new narcissists', as he memorably termed those who perceive the state of the world through the prism of their personal problems, are 'haunted not by guilt, but by anxiety'. In recording their inner experiences, they attempt to seduce others into giving them 'their attention, acclaim or sympathy' and to shore up their faltering sense of self. Personal life has become as warlike and as full of stress as the marketplace itself.

This may be good news for the self-assertive individual who is wary of moral scruples that may stand in the way of self-promotion. But it is bad news for everyone else – and most certainly for the prospects of human solidarity, the sole lever capable of hoisting the rest of us from the doldrums of humiliation and seething resentment.

The struggle to be included

As recently as 30 years ago, it could be seen that the sharpest inequality of wages tended to be accepted by those in the lower regions of the pay scale, provided theirs was a customary deprivation. Falling behind people they had hitherto treated as their equals was the thing that made people feel deprived. Now, much as then, deprivation means unhappiness. But the causes of humiliation, degradation and rejection are now at least as likely to include blows to social recognition and self-esteem as the discomforts brought about by material hardship. Deprivation still tends to be 'relative' and a benchmark is needed against which to measure one's own condition. One may feel deprived when falling below a standard of living enjoyed in the past, or when falling behind one's equals of yesterday who now, suddenly, surge ahead. What is, however, new is the status of today's benchmarks and the way they have added greater urgency and vigour to the pursuit of happiness.

Looking back, it can be seen that in stratified societies marked by a sharp polarisation of access to both material and symbolic values (prestige, respect, insurance against humiliation), it was the people situated 'in the middle' that tended to be most sensitive to the threat of unhappiness. The upper classes needed to do little or nothing to retain their superior condition; the lowest classes could do little or nothing to improve their inferior lot. But for the middle classes everything they didn't yet have appeared to be for the taking. Meanwhile, everything they already had and cherished could – in a single moment of inattention – be lost. More than any other category of people, the middle classes lived in a state of perpetual anxiety, oscillating between brief intervals of enjoyable safety and the horrors of approaching catastrophe.

Among reasons to interpret the advent of the modern era as a transformation promoted mostly by middle-class interests, obsessive concerns with the frailty of social standing and its defence loom very large indeed. When sketching the contours of a society knowing no unhappiness, utopian blueprints at the dawn of the modern era reflected predominantly middle-class dreams and longings. More than anything else, they visualised an end to uncertainty and insecurity. We may see this as an avant-garde of the times to come, experiencing the contradiction destined to become well-nigh universal in liquid-modern life. It foreshadows today's perpetual tension between security and freedom: equally coveted and indispensable for a happy life, but frightfully difficult to reconcile and enjoy simultaneously.

The middle classes have not, therefore, achieved their Utopia of the 'perfect balance' between equally coveted freedom and security. Instead, the instability of social location and the 'existential uncertainty' that were once endemic to the 'middle classes', have become a universal human condition. Not for nothing is television's *Big Brother* programme enjoying popularity that cuts across class divisions, presented under the rubric of 'reality TV'. This description suggests that off-screen life – 'the real thing' – is just like the on-screen saga of competitors playing their game of survival. No one is guaranteed to survive, permission to stay in the game is a temporary reprieve and team loyalty does not outlive its usefulness for the promotion of individual interest. That someone will be excluded is beyond dispute; the only question is who it will be. What is at issue is not the abolition of exclusion (a task that would favour joining forces and solidarity of action), but shifting the threat of exclusion away from self and on to others. In *Big Brother*, someone must be excluded each week; not because they have revealed themselves to be inadequate, but because it is written into the rules. Exclusion is in the nature of things – a 'law of nature', so to speak – against which it makes no sense to rebel. The only issue worth considering is how to stave off the prospect of being excluded for another week.

Meanwhile, back in our 'real' everyday lives, we are encouraged to actively seek 'social recognition' for what has been pre-interpreted as our individual choices. 'Social recognition' means acceptance by 'others who matter' that the form of life practised by a particular individual is worthy and decent, and, therefore, deserving of respect from other 'worthy and decent' people. The alternative to this social recognition is the denial of dignity: otherwise known as humiliation. As the sociologist Dennis Smith (2006, p 38) suggested in his recent book on globalisation: 'the act is humiliating if it forcefully overrides or contradicts the claim that particular individuals ... are making about who they are and where and how they fit in.' Smith adds that:

> *A person feels humiliated when s/he is brutally shown, by words, actions or events, that they cannot be what they think they are.... Humiliation is the experience of being unfairly, unreasonably and unwillingly pushed down, held down, held back or pushed out.*

In a society of individuals like ours, this is arguably the most venomous and implacable variety of resentment a person may feel and the most common and prolific cause of conflict, dissent, rebellion and thirst of revenge. Denial of recognition, refusal of respect and the threat of exclusion have replaced exploitation and discrimination as the formulae most commonly used to explain and justify the grudge individuals might bear towards society.

I would conclude that the list of conspicuous and worrying manifestations of 'social ills' produced by JRF's consultation, has its roots in the sociocultural and political transformations of the last decades. If this is the case, then the 'evils' in question are rooted in the form of life of the liquid-modern, thoroughly individualised society of consumers. Undertakings aimed at mitigating the impact of single social ills on the list may bring temporary and partial relief. But short of reforming the individualised society itself, they would hardly remove the cause of their proliferation and regeneration. To take just one example, appeals for the resurrection of 'family values' and family responsibilities that are currently so popular among politicians are likely to hang in thin air. According to social attitudes research, two thirds of English people believe that there is little difference between being married and living together, only a quarter think that married couples make better parents than unmarried ones and two thirds judge that divorce may be a positive step towards a better life (Ward and Carvel, 2008). We also have to acknowledge that in our individualised society, the role of parents is increasingly focused on (and all too often reduced to) providing children with their monetary entry tickets to the consumer market.

Notes

[1] Quoted from the 1997 Polish edition, *Resentyment i Moralno*, Czytelnik, p 49.

[2] Quoted from the 1997 Polish edition, *Resentyment i Moralno*, Czytelnik, p 41.

[3] http://commentisfree.guardian.co.uk/jeremy_ seabrook/2007/08/ the_perils_of_inequality_most.html

[4] http://commentisfree.guardian.co.uk/jeremy_ seabrook/2007/06/ children_of_the_market.html

References

Beck, U. and Beck-Gernsheim, E. (1995) *The normal chaos of love*, translated by Mark Ritter and Jane Wiebel, Cambridge: Polity Press, pp 3, 13, 53.

Drucker, P.F. (1989) *The new realities*, New York, NY: HarperCollins.

Ehrenreich, B. and English, D. (1979) *For her own good*, New York, NY: Knopf.

Frostrup, M. (2008) *The Observer Magazine*, 30 March.

James, O. (2008) 'Selfish capitalism is bad for our mental health', *The Guardian*, 3 January.

Lasch, C. (1979) *Culture of narcissism*, New York: Warner Books.

Lipovetsky, G. (1993) *L'ère du vide: Esais sur l'individualism contemporain*, Paris: Editions Gallimard.

Scheler, M. (1955) *Das Ressentiment im Aufbau der Moralen, Gesammelte Werke, vol III*, Bern: Francke Verlag.

Smith, D. (2006) *Globalization: The hidden agenda*, Cambridge: Polity Press.

Ward, L. and Carvel, J. (2008) 'Goodbye married couples, hello alternative family arrangements', *The Guardian*, 23 January.

Individualism

13

A wrong turn in the search for freedom?

Neal Lawson

> *It is the wish of all men ... to live happily. But when it comes to seeing clearly what it is that makes a life happy, they grope for the light. Indeed, a measure of the difficulty of achieving the happy life is that the greater the man's energy in striving for it, the further he grows away from it if he has taken a wrong turning on the road.* (Seneca, *On the happy life*, quoted in Bauman, 2008)

Social recession

Something profound has happened to society over the last 30 years, as two curious phenomena have come to light. The first is that as we are getting richer we don't seem to be getting any happier. The second is that we feel increasingly empowered as individuals, but increasingly disempowered as citizens. We can choose more of what we want in the shops, but feel more powerless than ever to shape the world around us. These phenomena combine to create a world that feels like it is out of our control. There is a sense that society is lacking direction that is mixed into a potentially lethal cocktail with an apparent inability to do anything about it. It is turning society into a toxic brew of intolerance, inequality, crime and violence.

'Social recession' is a useful phrase to describe this as it highlights the newly emerging understanding that society can suffer whether the economy is buoyant or, as at the time of writing, is experiencing an accelerating downturn. Social recession hits all social groupings, except the super-rich. An almost tangible sense of insecurity pervades our lives. Little is certain except an exhausting struggle to keep going on the 'earn-to-spend' treadmill of the consumer society. House prices are collapsing, basic food and utility costs are rising sharply and supposedly secure pension schemes are disappearing. It feels like there is nothing we can do. Employment also feels insecure. The concept of a job for life no longer exists. The growing pressure on our working lives is tangible – if the boss or other employees never go home then neither must we. In Britain we work some of the longest hours, yet enjoy fewer public benefits.

And the long hours culture is exacerbated by the desire to shop. We work to buy, but buying soon leaves us feeling empty. No wonder that the pressure of keeping up at work and on the high street is taking its toll. In the past we were known for what we did – what we produced. Now we are a society defined by what we consume. The number of bedrooms we have and the location of our home relay our social standing. Goods and services are not just valued for what they do, but for what they say about us. While we are never physically forced to buy, ever-changing styles and designs relentlessly coax us into buying more. If we refuse then we refuse to be 'normal'. This is a truly frightening concept: that we will fall off the treadmill into the abyss of the failed consumer. Yet it's not as if it's without fun or reward. Consumerism manages the cunning trick of repressing us through seduction. Why would anyone bother to fight against the joy of shopping when we obviously get a kick from it?

In the past it was the threat of unemployment or low pay that was used to discipline the workforce. Today in a consumer society it is the desire to desire that is the control mechanism for the reproduction of social values and norms. It is the seduction of consumption that keeps us working and buying and therefore ensures society stays in order and under control. Shopping buys us identity, meaning and purpose. But it does so only for the short term. For a society based on consumer one-upmanship means we are all prey to others getting ahead of us. As soon as our neighbour buys something we do not have, they put us in the shade – but only until we can out-buy them. We carry on shopping, like a donkey following the carrot dangled before its eyes, despite knowing it is empty, frivolous and meaningless. But what else is there to do? Being satisfied is not the objective of a consumer society. If that were the case, we would simply stop buying. We can never stop buying because that would mean the end of society as we know it.

But it is much worse for what Zygmunt Bauman (Chapter 12) calls 'failed consumers'. Every society has its poor whose shape and nature changes with the shape and nature of the society itself. The poor in a producer society were the unemployed; but because of the economic cycle at least some kind of periodic connection occurred with the rest of society. Today's poor enjoy no such benefits. Because they cannot properly consume, they are never needed. They are denied proper welfare and benefits because they will never be of any use to the rest of us. And they have no solidarity. They do not live in self-sustaining and supporting communities. Unlike the poor of the past, their goal is not to overthrow their oppressors but to be like them. The images of consumerism are all around them. Middle-class children are likely to be less concerned about the trainers they wear because they have other interests and ways to measure their success. But for those from sink estates, having the right brand or mobile is all there is. It is worth fighting and sometimes dying for.

In absolute terms this new poor may be better off, but it is the relative gap between rich and poor that matters – coupled with the emotional and psychological damage of being an outcast. Of course, the 'new poor' refuse to accept their lot. If they cannot consume by the rules, then the rules are broken. They steal or resort to fakes. But always their difference is apparent. Yet, if you follow the logic of a speech in July 2008 by the Conservative leader David Cameron, their poverty is also their fault (Elliott et al, 2008). They are lazy and idle – not part of the fraternity of 'hard-working families'. It is not society, the economy or politics that has failed them – they have failed themselves. In this sense, the poor have never been so excluded from the mainstream of society. They hold a mirror up to show the rest of us what failure looks like. In them we confront our potential abnormality and we despise them for it.

They have no hope because there is no collective infrastructure that would lend them hope. Consumption is now a private act. In a consumer society there is no tolerance, respect or compassion for others, just a possessive defence of our individual right to choose. Consumerism, the mindset of 'normality' in the 21st century, corrodes our social fabric. The consumer is king or queen. We are sovereign individuals: always right and in full possession of our rights. Money is to be spent now for instant gratification, not saved or directed towards long-term social needs. In this way, society enters a vicious cycle of decline. The sharper social differences get, the less likely it is that we seek common answers and public solutions. There is no empathy in a consumer society. Public spending is seen as wasteful and morally dubious. The less likely investment in the form of taxes becomes, the shabbier the public realm becomes and the less able it is to hold together the interests of different social classes.

Growing global market forces create new problems of community cohesion. Borders are opened up and due to profound economic imbalances this increases the flow of people between parts of the world. This creates tensions in the communities that become home to immigrants. In the past this was more containable because the infrastructure of the state could cope, but now public resources are stretched. New social housing is in short supply; we are also underinvesting in public transport and making impossible demands on health and education services. The situation is made worse by a crisis of national identity stoked by the decline of institutions that represent in part what it means to be British. The subjecting to the market of once-proud institutions like the BBC and Post Office eradicates tangible expressions of national identity. The result is that the market flattens everything.

Levels of anxiety reach new heights as we try the impossible trick of finding individual solutions to what are collectively created problems. We are reaching a tipping point in the social recession, beyond which society may not have the ability to recover the vital sense of common interest necessary for its sustainability. The further the market and its values encroach, the less space there is for community, society and the values that underpin them.

The triumph of neoliberalism

The political, social and economic history of the last 150 years has been defined by the struggle between the free market and the forces of society to better regulate and direct the economy. This struggle was the sharp point in the unfolding tensions between class forces and interests. Who would gain more – the owners of capital or those who worked by hand or brain? Governments of the Left and the Right came and went. Change was followed by consolidation and eventual consensus. After the post-war settlement there was cross-party agreement around relatively high levels of public service investment in welfare benefits, education and health: a mixed economy between the nationalised utilities and companies and the private sector grew.

All this unravelled in the 1970s: first under Labour, then decisively through Margaret Thatcher's leadership after 1979. The notion of a balance between the needs of society and the demands of the market no longer held. The imperative of her brand of neoliberal conservatism was the primacy of market forces as a moral necessity and an inevitable fact. The upshot was three decades of widening social inequality and what looks like diminishing social mobility. Despite strenuous efforts, New Labour has only offered a humanised version of what is still in essence a neoliberal project. If we want greater social cohesion and a more equal society, it is essential to understand why neoliberalism took such a strong political and cultural hold on the nation.

The neoliberal project was intensely political and was argued for in precise, coherent terms. But it was lucky in that the moment was right for a potential switch in the political direction of the country. The plan was rooted in the political economy of the Austrian school of economists, most notably Ludwig von Mises and his student Friedrich von Hayek. At the height of 'big' post-war government, this tenacious band of free marketeers developed a critique of state intervention and made the case for the liberalisation of the economy. In America, they infiltrated the universities and had a decisive influence on the creation of the Chicago School under Milton Friedman. In the UK, they found their voice through the creation of new think-tanks like the Institute for Economic Affairs. The moment for neoliberal advance came via sweeping economic, cultural and social changes in the 1960s and1970s. The forces of economic and therefore social centralisation were unwinding. The 'big government' era of Fordism was reaching the limits of performance and effectiveness. In the East, the Soviet model was being found wanting. In the West, social democracy was struggling to meet the pressures of these new cultural times and economic downturn because of the oil price shock.

Right on cue came Mrs Thatcher, extolling the virtues of the free market, the small state, low taxes, weaker unions and the privatisation of industries and social housing. The neoliberal project was vast in its ambition. Not just to restructure the economy but also to use the economy to change the way people felt and behaved. Mrs Thatcher famously said:'Economics are the method but the objective is to change the heart and soul.'[1] She knew that in all of us there is the propensity to be caring, compassionate and cooperative as well as possessive, individualistic and greedy. She knew, too, that people could be bent and shaped by institutions that favoured one set of characteristics over the other. Her years in power were an exercise in destroying the institutions of society and promoting the institutes and practices of the market. As she famously said, 'there is no alternative' (otherwise known as 'TINA').[2]

Britain still lives in the shadow of TINA. New Labour's election in 1997 marked not a different political phase but a new part of the same neoliberal project. Indeed, New Labour's coupling of economic efficiency with social justice meant that the promotion of the market could be justified in almost any sphere. As only Nixon could go to China, so only New Labour could embrace the market, going further than Mrs Thatcher ever dreamed or dared. The thinking was simple: market systems were deemed efficient because they closed the gap between producers and consumers, enabling quick and easy signals to flow between the two. This meant cutting out mediating organisations that required dialogue, debate and consensus-building to function. Trades unions, local government, professional bodies and community groups all slowed the decision-making process and were deemed inefficient. The *agora*, the term the ancient Greeks used for the public sphere, was a luxury that a competitive economy could do without. Democracy was suddenly part of the problem, not part of the solution. This was to be a project built on agoraphobia – a fear of public spaces. It was no accident that the early flowering in New Labour circles of the politics of community and stakeholding quickly withered on the vine.

New Labour now looks as if it is buckling under the weight of its own contradiction. An essentially neoliberal project cannot be housed forever in an essentially pro-social political movement. But it means that the possibilities for change are presently restricted. All three main parties huddle on the same narrow territory. The state must be further commercialised, benefits payments more stringently applied, wherever possible taxes lowered, the market left to its own devices, regulations minimised, labour markets kept flexible. But elements of the state like law and order are strengthened to deal with the antisocial consequences of the free market. As long as the consensus holds, democracy and the chances of an alternative are diminished.

This is not, however, some neutral point of equilibrium that has been reached, but a settlement in favour of free markets and those who benefit most from them. It is not that markets are morally wrong – they are just a mechanism to seek profit. We may desire a balance between the dynamism of the marketplace and the need for a space to be social and equal. But markets simply do not 'do' balance. The demands of shareholders, investors and the fear of competitors mean that they have to keep on finding fresh sites for profit. It is for society and the state to erect the regulatory and moral barriers that can keep the market in check. But it is those barriers that have now been discarded.

The march of the market means that politics now does less and less. It used to deal with the big things in life. But now it only exists to serve the interests of the market. Fewer people take an interest in politics because the common perception is that whoever you vote for nothing really changes. Those who do bother to vote have more of an interest in the economic and social status quo, so only their views are targeted. As democracy goes further into retreat, the field is left open to the market. And if collectively we cannot do anything then we might as well go out and spend, spend, spend. The market is now the master and society is its servant.

The solution

Anyone who wants a more equal and democratic society has a problem. The market is not the answer, as the experience of the last 30 years testifies and the crisis of 2008–09 has proved. But the old centralised state is not the answer either. The solution lies in going back to the cultural crossroad of the 1960s, when notions of freedom became largely individualised. Instead of railing against individualism per se, progressives need to recognise that all aspirations start from people. However, it is the context in which they are formed and the means by which they are secured that matters. What is required is a redefinition of freedom. Instead of viewing it only through the prism of limited individualism and consumerism, freedom needs to be recast in more expansive terms to give people real autonomy, defined as control over their lives. This requires three things.

First, it demands equality. In theory we are free to do whatever we want, to buy what we want and become what we want. In reality we need the resources to make anything happen. At a frivolous level, I am free to eat at the Savoy Hotel every day of the week but the reality is I can't afford it. More importantly, to have a job interview I need the right clothes and the bus fare, as well as the right qualifications and training. We need sufficient equality to ensure we have maximum freedom. Equality is not about treating everyone as if they are the same; it is about ensuring that everyone has sufficient resources to be as free as possible.

Next, a modern definition of freedom demands solidarity. The solution to changing more and taking back control of our lives is only to be found by acting in concert and cooperation with others. It is as social citizens that we make our world. The challenge is to find a way of doing collectivism differently. The unaccountable and bureaucratic state should concern progressives as much as the unaccountable market. At every level the state needs to be democratised, humanised and where possible localised to ensure that it is people power that makes decisions.

All the problems we face demand more collectivism not less. The credit crunch, the problems with financial services regulation, the shortage of affordable housing, pensions, long-term care, transport, the closure of post offices, the need to regulate labour markets and of course climate change all demand greater collective co-operation. None of them are issues we can solve alone as individual consumers. In no instance is anyone saying the answer lies in more freedom for the market. The market is the problem, not the solution.

But in all this there are contradictions and tensions that need to be worked through. Not just between short-term and long-term goals and differing class interests, but also between a desire for diversity through localism and the need for equality. Difference and equality clash. By rightly allowing a thousand flowers to bloom in different communities so that people can become directly involved in institutions that influence their lives, we open up the potential for a 'postcode lottery' with different outcomes in different places. The management of this paradox represents the third strand of the reformulation of freedom, which is to dare more democracy. Democracy allows people to live the tensions and the problems of the diversity/equity divide. It enables them to share in the management and containment of them through proper deliberative processes, both in public services and in their community.

This external tension between a need for difference and a need to belong, which must be based on some level of similarity, is mirrored in our own personalities and characteristics. These competing desires can be seen as the motor of human history as we continually swing between more communitarian needs and then more individualistic desires. Too much of one leads to increased demand for the other. Progressives must not ignore the pull of individualism, but set in place institutions and cultures that allow a reasonable balance between collective action and personal initiative. Democracy is the means by which this process can be mediated. It is no accident that the high point of equality in Britain in the 1950s and 1960s coincided with the high point of democratic participation. The two go hand in hand as it is in the democratic sphere that we meet each other as equal citizens.

The crucial step all progressives need to make is the recognition that democracy is not just a means to an end – the delivery mechanism for state power – but an end in itself. Democracy delivers, and is, 'the good society'. More equality and greater solidarity, facilitated by democracy, provides the basis for a more compelling vision of what it means to be free. To realise this vision, requires two important steps. The first is the development of an alternative political economy. Progressives need to envisage and then construct a new architecture to manage global competitive markets in the interests of society. This feels like a very tall order. But just as progressives had to find solutions to the lack of demand in the economy during the slump of the 1930s (which led to the creation of Keynesian demand management and global institutions to manage trade) so today we, again, need to build institutions to ensure that capitalism is saved from itself and that economies are made to work in the interests of society, not the other way around. To do otherwise is to be left addressing the symptoms of unregulated markets without touchiing the causes. We need to recognise the need for a balance between economic and social needs.

The second step towards a new progressive consensus rests on accepting that fears of the unaccountable market are only trumped by fears of the unaccountable state. The market provides some compensatory relief from the drudgery of trying to survive life in the 21st century, but our experiences of the state are rarely rewarding. Efforts to make the state more accountable and responsive to our needs have been tried through the choice and competition agenda, but it doesn't work. There is, or should be, a public service ethos based on fairness. This should also acknowledge that public services ought to be delivered by workers who are trusted rather than cajoled by markets or policy makers. The wrong turn taken with public services has left the profound paradox that investment is at record levels, but so also is public dissatisfaction.

At both the macro and micro levels, the state needs to be renewed by democratising it. A properly written constitution, a fully elected second chamber, devolution and localism, a limit on campaign expenditure and a fair voting system would all go a long way to reviving confidence. Yet democratic reform needs to extend beyond Parliament. Public services themselves need to be democratised, so people feel ownership of them and so they become more efficient and responsive. If patients of a general practitioner were balloted every year on whether their doctor should keep their job then the pressure to provide a good service would be far stronger. Thus, real freedom is to be found through the design and redesign of the institutions that have the ability to help us shape our lives, such as schools, hospitals and local government. As we strengthen democracy so we reinforce society's ability to regulate the market, creating a virtuous circle.

A renewed sense of direction

The growth of individualism and the crisis of community cohesion, social justice and democracy itself have their roots in the way the cultural revolution of the 1960s was skilfully deflected by the right into a crusade for freedom based on free markets. But free markets do not create free people – at least not for the vast majority. Left unchecked they create social evils and a social recession. The 'new Right' had the imagination and ambition to believe that a different world was possible from the post-war welfare settlement, which had seen social mobility increase and inequality fall. Progressives today have stopped dreaming that a better world is both desirable and feasible and too many have swallowed almost whole the line that nothing other than accommodation to the market is possible. But progressives have to be relentless in the search for the answer to the manifest problems of society. Realism always starts with utopian visions because that is the only way we can know what we are being realistic about. The National Health Service started as a dream, and if floated as an idea today would presumably be denounced by 'pragmatists' as an impossibility. As such, pragmatism has become a meaningless term: it should mean that we know where we are going but are just being clever about how we get there. It is time to be properly pragmatic again – to have a vision and a task to change the world.

Notes

[1] Margaret Thatcher, interview with Ronald Butt for *The Sunday Times*, 3 May 1981.

[2] Margaret Thatcher, press conference for American correspondents in London, 25 June 1980.

References

Bauman, Z. (2008) *The art of life*, Cambridge: Polity Press.
Elliott, F., Riddell, P., Davidson, L. and Coates, S. (2008) 'David Cameron tells the fat and the poor: take responsibility', *The Times*, 8 July, www.timesonline.co.uk/tol/news/politics/article4290298.ece

14

Individualism and community: investing in civil society

Stephen Thake

Social evils in the 21st century: reframing the debate

The Joseph Rowntree Foundation's consultation exercise has unearthed a chaos of social evils. This raises a concern that by concentrating on a multiplicity of social evils, we are focusing on symptoms rather than causes. The 'evils' identified – ranging from individualism and consumerism to loss of social solidarity – all strike me as symptoms of our bewildered response to rapid technological and scientific advances, climate change, globalised economic activity and the eastwards shift of economic power.

The pace of change has accelerated in our lifetime and presents challenges to the agencies of the state, commerce, organised religion and the media; challenges that they have failed to respond to adequately or fast enough. A failure of agency has led to a withdrawal of authority from and trust in those institutions and people responsible for managing them (Figure 14.1). All this helps to explain the retreat into individualism. Consumerism, like comfort food, has become displacement behaviour to mask the stress. The consequence is that we consume more than we need, and thus contribute to the larger forces driving the destructive dynamic.

My proposition is that it is important to understand the existing dynamic in order to establish agencies that are better able to manage technological and economic changes and their environmental consequences for the wider good. That requires intervention at all levels. But change at the local level is capable of engendering new forms of action and solidarity that in turn provide the drivers that can reinvigorate existing and establish new forms of agency. It is, therefore, important to support behavioural change at a local level that is consistent with addressing the larger issues.

Figure 14.1: Social evils as symptons of the consequences of failure of agency to respond to global change

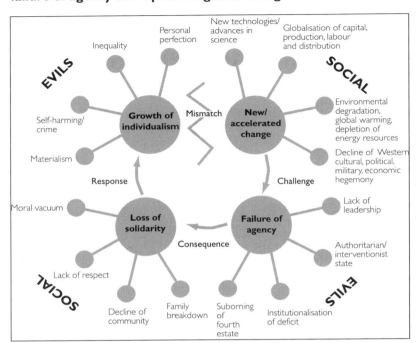

Scale of change

In 1904, when Joseph Rowntree set up his philanthropic trusts, the earth was thought of as a solid object. Germany and Great Britain, the pioneers of the first Industrial Revolution, were still engaged in a competition to carve out and control a world dominated by the concept of physical empire. The First World War was still over the horizon, as was the Great Depression and the rise of totalitarian socialism and fascism. Since then the face-off between the US and the Soviet Union, the leaders of the second Industrial Revolution, has come and gone. The theories of relativity and quantum mechanics have revolutionised science and moved it beyond the comprehensible concepts of Newton, Hooke and Faraday. Innovation has taken on a life of its own with a myriad of advances taking place and being transported around the globe at ever-increasing speed. The driving forces of progress have become distanced from us, beyond our control and yet impact on our daily lives.

In the last 50 years, the third Industrial Revolution, in which de-mechanisation, miniaturisation, hydrocarbons, computers, telecommunications and containerisation have all had a part to play, has seen the geographical centre of gravity for economic growth shift to the Pacific Rim. We are now in the throes of a fourth phase of industrialisation, which brings together the models of production developed through the first three phases with the unexploited labour markets in China and the Indian subcontinent. This is bringing about profound changes in the world order.

The benefits and costs of change

Changes in science, technology, organisation, production and distribution have offered progressive governments the prospect of eradicating want and disease. These same advances have facilitated huge increases in wealth worldwide. For the first time in the history of humankind, the prospect of creating a basic standard of living and healthcare for the poorest has become a possibility. But implementing that vision has come with social, physical and economic costs.

In developing economies, industrialisation has brought upheaval, including massive population movements and rapid urbanisation. It has created the overcrowding, squalor and polarisation of wealth and poverty that epitomised the first generation of industrialised cities 150 years ago. In developed economies, per capita income has grown even faster. But that increase has also come at a price. The transition from an industrial to a service economy has resulted in the demolition of large swathes of our cities with the dislocation of labour markets, communities and families. Manual workers have been spun out of the system while the options for other groups have been closed down. Here too, polarisation between rich and poor has grown.

If we take the social evils originally listed by Joseph Rowntree, we may feel a superficial sense of satisfaction that war and slavery have been eradicated; until we remember that more people have died in wars in Africa and Asia in the last 60 years than were killed in the two world wars combined. Similarly, we might feel compelled to acknowledge that the wealth generated through globalisation is a product of the exploitation of labour in far-off locations, with the trade routes policed not by gun-ships but by the World Trade Organization. The surplus wealth created by new forms of production and distribution has meant that many, in Western society, have moved from meeting basic needs to having a surfeit. However, to feed this way of life now means that the supply of energy and the control of raw materials are increasingly replacing labour and capital as key resources and pollution arising from the greater use of fossil fuel energy has taken global warming to its tipping point.

The failure of agency

The destructive aspects of the global dynamic have put national governments under pressure. For 100 years through to the 1950s, civil society through trades unions and mass political parties struggled to secure an equitable distribution of the wealth created. However, just as a consensus over the benefits of a mixed economy had been secured, the mode of production shifted from being predominantly national in form to becoming increasingly global. The global corporations that operate in the unregulated space beyond the control of state governments move much of the wealth created offshore. Held by banks, hedge funds and sovereign wealth funds, these take on a life of their own, with the capacity to distort and destabilise the financial systems.

The architecture of the international regulatory framework is, as the international banking crisis of 2008 demonstrated, non-anticipatory, incomplete and the intervention mechanisms weak. Domestically it has been difficult for national governments to admit that they are unable to protect their populations from the uncertainties of the new world order. Powerless to halt the process, they have sought to manage change in order to maximise the benefits while mitigating the dis-benefits.

Governments at all levels have sought to professionalise their interventions. In doing so, they have corporatised and distanced themselves from the communities they serve, while at the same time penetrating deeper and deeper into people's daily lives. Yet the levers at their disposal are limited. Their responses are seen to be inadequate and clumsy, giving rise to unintended consequences, or simply irrelevant. Many communities feel abandoned, neglected or betrayed. It is no wonder that politicians become cautious and risk averse. Commitments are chosen carefully. Being careful with the truth becomes a way of life. This has led to a crisis of agency and the withdrawal of authority. Politicians, although they might be better equipped and more professional than their predecessors, are held in lower esteem and are required to be more accountable for their actions.

Loss of solidarity

The failure of agency has resulted in a decline in participation in the political process. The bonds that held together the alliances at the heart of mass political parties have loosened. Both voting at elections and membership of political parties have declined. The loss of solidarity is evidenced in other ways, too.

Community activity has been built around three pillars: the workplace, the family and faith. All have experienced considerable change over the last 50 years, with a significant knock-on effect on community activity and community capacity. Many of the manufacturing industries have gone and with them work-based community activities. Those industries that have thrived have jettisoned their commitment to community because it does not contribute to the bottom line.

In addition, the nature of the workforce has changed. It now takes two working adults to generate sufficient income to maintain a tolerable quality of life. This has brought enormous benefits in terms of gender equality and growth of income. But it has also been at a cost. For those with children, life is dominated by getting food on the table as quickly as possible and the never-ending juggling of childcare. Adults and children have to get by with less of each other; family life is hollowed out. And affluence, as economic recession now emphasises, is precarious. With the perpetual fear of illness, accident or job closure, everything can fall apart at a moment's notice. There is little time for community activity. Simply getting by is a draining and full-time occupation.

Faith communities have been a third pillar of community engagement. Yet the last 50 years have witnessed an unprecedented commercialisation and secularisation of society. Congregations have aged and declined to such an extent that many churches struggle to keep their doors open and their roofs watertight. There is diminishing energy for community activity and outreach.

Retreat into individualism

At the local level, an individual, uncertain of their future, will do everything possible to avoid being tumbled out of the system and to protect those closest to them from a similar fate. It is not surprising that those with 'pointy elbows' and inside knowledge will manipulate systems for individual gain, and that cities become partitioned between neighbourhoods of affluence and flight. Others, for whom flight is not a realistic option, batten down the hatches and hope to survive in quiet disengagement. This has been the strategy of many older people, who now find that their fixed incomes and plans have been overtaken by events. Those who are left behind and who conclude that the struggle is too great, may blur the pain by retreating into the comfort of food, alcohol and substance dependency. For others, noticeable for the first time among the young, depression, self-harming or suicide has been an outcome.

A retreat into self is not limited to the individual. At a national level, it can give rise to greater protectionism, appeals to national values and holding at bay those who do not hold those values. Within nation states it can give rise to the re-emergence of geographical and cultural fault lines, with similar appeals to local identities and distrust of 'the other'. At a time when there is a premium on cooperation and collective action to address large-scale and common threats, a myriad of individual choices and actions contribute to a multi-speed society and a multi-speed world, where divisions become wider and more entrenched.

Investing in a counter-dynamic

There is, nevertheless, a perverse sense in which an invitation to focus on social evils is comforting. Social evils lie outside ourselves and are located in others. It is government, the media, big business and religion that we hold largely responsible. Although individuals have choices to make, 'social evil' implies that they are powerless in the face of the failure of existing agencies to foresee, forestall, manage or reverse these forces. Yet the shirts on our backs, the shoes on our feet, the iPods in our ears, the cars we drive and the flights we take are all products of Western hegemony, globalisation and technological change. We benefit from the products of these processes while distancing ourselves from the negative consequences.

It is especially interesting that technological change, globalisation, exploitation of labour, environmental degradation and the dominance of Western culture have not generated the same level of outrage against slavery, squalor and poverty that existed in Victorian Britain. Then, they were national issues, which the political and intellectual leaders felt they could control. Now they are global and beyond our control. We are, therefore, not complicit. We can live the good life and the world can 'go to hell in a handcart'.

Yet the pictures taken from Apollo 17 spacecraft in the early 1970s provided another vision of the earth. Those images of a fragile globe hanging in space led to a profound shift in outlook. There was greater understanding that the world's resources are finite and that the future of the human species is intertwined with that of our planet. It made it easier to understand that consequences of global warming wash back on everybody. And to address those issues we need to change our view of ourselves in relation to the world. That means reassessing the idea of the primacy of humankind. We need to be humble enough to accept that we are, in Stephen Hawking's definition, 'an advanced breed of monkeys, on a minor planet of a very average star' (*Der Spiegel*, 17 October 1989).

The advances of science cannot be undone. Instead, we need to learn to harness scientific and technological change to create equilibrium in the use of the world's resources. We must use globalisation of production, labour and distribution as a means of understanding and respecting other people's cultures and traditions. It requires a change in outlook as radical as that epitomised by the shift from medieval ecclesiasticism to modern enlightenment. The consequences, however, of not making the transition are now all too evident.

In a cosmopolitan world, the actions of all – individuals, solidarities and agencies – need to be congruent with, and contribute to, harnessing scientific and technological advance to positive ends. But there lies the rub. We might be able to articulate the outcomes (see Figure 14.2), but there is less understanding of how to bring them about. We can hold an articulate debate about social evils, but if we want to change the dynamic, we must develop a comprehensive and shared debate about social virtues and what drives them.

Figure 14.2: Developing a counter-dynamic that supports social virtues and generates positive global change

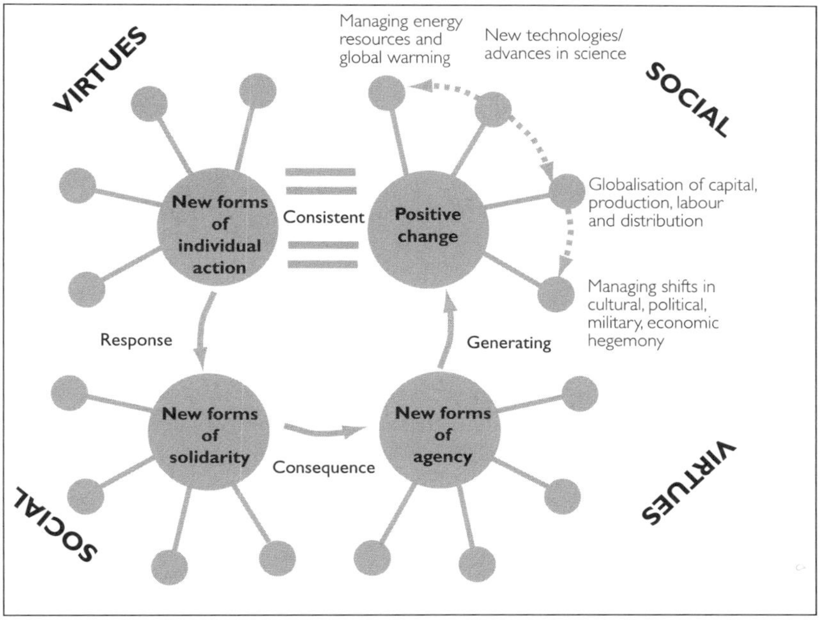

We need to develop and embed a confident narrative for personal and group behaviour relevant for the 21st century. I believe that this narrative will be built around the 'we' rather than the 'I' and around what we share in common, not in what we own. I am, therefore, arguing for a counterintuitive response to the current crisis of confidence on the world stage. In addition to creating a new global architecture, saving the banks and propping up the car industry, we need to invest in civil society.

Through investing in civil society, we can support a multiplicity of individual behaviour changes that can generate different forms of solidarity. These, in turn, can reinvigorate existing and create new forms of agency that are better able to manage the challenges that we face.

New forms of individual action

Individual well-being and social cohesion do not come from on high. We learn by doing. Individuals are already asking themselves simple questions: can I buy fruit and vegetables in season, eat smaller portions of meat, travel by train rather than plane, ride a bike instead of driving a car, separate my wet from my dry waste, choose low-energy appliances? We, likewise, need to start asking how many pairs of shoes we need, how many suits, jackets and shirts, how many changes of sheets and whether we really need to buy new.

In answering these questions we need to recognise our interdependence and ask the more fundamental question and understand how our actions impact on those who live on the margins – on Pacific atolls, on the streets of India, in factories in developing economies, on the ice fields of Alaska, on rural farms, but also the old, the young, people from minority ethnic communities and women. Individual changes may not attack poverty head-on but they do establish boundaries on excess. And they establish the base for communal activity and the moral authority to address examples of outrageous behaviour and consumption. Countering individual excess is a question of social justice and environmental sustainability for ultimately we are all our brothers' keepers.

Solidarity at the local level

There are an estimated 750,000 non-profit organisations in the UK. They operate in the space beyond government or the private sector, and the variety of activities they get involved in is forever changing. They range from global networks right down to small groups run entirely by volunteers. In total, they control revenue budgets of over £35 billion per annum and own capital assets valued at over £65 billion. Among them are 500,000 or so community-based organisations. Some are substantial with long track records; others flourish for a particular purpose and then fade. They differ from their larger counterparts because they are smaller and more local. They grow out of a self-help tradition and, as they are one-offs, they are less constrained by the need to maintain internal consistency that besets larger agencies. They can respond more rapidly to emerging needs and can experiment with new ways of doing things. At a local level, such organisations build social, cultural and economic capital and are active in neighbourhoods within every town and city.

Community-based organisations make an important contribution in neighbourhoods where poverty has become endemic. Labour markets are often under severe pressure, including a continuing export of jobs. Here, a new landscape has opened up that is beyond the reach of the public sector and outside the remit of the private sector. These are communities living with high levels of stress, whether measured, on the street, in terms of crime, vandalism and civil disorder, or, within the home, in terms of domestic violence, substance abuse and poor health. Community-based agencies provide safe havens where confidences can be shared, trust can grow and healing can take place. Not least, they develop meaningful long-term relationships and partnerships. They are able to cope with variety and develop dialogues between generations and between communities. They can be a hive of activity from the early hours to late at night, at weekends as well as on weekdays, high days and holidays.

Such organisations are not limited to poor neighbourhoods. They are, however, organising themselves in many different and exciting ways that include food cooperatives, time banks, housing cooperatives and the co-ownership of 'heat and power' plants and wind farms that pump surplus electricity back into the grid. The task ahead is to enable these collective initiatives to reach and pass the tipping point where they become recognised as a market in their own right.

Investing in civil society

So what are the practical steps that need to be taken to invest in a civil society capable of thriving in the 21st century? First, we need to invest in grassroots activity in the form of a 2% precept on Council Tax. If we accept local precepts levied on every household to pay for the police, we should be prepared to do it for community benefit. This would provide a realistic budget to support the work of community-based organisations. The resulting funds would be allocated to and disbursed by independently constituted community councils. Free from party politics, they would also be responsible for taking the lead on community-led participatory budgetary and physical planning.

Second, we need to expand the 'commons'. Land and buildings 'belonging' to local authorities and other public sector bodies ought to be treated as assets held in trust on behalf of civil society. A proportion should be reallocated to civil society organisations to provide a secure base for their operations and to bring about social change. But the ownership and management of buildings also brings longer-term responsibilities and liabilities. The transferred properties that have limited income-earning capacity, such as community centres, should be accompanied by assets that have greater income-earning capacity, such as local shops and workspaces.

Third, the proportion of public services commissioned from the civil society organisations should double over the next decade. We continue to conflate the financing and delivery of public services because we have yet to fully understand the benefits of local production, or to explore a proper balance between delivery by state, private and third sector agencies. We need to acknowledge the scope for new forms of delivery agency that are embedded in the traditions of mutuality, cooperative ownership, co-production and self-help. This should create a market in its own right where social enterprises can thrive either on their own or as part of hybrid organisations providing publicly funded services and self-funded community activities.

However, funding a thriving civil society should not be seen only as the reallocation of public sector assets and services. There have to be major advantages for local authorities too. A strong civil society will provide local authorities with the space to focus on their overarching role of bringing together and integrating the activities of market, state and civil society agencies to develop and implement the local strategies that create a thriving economy and deliver efficient services.

At the national level, meanwhile, there needs to be a root and branch review of existing charities and foundations. There are many that were established for purposes that no longer exist. There are others that are the fiefdoms of their self-perpetuating trustees. There needs to be more openness, transparency and accountability and a shift from philanthropy to mutuality. We need to segment the market and distinguish between grant-giving charities, the larger voluntary sector organisations and local and community-based organisations. They serve different markets and require different approaches if they are to thrive.

The ability of community-based organisations to raise their own finance also needs to be enhanced. In this context, community foundations, community shares and community bond schemes need to be developed further. But we also need to make better use of the Big Lottery Fund (BLF). Once its preoccupation with funding the 2012 Olympics is over, it should, like the Bank of England, be freed from central government interference. The BLF should no longer be used by governments to deliver their unfunded objectives. Instead, it should be specifically charged with supporting a thriving and sustainable civil society.

The private sector has a role to play, as well. It is now accepted that the funds held in dormant accounts by banks and building societies do not belong to them. However, they do not belong to government either, and should not be appropriated to pay for programme areas, like youth services, from which public service providers have conspicuously withdrawn. The funds should, as recommended by the Commission on Unclaimed Assets, be transferred to an independent social investment bank that channels investment funds to local communities through a series of specialist independent intermediary bodies. The concept of dormant accounts should also be extended to the public sector. The government holds huge sums of uncollected national savings and premium bonds. These should be put into the pot as well.

Conclusion

In a world beset with problems beyond our immediate control, I have deliberately focused on the individual, the practical and the day to day: areas over which we do have some influence. It is a direction of travel that offers hope. By investing in communal activity, we create local support networks and establish points of reference between the state and the individual. It can release unrealised energies and redirect others to bring about a myriad of actions. On their own they will not solve the larger issues, but without them we will not be able to bring them to resolution. It might be that those larger issues, as some fear, have already passed beyond the capacity of human society to bring under control. If that is the case, building the social and cultural capital that will be created on the journey will mean that we are better able to cope with the consequences.

Inequality

15

Opportunity and aspiration: two sides of the same coin?

Chris Creegan

My starting point for this chapter is the notion of 'truncated opportunities': the idea that over the course of life, opportunities can be lost, limited or wasted through circumstances over which we have varying degrees of control. In order to address the inequalities created and exacerbated by truncation of opportunity, we need to reframe the relationship between opportunity and aspiration. And in doing so, we need not only to think about the opportunities and aspirations of individual citizens, but of society as a whole.

The idea of 'truncated opportunities' is not merely abstract. It comes from eliciting the voices of people we do not usually hear, even though we often hear about them. We design interventions for them. We talk to them in relation to services − as recipients, non-recipients and potential recipients. We even have labels for them. Some they partly use themselves, like 'carers'; and others we have bestowed upon them, as in 'NEETs' (people not in education, employment or training). Sometimes we remember that they are people first (as in 'people with learning difficulties'), but on other occasions we do not (as in 'the unemployed', 'the homeless' or 'the elderly').

But how often do we ask them about their lives? As social researchers or policy makers, or even practitioners, how often do we ask people to tell us about their hopes, fears and aspirations beyond whatever aspects of deficit bring them into contact with government or welfare organisations? From my experience as a social researcher, the answer is not very often. I have, of course, conducted some fascinating research with people whose voices might not otherwise have been heard, including vulnerable young people, unmarried parents and people facing discrimination at work. But the bounded nature of social research can be frustrating. At the end of an interview, the digital recorder goes back in the researcher's bag, the consent form is signed and the respondent is reminded of the confidentiality and anonymity of the process. For all that I might want to stay behind and continue talking, I do not, because that would corrupt the research process both ethically and methodologically. It is not normally my role.

Thanks, however, to the Joseph Rowntree Foundation's (JRF) project on 'social evil', I became part of a team whose specific commission was to obtain the views of people whose voices often go unheard in conventional research. Included among them were people with learning disabilities, ex-offenders, carers, care leavers, other vulnerable young people and people with experience of homelessness and unemployment (see Chapters 4 and 5). Beginning with a simple, open-ended question – 'What do you think are today's social evils?' – our task was to get them to talk on their own terms. In order to understand what lay behind their initial responses, we had to enable them to talk about things that had happened in their lives. Thus, people talked to us in the context of their own hopes and aspirations that had not been realised. They talked of opportunities and chances that had been limited, lost or even wasted. This is what led us to adopt the term 'truncated opportunities'.

It is important to emphasise that the notion that emerged from the accounts of those we spoke to is not simply about inequality of opportunity, poverty or life chances; even though it is related to all of those things. The participants were mostly poorer people, not merely in terms of income but also in terms of participation and access to services. They were people who had experienced inequality. In some cases they were people who, by any standard, had faced unequal life chances from the very start. But the stories of loss, waste and limiting of opportunities that threaded through their lives had been triggered at different life stages. They related to both external (or societal) and internal (or personal) constraints to opportunity. External constraints could include lack of affordable housing or worklessness, while internal constraints could include caring responsibilities or mental health problems.

Their opportunities were not only curtailed by being born into poverty or with learning difficulties. They had also been lost or wasted across the course of life because of circumstances that had arisen (such as having to care for someone or becoming homeless) or through personal actions (such as drug and alcohol misuse). The extent to which the impact of reduced opportunity had been mitigated, either within the personal or public domain, varied considerably.

Three further points arise from the accounts of truncated opportunity revealed by our research. First, establishing the counterfactual in relation to restricted opportunity is difficult. How can we know what the outcome would have been if opportunities had been given or taken? Second, if we were able to mitigate truncation of opportunity, would the opportunities given to people enable their aspirations to be met? Third, it is worth reflecting that truncated opportunities may not always be experienced as negative. As one door closes in life, another door may open. To explore the issue further, I want to briefly present to some illustrative examples of lost, limited and wasted opportunities and an example of the role of aspiration in contemporary Britain.

Opportunities lost: older people

Opportunities can be lost in later life partly because major life events such as widowhood can cause 'cycles of decline' (Social Exclusion Unit, 2006a). Over the last few years a whole series of strategy documents has been produced by government concerning older people, including *Opportunity age* published by the Department for Work and Pensions in 2005 (HM Government, 2005) and *A new ambition for old age* published by the Department of Health in 2006 (Philp, 2006). But how much attention have they received?

The English Longitudinal Study of Ageing (ELSA), a large-scale survey of people aged 50 and over in England, was used by the government's Social Exclusion Unit to examine the key risk factors, or indicators, of social exclusion among older people (SEU, 2006b). The results, published in 2006, were shameful. Over two million people of pension age live in poverty. Around 30% of people over the age of 65 did not see any friends at least once a week. Approximately one third of people living in 'non-decent' homes were aged 60 years or over.

The loss of opportunities for people in later life has a multiplicity of negative impacts on their health and well-being, their exclusion from social networks and cultural activities and their participation in wider society. The consequences, though, are surely much greater than the impact on older people themselves, because society loses too. By focusing more on older people's (real) need for care than on their potential contribution, we are all the losers. Older people surely have a wealth of experience, knowledge and wisdom that everyone can benefit from. By tapping into it we would enable them to flourish, notwithstanding the frailty and need that often comes with old age.

Opportunities limited: carers

The responsibility of caring for someone can happen at any stage during life. At one end of the spectrum, it is estimated that 1.5 million people who are over the age of 60 are carers in Britain (Buckner and Yeandle, 2005). Many have spent years bringing up children only to find, as retirement approaches, that what life holds in store is looking after an elderly parent. Over 8,000 carers are aged 90 years and above, and 4,000 of these much older carers provide 50 or more hours of care each week. Older carers are often in poor health themselves, usually living with a partner who is sometimes still in paid work, and highly concentrated in areas affected by socioeconomic deprivation. At the other end of the age range, Carers UK (2007) estimates that there are around 175,000 young carers in the UK.

Among the many negative impacts of the caring role are limited opportunities for social and leisure activities and limited horizons and aspirations (Dearden and Becker, 2004). For older and younger people alike, it can be an isolating and excluding experience. The carer role is one that many people choose out of love for a partner or family member, but it is also one they get tied into as a result of obligation and the lack of viable alternatives. Carers UK estimates that 80% of carers are of working age, but that 58% of them give up work because of their caring responsibilities. As well as giving up work and sacrificing their pensions, carers are having to sell their homes, cut back on food, heating and clothes and sacrifice their pensions. This leaves many deeply anxious about their financial future (Carers UK, 2007). An Institute for Public Policy Research (IPPR) report estimates that carers unable to work lose out on £5 billion per year of potential earnings (Moullin, 2008). Yet Carers UK (2007) estimates that carers' support is worth £87 billion per year to the state.

Opportunities wasted: drug and alcohol addiction

NatCen (National Centre for Social Research) has recently been involved in a Drug Treatment Outcomes Research Study (Jones et al, 2007) designed to update existing knowledge on the effectiveness of drug treatment in England. Using a sample broadly representative of all drug treatment seekers, it found that most (77%) were unemployed and 38% had left school before the age of 16. Crack cocaine use (44%) was associated with higher levels of criminality, poorer health and recent psychiatric treatment. We may be living in a classless society where political ideology is concerned, but in the illegal drugs market the class system is alive and kicking. At the extremes, drug use for middle-class people is more likely to be 'recreational' and relatively harmless. But for working-class people it has greater potential to become a way of life associated with a vicious cycle of criminal behaviour, in which they are both perpetrator and victim. Moreover, some middle-class people seem to want protection from the rampant criminal behaviour associated with drug misuse, while simultaneously claiming the freedom to dabble in illegal drug use at the weekends with impunity.

It could be argued that such confusion is confined to a small minority. But if we substitute alcohol for drugs, the confusion arguably becomes greater. It has been suggested by one commentator that ministers are happy to crack down on the many thousands who use cannabis socially, but as long as 'booze' remains the drug of choice of *Daily Mail* readers, they will not dare to criminalise middle-class people whose fix is available at bargain prices in supermarkets (Smith, 2008). For the late playwright Simon Gray, alcoholism resulted from drinking several bottles of champagne a day over many years, until the doctor ordered him to stop. He denied any regret over his drinking years, insisting that a lot of his plays had been written under the influence. 'I think it somehow liberated one,' he added (Barber, 2004). But such accounts are the exception and give the lie to the appalling waste that alcohol addiction generates. Moreover, the real casualties of alcoholism, whose lives are blighted rather than liberated, are those whose drink of choice is cheap cider rather than champagne.

If drug and alcohol misuse are social evils and truncate opportunities, what should we do about them? If the real problems are poverty and inequality, does it matter what approach we take to prohibition and enforcement? Whatever your point of view, it is clear that the confused narrative at the heart of the national debate about drugs and alcohol requires a cultural shift to tackle the waste caused by misuse. Unless this happens, misuse will continue to lead to wasted opportunities and will do so disproportionately among those who are less well off.

Aspirations: housing tenure

The phrase 'poverty of aspiration' has become common currency in the past few years. That it exists and helps to perpetuate cycles of poverty and inequality is surely undeniable. But aspiration can also fuel individualism, greed and consumerism. At the beginning of the 21st century, we have somehow lulled ourselves into a false consciousness whereby those who 'have' can have more and more, and where aspiration has no limits because its realisation has no impact beyond our own lives. Apparently we can acquire more without having to pay any more and no one will come to any harm as a result. Perhaps the most potent symbol of this is the current housing crisis in the UK. The private housing market in the UK is, according to some commentators, on the brink of collapse – 'a "house of cards" that is set to implode after years of reckless mortgage lending, chronic oversupply of new flats and widespread fraud' (Pagamenta, 2008).

Yet politicians of all political persuasions have argued in recent years that home ownership offers a route to a more equal as well as a more prosperous society. For example, Yvette Cooper, while Minister for Housing, had this to say:

> *Promoting home ownership is often seen as being about aspirations. It is.... But it is also about addressing inequalities. And when done alongside extending housing supply and improving access to social housing too, it forms a vital part of a programme to widen life chances for all. (Cooper, 2005)*

But her assertion that promoting home ownership is about addressing inequalities is, in reality, questionable. In one sense, equality in the housing market might be taken to mean that everyone would have the opportunity to own their own home. But in another sense, it exposes a fundamental fault line that has long been at the heart of housing policy: rental housing, particularly subsidised social housing, is seen as inferior to home ownership. Far from being aspirational, it is seen as an option for those who are not lucky enough to be able to afford their own home.

During the housing boom – now passed – some people made huge profits by selling their houses. For those who were lucky enough to sell before the current crisis, those profits materialised. For those who did not sell before the crisis, 'tomorrow has arrived and consumers are sitting on £1.4 trillion of debt, the highest for any country in the world' (Macwhirter, 2008). But for those in social housing there is a different sorry tale. The socioeconomic characteristics of those living in different housing tenures have changed dramatically in the last 25 years. Those in social housing are now disproportionately represented in the lowest income groups, have much higher levels of unemployment and long-term economic activity. They face multiple barriers or difficulties in the labour market, including ill-health (Hills, 2007). We can also be pretty confident that home ownership affects the causes of social mobility, including educational attainment and childhood poverty, while social housing has become associated with downward mobility (Nunn et al, 2007).

This is all a far cry from the post-war vision for housing, which recognised the need for mixed neighbourhoods. How did it come to this? It is difficult not to draw the conclusion that individualism and greed have fuelled these changes. Those of us who could afford to were happy to see the value of our homes rise exponentially, and in some cases use the profits to buy second properties. Our greed was such that, not content with being a nation of homeowners, we seemed to want to become a nation of landlords. Yet we knew this was a divided nation, in which those inside the market understood that our actions were pricing others out. Is it really so absurd to suggest that middle-class people might in some circumstances actually prefer to opt for social housing as a choice that fits with their aspirations in terms of quality of life? In the recent past, the answer appears to have been 'yes', at least in part because of the potential for increased personal wealth (and perceived security) attached to home ownership. Perhaps now, as we experience the second housing crash in 20 years, we might pause to think again about what sort of housing policy would really benefit the whole of society, as opposed to one section of it. The failure to develop a credible and equitable housing strategy was one of the biggest disappointments of the Labour government from 1997. A new vision for housing, which includes a radical overhaul of both the private and social housing sectors, and places different housing tenures on an equal footing, not merely in terms of location but also in terms of opportunity and aspiration, is long overdue.

Alleviating truncated opportunities

Threaded through the reduced opportunities discovered by our research is a shared experience of the impact of class, poverty and inequality on opportunity. For me this raises the question of how far we have really moved on from the predicament identified by Joseph Rowntree a century ago.[1] He argued, then, that 'philanthropic effort was directed to remedying the more superficial manifestations of weakness or evil, while little thought or effort was directed to search out their underlying causes'. My concern is twofold. First, there is increasingly a mismatch between our individual aspirations and the opportunities that can realistically be afforded to us if we genuinely aspire to a more equal society. Second, we appear unwilling as a society, and unable through our political system, to really confront the relationship between poverty, inequality and truncated opportunities. And so our philanthropic efforts continue, well intentioned and sometimes very well resourced. But there is an implicit acceptance that loss of opportunity is inevitable and that a degree of inequality is quite simply 'okay'.

The reality is that, whether loss of opportunity is caused by something done to you, something that happens to you or something that you choose to do, the limitations imposed are greater and the escape routes are fewer if you are already disadvantaged through poverty and inequality. This is particularly the case if that disadvantage is chronic and multiple. So why can't we do more as a society to alleviate the truncation of opportunity? The JRF social evils consultation revealed a strong sense of unease about some of the changes shaping British society. Among the key concerns highlighted by respondents about how we seem to live our lives today were a decline of community and values and an increase in individualism, consumerism and greed.

My contention is that it is our collective failure as a society to take responsibility for these concerns that renders us incapable of dealing with 'truncated opportunities'. This is not to deny the importance of individual agency and responsibility. And of course disadvantage does not negate responsibility. Indeed, respondents in our research spoke eloquently about their own sense of personal responsibility and disappointment with their actions. Neither is it to suggest that the interventions we have collectively designed as a society to respond to the manifestations of poverty and inequality are not well intentioned or necessary. Arguably, we all have a responsibility, regardless of circumstance, to ensure that our aspirations are not shaped by individualism, consumerism and greed. But we need to bear in mind that for some of us the relationship between opportunity and aspiration is a more level playing field than for others.

I do, however, suggest that until we can reconcile the problems of individualism, consumerism and greed, which are at the heart of the current social, economic and political settlement in British society, life opportunities will continue to be lost, limited and wasted. The lives of poorer and more vulnerable people will be disproportionately affected and we will continue to turn the other way. This leads to the inescapable conclusion that 'some lives', as the late David Widgery movingly conveyed (Widgery, 1993), are ultimately expendable. We must remain alert to the pernicious effect of poverty of aspiration. But we must also reframe the meaning of aspiration. So when we talk about poverty of aspiration, we need to think not merely about reshaping the aspirations of individuals, but also our collective aspirations as a society. Without a shared aspiration for equality, individual opportunities will continue to be truncated. That means facing up to the consequences of individualism, consumerism and greed, individually and collectively.

Unheard voices

My final argument returns to eliciting unheard voices. If any of this is to happen, we need to find new ways of ensuring that we elicit the voices of those who have experienced truncated opportunity and that we hear them. In a small but far from insignificant way this is what the JRF set out to do with its social evils project. But how might we do it as a society? The government's 2008 White Paper *Communities in control* (DCLG, 2008) was focused on empowering citizens and provided a welcome emphasis on active citizenship, and improving local public services by involving users and strengthening local accountability. But such measures aside, my view is that taking a hard look at who votes and whether their votes really count is an important place to start.

In the ever-more competitive race to chase the middle-class vote and occupy the centre ground of British politics, those at the margins all too often go unheard. Their votes, like their opportunities, have become expendable. It is true that since 1997, Labour's focus on social exclusion, and latterly on chronic and multiple exclusion, represents a serious and genuine attempt to improve life chances and opportunities, and create a more equal society. It is also true that the recent emphasis on social justice by the Conservative Party is a welcome step. But have such developments placed sufficient emphasis on enabling the active citizenship of those who are socially excluded? Worryingly, another reason why their voices go unheard is that they don't necessarily even vote in the first place, or see any point in doing so. Indeed, it has been argued very persuasively that what should concern us most is not falling turnout in elections, but unequal turnout.

Put simply, as it has by Ben Rogers of the Institute for Public Policy Research: 'Elections are about influence. Voice is power' (Rogers,

2005). He rightly argued that the need to boost turnout among disadvantaged groups means that the time has come to give serious thought to compulsory voting – or at least compulsory attendance at the polling station or completing a postal form. Why? Because the evidence suggests that by increasing participation at the ballot box, compulsory voting narrows the gap between the rich and poor vote. The 'gain to democracy' would, in Rogers' view, be great, while the 'loss to liberty' would be negligible. We are rightly proud of the British democratic tradition. But at the beginning of the 21st century, we are sleepwalking into a democracy that is deeply eroded: a democracy where some voices simply don't matter. We need a democracy where everyone's voice is heard and where our individual aspirations for a better life for ourselves and our shared aspirations for equality are not seen as mutually exclusive, but two sides of the same coin.

Note

[1] www.jrf.org.uk/centenary/memorandum.html

References

Barber, L. (2004) 'I wrote a lot of my plays drunk: it liberated me', *The Observer*, 4 April.

Buckner, L. and Yeandle, S. (2005) *Older carers in the UK*, Sheffield: Sheffield Hallam University.

Carers UK (2007) *Real change, not short change: Time to deliver for carers*, London: Carers UK.

Cooper, Y. (2005) 'We have not yet gone far enough', in *Why life chances matter: The interim report of the Fabian Commission on Life Chances and Child Poverty*, Fabian Ideas, vol 616, London: Fabian Society.

DCLG (Department for Communities and Local Government) (2008) *Communities in control: Real people, real power*, London: The Stationery Office.

Dearden, C. and Becker, S. (2004) *Young carers in the UK: The 2004 report*, London: Carers UK.

Hills, J. (2007) *Ends and means: The future roles in social housing in England*, CASE Report 34, London: Centre for Analysis of Social Exclusion, London School of Economics and Political Science.

HM Government (2005) *Opportunity age*, London: Department for Work and Pensions.

Jones, A., Weston, S., Moody, A., Millar, T., Dollin, L., Anderson, T. and Donmall, M. (2007) *The Drug Treatment Outcomes Research Study (DTORS)*, London: Home Office.

Macwhirter, I. (2008) 'Crash: the housing crisis is just beginning', *New Statesman*, 5 June.

Moullin, S. (2008) *Just Care? A fresh approach to adult services*, London: IPPR.

Nunn, A., Johnson, S., Monro, S., Bickerstaffe, T. and Kelsey, S. (2007) *Factors influencing social mobility*, DWP Research Report 450, London: Department for Work and Pensions.

Pagamenta, R. (2008) 'UK housing market close to collapse, analyst says', *The Times*, 21 February.

Philp, I. (2006) *A new ambition for old age: Next steps in implementing the National Service Framework for Older People*, London: Department of Health.

Rogers, B. (2005) 'Turnout is really about class', *The Guardian*, 14 May.

Social Exclusion Unit (2006a) *A sure start to later life: Ending inequalities for older people*, London: Office of the Deputy Prime Minister.

Social Exclusion Unit (2006b) *The social exclusion of older people: Evidence from the first wave of the English longitudinal study on ageing (ELSA)*, London: Office of the Deputy Prime Minister.

Smith, J. (2008) 'Success is no antidote to addiction: what the West London siege tells us about class', *Independent on Sunday*, 11 May.

Widgery, D. (1993) *Some lives! A GP's East End*, London: Simon & Schuster.

16

Five types of inequality

Ferdinand Mount

The subject of inequality has come back to nag at our consciences and baffle our political energies. Of course, it never really went away. Ever since the Second World War, in the guise of equality of opportunity, it has been the guiding motive of successive British governments. The general sense of a shared mission led to something dangerously close to complacency. We were slowly moving in the right direction and the only argument was about the average speed and right time to change gear. Now we are not so sure of ourselves. The statistics tell us that social mobility has more or less ground to a halt. Incomes seem to be polarising and our society is divided into what I call 'uppers' and 'downers': the former full of confidence and looking to the future, the latter desperately trying to cling on to what little they have got. Behind the statistics we glimpse the formation of a demoralised underclass, deprived in both cultural and material terms, and a good deal larger than we hoped.

Inequality is tricky terrain, rather like parts of a First World War battlefield: a swamp sown with unexploded bombs and crossed by ancient trenches; some now crumbling and unoccupied, others still fiercely defended. Arguments about equality have gone on so long, and aroused such fierce feelings, that anyone venturing into this particular no-man's land needs to tiptoe. Much of the confusion is due to the assumption shared by many of the combatants that equality and inequality are simple and easily defined concepts. To begin to untangle the muddle, I suggest that we divide inequality into five rough types:

- *political equality*, in which I include civic equality and equality before the law;
- *equality of outcome or result*, by which I mean primarily equality of income and wealth;
- *equality of opportunity*, these days often called equality of access or of life chances;

- a less examined idea, *equality of treatment*, which can be taken to include or at least help to generate equality of agency and responsibility; and
- something that is not often recognised as a kind of equality at all, *equality of membership in society*.

These may overlap or conflict, but defining them will help us to see how remedies for the injurious aspects of inequality will, themselves, need to be quite intricate.

Political equality: the long struggle

Equality is a core principle of Western civilisation. This is true both of our dominant political tradition and of our dominant religious tradition. The equality of all humans in the eyes of God was a crucial founding principle of Christianity. We may acknowledge that states that converted to the new faith made little or no effort to carry this principle into practice by altering their social arrangements or the secular power of the king. All the same, the ideal of equality remained lodged in the mind as a prick to the conscience and occasionally a spur to reform. Slowly over the centuries, certain egalitarian practices gained hold: the equality of all men before the law, then much later equal rights to political participation. In Britain that process was not completed until 1930, when women under the age of 30 were enfranchised. The achievement of these legal and political equalities levelled up all adult citizens in their relations with the authorities and the political system. But economic and social equality remained a long way off.

Equality of outcome: the conflict with liberty and dynamism

In recent years equality in all its aspects has reached the status of being the 'number one goal' in much social and political discussion. Yet, as Sir Isaiah Berlin pointed out, no single principle of social action, however irreproachable, can hope to enjoy supremacy. Other principles, no less morally desirable, may come into conflict with it. Two principles may be stubbornly incommensurable; the best you can do is to work out a compromise between them. Equality often conflicts with liberty, for example. The government cannot engineer greater equality in economic relations without damaging the freedom of the more thrusting citizens to get ahead.

Like many on the Left before and since, R.H. Tawney argued in 1931 that this isn't necessarily so. In a well-structured society, he says:

> *a large measure of equality, so far from being inimical to liberty, is essential to it. In conditions which impose co-operative, rather than merely individual effort, liberty is, in fact, equality in action, in the sense, not that all men perform identical functions or wield the same degree of power, but that all men are equally protected against the abuse of power, and equally entitled to insist that power shall be used, not for personal ends but for the general advantage. (Tawney, 1931, p 168)*

Within this last sentence, the strains of pressing his argument begin to show. 'Co-operative effort' is to be 'imposed'; 'all men' are 'entitled to insist' that power is used for 'general advantage'. This is clearly a society in which the state calls the shots. It is this line of argument which provoked Berlin's famous retort that:

> *[N]othing is gained by a confusion of terms. To avoid glaring inequality or widespread misery I am ready to sacrifice some, or all, of my freedom: I may do so willingly and freely: but it is freedom that I am giving up for the sake of justice or equality or the love of my fellow men. I should be guilt-stricken, and rightly so, if I were not, in some circumstances, ready to make this sacrifice. But a sacrifice is not an increase in what is being sacrificed, namely freedom, however great the moral need or the compensation for it. Everything is what it is: liberty is liberty, not equality or fairness or justice or human happiness or a quiet conscience. (Berlin, 1958, p 10)*

Just as principles may conflict, so may goals. If we increase income taxes to a level where all incomes after tax are approximately equal, then any rational person will conclude that there is no point in striving to increase their income in this society. They will either take life easy or emigrate.

Rather than trying to offer a grand overall programme, I shall try to throw out suggestions that might help to remedy the different types of inequality where they pinch the most. But first we need to get our history straight. It is common ground, I think, that the equalities that are already achieved came from that deep urge to recognise the equality of all human beings as citizens and as children of God. We can see, for example, how the abolition of slavery and the fall of apartheid derived from those impulses. The same is true of the progress towards sexual equality. It started with the suffragettes and ended with equal pay and pensions.

Does the same consensus apply when we consider the history of progress towards equality of incomes? The heroic narrative of the Labour Party and its allies is that the progressive forces in British politics won a gruelling struggle to equalise incomes through the tax system. This, I am afraid, is not quite how it happened. It was war, not socialism, that was the great leveller. Income tax was first introduced on a serious basis to pay for the Napoleonic Wars. Even after Lloyd George's 'People's Budget' in 1909 it only stood at 1s 2d in the pound. Yet following the declaration of war in 1914, things moved rapidly. By 1917, the income tax rate was 5s in the pound. After the Second World War was declared, income tax took another giant jump, reaching 10s in the pound in 1942. That figure inched down slowly after the Second World War, but in 1969, the rate was still as high as 8s 3d. It took another 25 years before it came down to the equivalent of 5s – by then a decimal 25p – in the pound.

In an Epilogue to *Equality* in 1952, Tawney rejoiced at 'a somewhat more equalitarian social order' (Tawney, 1952, p 222), but did not really acknowledge that this direction had been imposed by wartime emergencies rather than an internal political imperative. It is not clear that income equalisation for its own sake has ever taken as firm a grip on British politics as its enthusiasts imagine.

Equality of opportunity: the new ideal

What has taken root is something that fits better into the category of equality of opportunity and the view that every citizen has a right to a decent start in life. After the First World War, there were to be homes, schools and hospitals 'fit for heroes' and the children of heroes, too. Between the wars a succession of health and education Acts were passed, mostly by Conservative-dominated governments. During the Second World War, the Churchill coalition produced blueprints for amalgamating the network of publicly provided schools, hospitals and pensions into nationally controlled and funded services. I mention this not to undermine the Attlee government's proud claim to have introduced these national services, but to point out how two wars had introduced a new consensus that the state had a duty to ensure a decent minimum standard of living for its citizens and a start in life that would enable them to make the best of their talents. Equality of opportunity, rather than equality of outcome, was the guiding principle.

Inequality of income diminished as the share of national income taken by the government continued to rise. The government's share of national income surpassed 40% in the late 1970s, then diminished under the Thatcher government by about 5 percentage points. These were then put back on during the Major and Blair years. But the revival in government expenditure had little or no effect in equalising incomes. The gap between the lowest and the highest has widened in the last few years. So whatever else may have been a priority for New Labour, income equalisation was not. Equality of opportunity has, however, been embraced with the same fervour as it was by R.A. Butler and the more go-ahead Tories in the 1940s and 1950s.

In the years immediately following the Second World War, inequalities of outcome were not so conspicuous and consequently did not grate as much. But, as the engine of prosperity picked up steam, gaps began to open between the frontrunners and the pack. In the 1960s, amid the hum of dishwashers and the forest of television aerials, growing prosperity gave the income gap a higher profile. In recent years, there has been even stronger statistical evidence for the stretching out of incomes. In particular, there has been polarisation at both ends of the scales: the post-tax incomes of the top decile are further and further removed from the incomes of the bottom decile.

My anxiety here is directed at the income tax system, which seems to have developed a sort of 'middle-aged spread'. Before the Second World War, nobody below the middle classes, broadly construed, paid any income tax. Now the paunch of the public purse has sagged. It is true that the rich pay more tax than they used to, because they actually pay the advertised rates instead of using every legitimate dodge to evade them. But it is also true that the poor pay too much tax. A single person with no children on £10,000 a year pays £1,415 in tax, then receives £1,138 in tax credit – a net outgoing of just under £300. If they struggle up to £15,000, their tax rises to nearly £3,000 a year and their tax credit disappears. Thus, they pay three fifths of their extra income in tax, a marginal rate of 60%.

The remedy for this fiscal sag is a simple one: to raise personal allowances much closer to average earnings and so float lower earners clear of income tax altogether. This helps higher earners, too. But I would recoup much of this by removing, or partially removing, the cap on National Insurance contributions for higher earners. The National Insurance system is a curious muddle, accumulated over the years from half-hearted efforts to graft earnings-related elements onto the original flat-rate scheme. Why not acknowledge it as a progressive tax on earnings for the special purpose of providing decent flat-rate benefits for our fellow citizens in sickness and retirement?

There is one other measure of financial equalisation that would merely restore us to the way things were 30 years ago. The Council Tax was a compromise that rescued us from the calamity of the Community Charge, or Poll Tax. But unlike the preceding household Rates, it is not fully progressive. A house in 'Millionaires Row' pays the same as a decent semi in a nice area. Introduce a few more bands at the top end and the demand on the lower end will be that much less. Combined with my proposed changes to National Insurance, this could produce a considerable amount of revenue to help the worst off without unduly compressing incentives.

Inequality of income, although an irritant, is clearly not the major motor of the present discontents. This for the reason that inequalities were as large, if not more so, in earlier decades such as the 1930s, when it seems resentment about inequality was not so sharply felt. Meanwhile, the current Labour government maintains its focus on equality of opportunity and on its subset, equality of access. Everyone must have access to art and music, to sport and the countryside, to technical and professional skills, to home ownership and capital accumulation, to name but a few. The difficulty, of course, is that government is not in a position to wave a magic wand and, say, create a network of music teachers and academies where every child has the opportunity to learn an instrument to high standards. Most such opportunities depend on flourishing intermediate institutions, which provide the opportunities or underwrite them. The trouble is that governments over the past 30 years have undermined the independence and the self-confidence of almost every intermediate institution in the land – local authorities, professional associations, schools and universities. It is only by reviving the freedoms of self-management that genuine access to the best can be made available.

There are other kinds of access that are not so often mentioned. Let me give an example, which some people have considered eccentric, but which seems, to me, quite significant. In other European countries it is easy enough for people of modest means to buy a patch of land and build a house for themselves; completing the job as funds and time become available. In Britain, such a sight is a rarity. The ownership of building land is largely confined to public authorities and big developers. Indeed, the planning system frowns on piecemeal development and restricts the supply of land, thus sending its price sky-high. In this case, as in many others where access is concerned, government is the problem rather than the solution.

It is obviously desirable that we strive towards equality of access. Yet we cannot really claim that access is denied in many of the cases we have been thinking about. Museums are free, schools arrange specialist teachers, the footpaths are open, Radio 3 is on air every day, sports clubs are eager for recruits and the number of university places has doubled. In the final analysis, I cannot pretend that inequality of access is any more crucial than inequality of income to the malaise we sense, but find hard to pin down.

Equality of treatment

Equality in accessing public services such as health, education, housing and social security sounds a straightforward enough goal. Yet in carrying out the necessary social engineering, government is compelled to discriminate; to treat its citizens unequally. This may be benignly intended and to some extent unavoidable, but it almost inevitably sets up consequential inequalities of respect and agency. If some people are seen to be in control of the important decisions in their lives and others have most decisions taken for them, even for the best of motives, you cannot expect the high-powered to have much respect for the low-powered. Nor can you expect the low-powered to have much respect for themselves. So how are we to give the condemned and excluded a real stake in society and a genuine sense of participation and self-worth? Is not equality of treatment often easier and more effective than carefully targeted benefits? Would it not be better to have flat-rate systems of child benefit and retirement pensions, at generous levels, and get rid of the means-tested network of credits and benefits that are so uneven and humiliating in their application?

Equality of treatment must be an underlying principle, too, in our efforts to break down the mono-tenured ghettoes of our larger council estates. I say 'break down', but not 'knock down'; many of them are decent, even handsome places. But as they have dwindled in numbers over the last 20 years, so they have concentrated the most depressed sectors of society: the workless, the incapacitated and the 'monoglot' immigrants. 'Abandon Hope All Ye Who Enter Here' could just as well be written over the gates of the worst estates as over the gates of hell. Every variation of right-to-buy, shared ownership, social landlord and cooperative solution is worth looking at. But the people who should do the looking are local councillors, not ministers in Whitehall whose endless regulations intensify the sense of remoteness and powerlessness.

Equality of treatment bleeds into equality of responsibility. They are – or ought to be – part of the same transaction between the citizen and the state, or between the citizen and their home town. In receiving benefits, people should also think of themselves as taking on responsibilities. Benefits that are tossed out without reciprocal expectations are a deprival of participation and a denial of agency. An extreme example is the system where Housing Benefit has been paid direct to landlords without passing through the tenant. An experiment of giving the money to the tenant has been introduced in several local authorities, and landlords are up in arms. Well, tough luck. If we act as though tenants cannot be entrusted with even that much responsibility, we really are treating them as infants. The same is true of out-of-work benefits, notably Incapacity Benefit, where the numbers drawing it for reasons of mental distress have ballooned. Handing out the cash without making any serious collaborative effort to find work for the recipients is not only an insult to those who slog away for wages not much higher than the benefit, but also to condemn the claimants as effectively unemployable.

This leads me on to mention other areas where equality of agency may be restored or bolstered. Some variety of school voucher or 'ticket', envisaged in a section of the 1870 Education Act that never came into force, would give less well-off parents a locus in the educational process that their existing limited choice of schools does not offer. These are familiar topics among libertarians. They are even gaining ground in such impeccably social-democratic nations as Sweden and the Netherlands, which have demonstrated that it is to the worst off that these devices offer the best chance of both voice and exit.

Equality of membership

My concluding thoughts concern three areas of social life that are not usually thought of as having anything to do with equality at all. Yet in my view they provide the surest underpinning for the more familiar types of equality. They all came for a while to be regarded as old-fashioned and irrelevant to society today, but have recently, rather surprisingly, come back into play. They are, first, the overt encouragement of 'Britishness'; second, the revival of faith schools; and third, the restoration of financial incentives for marriage.

A few years ago, none of these would have been regarded as an appropriate topic for polite society to discuss. They were unsuitable elements in an individualistic, secular, modern-minded society in which the cake of custom had crumbled into dust. And even now the justifications given for them are somewhat hesitant, as though the justifiers were trying to make out an argument in a language they had not spoken for years. Re-stressing the importance of being British will, it is said, cement the allegiance of new immigrants, especially Muslim immigrants. The revival of faith schools will improve the general level of exam results. And if more people are encouraged to get married, levels of delinquency and social misery will be reduced.

All these things are probably true. But these are only instrumental by-products. There is a much more sweeping and enveloping effect on those who commit themselves to such reinvigorated social institutions. What happens is that they are admitted, on equal terms, to membership of a community. The oath of allegiance to the Queen, which, it is suggested, schoolchildren should now take, is not a humiliating crawl, as republicans think. On the contrary, as members of the armed forces and other public officials readily assume, it is an admission into a community in which equal members are equally bound by lasting ties of loyalty. Many secularists are indignant that some parents should feign religious commitment in order to get their children into a popular school. But from the point of view of society, what matters is that those parents have associated themselves with a particular form of community. They have enlisted in what Edmund Burke in the 18th century described as 'little platoons'. In the case of marriage, the couple are forming their own 'little platoon', which, as soon as it is formed, enjoys equal status with every other such couple-dom. Just as all of us are equally subjects of the Queen and all members of a faith are equal in that membership, so every family is equal in value. Indeed, there is no more obvious way for a prince or politician to remind us that they share our common humanity than by parading their family.

Discussion of equality tends to take place in terms of the advantages and disadvantages enjoyed or endured by individuals. Yet the most precious forms of equality may be those in which the individual is not atomised but freely conjoined. Where the individual exhibits psychic damage and distress, it may be precisely because they are not in any body beyond their own. They stand unprotected against the realisations of their own frailty and failure.

New routes to fairness

We need to make it possible for everyone to lead a life that they can consider worth living and which can give them a legitimate sense of self-worth. But I doubt whether the most robust measures taken against the more material inequalities of income and opportunity will do much to cheer up the desolation among the 'downers' in our society, unless we recognise the importance of equality of membership. Neither Left nor Right has ever really got hold of this principle: the Right because it tends to give priority to subjection to authority over shared belonging; the Left because it is often suspicious of existing local and national institutions and would prefer to replace them by an international working class. Both ideological wings fail to grasp that inequality is a *complex* evil. To remedy it, one must engage in various separate enterprises: to work for distributive justice; that is, a tax system in which the burdens are fairly shared. It is, after all, possible to argue that if the *ancien* fiscal regime had been remotely fair, there might never have been a French Revolution.

But there are other sorts of fairness that must be addressed: equality of opportunity, bringing about a society that equalises life chances so far as possible and opens up every career to talent from every social level; equality of responsibility, with a welfare state that is not blatantly divided into agents and patients, the doers and the done-to; and finally equality of membership. The last of these is by no means the least, for, as St Paul told the citizens of Ephesus, 'We are members one of another'. That, too, was a message about equality.

References

Berlin, I. (1958) *Two concepts of liberty*, Oxford: Oxford University Press.

Tawney, R.H. (1931) *Equality* (1964 edition), London: Allen & Unwin.

Tawney, R.H. (1952) 'Epilogue', in *Equality*, London: Allen & Unwin.

17

The poor and the unequal

Jeremy Seabrook

In India, shortly after a policy of economic liberalisation was introduced in the early 1990s, I attended a seminar conducted by a Westerner who was instructing the government in the mysterious arts of deregulation. He spoke enthusiastically of the 'creative imbalances' that would be a prerequisite for development. This was a euphemism for even more gross inequalities than those that have historically disfigured India. The consequences may now be seen, on the one hand, in the suicides of at least 140,000 farmers engulfed by debt; and on the other, in the extravagant palace constructed by Mukesh Ambani in Mumbai – a 27-storey structure with its own helipad, pools, elegant rooms, private theatre and staff of 600.

Meritorious or meretricious?

It is sometimes hard to distinguish between 'natural' inequalities, that is to say the unequal distribution of positive human characteristics – intelligence, creativity, beauty or strength of personality – and those that are socially determined – power, wealth or privileged education. Most discussion about 'equality' focuses on the latter, since it is virtually impossible to alter natural attributes that favour some people in the world over others.

Attempts to reduce inequality base themselves on raising the life chances of the socially disadvantaged, so, in that tiresome cliché, they can compete on a 'level playing field' with more fortunate peers. 'Equality of opportunity' is supposed to compensate for all social, educational and cultural handicaps endured by those not born to privilege. This is a shallow and meretricious approach, since the only way in which actual equality of opportunity could be achieved would be by raising everybody to the level of the most advantaged. The idea that 'education' can make good all deficiencies is a sentimental, or ideological, fiction.

Establishing 'equality of opportunity' is the flimsiest justification for a society that likes to think of itself as rewarding 'merit'. For its notion of merit is overwhelmingly concentrated on those favoured either by birth or by endowment. In other words, society more or less faithfully reflects profound natural and human-made inequalities. When people rise in what is labelled a meritocracy, the meritorious look with complaisance on the rewards that their ostensible worth bestows on them. Although they may be troubled by a perceived lack of 'meritoriousness' in those from whom rewards are withheld, they rarely contest the basis on which their own good fortune has been constructed.

It is difficult for those at the bottom of a highly stratified society to view this assessment of their worth (or lack of it) with equanimity. Some will, of course, acquiesce and adapt their expectations and lifestyle to the humble position to which the market has summoned them. But if many able, competent and intelligent people find that they are assigned an undeserved lowly status, they are unlikely to go meekly about their business without some form of protest. It may be that the considerable levels of crime, violence and dealing in prohibited substances is a consequence of significant portions of the poor taking into their own hands remedies for their exclusion and alienation. It may also be that the inability of the authorities to do much about it is less a reflection of their impotence than of a collusive tolerance. Private remedies for economically and socially induced wrongs are deemed more acceptable than the alternative, which would be collective, solidarity-based movements of poor people themselves working to change the society that determines their condition. Indeed, the consistent disgracing of collective action over the past two generations has been a major contributor to the unequal society. Such action was informed by a non-defunct impulse towards socialism. Its discrediting has led to the breakdown of belonging, social incoherence and that intense individualism which also now troubles policy makers and politicians.

One day we may come to look back with incredulity on societies that, given the vast differences in ability, competence and intelligence of their people, chose to enshrine and aggravate these distinctions by replicating them in social hierarchies. People may wonder that such primitive thinking endured for so long in a future time when talent and distinction are recognised, but efforts are also made to compensate the vulnerable, the unskilled and the underendowed for disadvantages for which they are not personally responsible.

Poverty and disempowerment

The issue of accepting personal responsibility for socially determined circumstances has an important bearing on the difference between the poor and the unequal. In societies where a majority are poor and cannot provide enough for themselves and their families, people know that their experience of need is not their fault. Efforts were made in the early industrial period to blame the poor for their poverty; they were said to be idle or improvident.

Yet despite attempts to make the poor responsible for their own condition, people fiercely repudiated this version of the world. They did so by organised resistance in the workplace and in the dingy neighbourhoods and grimy industrial suburbs of Britain. Reformers and philanthropists supported this project. Some of the upper class did so out of a sense of *noblesse oblige*, others because they were animated by a moral or religious sense of justice. The story of the rise of the trades union movement, friendly societies and mutual help organisations, is a matter of record (as, indeed, is their more recent decline). As long as people were aware that their poverty had its roots in society, they retained a sense of latent, if not actual, power. In the long shadow cast by the French Revolution, it was clear to ruling elites that if the poor chose to exercise their brute power, they could conceivably overturn a system from which, it seemed well into the 19th century, they were destined to remain estranged.

By contrast, the dissolution of collective resistance, the weakening of trades unions and the decay of community has taken place at a time of vastly increased prosperity. The vast majority of the people in Britain today are not poor, but have something very tangible to protect. This has at least two important consequences. First, it ensures that only a small minority would now conceivably vote away a system in which most people are beneficiaries. Second, where individuals once resisted taking responsibility for their poverty at a time of mass misery, no such reluctance exists when it comes to taking credit for their prosperity. In other words, an ideology that was fiercely contested in the early industrial era now has an easier passage at a time when people are only too ready to claim that their good fortune is a result of work, diligence or worth. In consequence, they are also more ready to accept the idea that the poor are also authors of their own fate, and to censure them accordingly. Nothing, it seems, is forgotten so swiftly as poverty.

This is the context in which poverty is treated as a residual problem. The theory is that, with time, the excluded and marginalised will all be caught in the tender clasp of a capitalism that once made privation the experience of most people. This has clearly not happened. The poor, now a minority, are disempowered in a democracy where most people are well to do. The limits of their electoral power ensure that they can do little to alter unjust social or economic structures. This widespread sense of impotence may lie at the heart of declining participation in elections.

Myth and the 'magic' of markets

Mass poverty in the 'developed' world has been much mitigated; but growing inequality is an unintended consequence of this improvement. Rising living standards have occurred for a number of reasons: first, the wealth accumulated from colonial extraction; second, the organisation of the industrial working class and its growing political power; and third, the threat to capitalism from the socialist heresy. Until the 1960s, it was not clear that the Soviet system would fail to vanquish its rival. Self-preservation demanded that capitalism show itself to be more just and clement than its global competitor. This was achieved by spectacular economic growth, distributed according to the formulation that as the rich grew much richer, the poor might become a little less poor.

Unhappily, the rate at which the rich have improved their position exceeds the pace at which the poor rise. Greater inequality is written into the very scenario on which perpetual improvement is based. Governments have sought to lessen the gap, but their intervention cannot keep up with the promiscuous way in which the free market spreads its rewards. Although people are kept out of absolute poverty, the bottom 20% lag further and further behind the top 20%. Globalisation means that rewards are increasingly articulated to a single transnational standard. This justifies excessive remuneration to the already favoured, on the basis that if top talent were unduly taxed, they would relocate overseas.

Thus, the pattern of economic growth that prevails now in almost every country on earth leads to growing inequality. Optimists sometimes wish this away with another glib, but pervasive cliché, that a rising tide lifts all boats. This homely image is yet another version of the discredited 'trickle-down' theory. Some boats plainly leak, while the fate of those without boats is unrecorded. Moreover, in storms many boats simply capsize.

So universally accepted is this interpretation of the world that economic imperatives are now regarded with a profound fatalism. Societies that pride themselves on their mobility and capacity for innovation are suddenly powerless to do anything about inequality.

As soon as redistribution is mentioned, the defenders of the present order reach readily for myth and fable, citing the sanctity of the life of geese that lay golden eggs and the 'magic of markets'. The economy, it seems, is now the only site in a secular society where miracles still regularly occur. Yet we see the most dynamic societies the world has ever known throwing up their hands in the face of inequality: a supposed economic necessity, elevated into an underlying principle of life. Such societies quite readily promise us transcendence in areas of experience that religion and common sense alike have declared to be immutable – from ageing to the impossibility of paradise on earth. Yet they show an obdurate inability to act in areas that have previously been thought to be well within human power – such as the establishment of economic justice and regulation of the relationship between rich and poor.

The rulers of Britain have rarely had any great quarrel with inequality. Of greater concern has been the geometry of society: the pyramid at the base of which the poor were dangerously concentrated. The changes we have seen have altered the shape of society, from pyramid to rhomboid; or perhaps we might say, diamond. This is a more satisfactory economic morphology, since it means that the majority are now concentrated in the middle, and the poor have become a minority. As the squat pyramid was extruded into a diamond shape, threats to security from the density of disaffected poor people appeared to subside. The problem today is that this shape has become more elongated. While extravagant rewards are reaped at the top, those at the bottom live at a level of deprivation that makes inequality as unacceptable as the poverty of the majority in earlier times.

These awkward developments should be the starting point of any useful discussion of equality; although 'fairness' is, perhaps, a better term, since it is one to which most people respond. It is, after all, the protest of childhood at unjust treatment. 'It's not fair' is a cry that resounds in the ears of parents worldwide. If inequality cannot be eradicated, can we consider a fairer distribution of wealth, goods and services?

Inequality, globalism and delusion

Before we wonder how this is to be accomplished, it is necessary to demolish some myths that prevent us from moving beyond the brutal proposition that only if the rich become much richer may the poor become a little less poor. The sanctification of an extremely narrow version of what wealth is should be the first casualty in any struggle against inequality. The reduction of the richness and diversity of the world to money is, perhaps, the greatest limitation on our ability to distinguish the roots of artificially sustained impoverishments. In daily speech we refer to a wealth of experience, the richness of life, the resourcefulness of people, the treasures of the mind. In doing so, we acknowledge aspects of living that have not been enclosed, transformed into a commodity or service and sold back to us. Rather than acquiescing in the invasive power of the market to penetrate ever more deeply into these inner spaces, we might perhaps declare certain areas off limits.

We would, thus, protect all the freely offered acts of mercy and kindness, the services and small gifts that we, unbidden, share with our neighbours, and with it the vast storehouse of our common humanity, which is under assault as never before. The only resources that are boundless are not, alas, the rapidly depleting riches of the earth, but the ingenuity, inventiveness and contriving of people. While we stand agape at the array of goods conjured before our wondering eyes in the display cases of the world, we are complicit in our own powerlessness. Life and dynamism have deserted us and become invested in shimmering commodities, the desirability of which is designated by price, even when they were once cherished and acknowledged to be priceless.

Inequality has historically always seemed more abstract than poverty, which is why the latter has been the primary focus of campaigners and social reformers. In the process, poverty has become institutionalised. It has, indeed, become an amicable companion to wealth, since without a focus on the poor, how will the urgencies of perpetual growth and expansion be sustained? By setting the poverty line at 60% of the median wage, poverty is immortalised. It serves as a spur to even greater feats of production and expansion, to yet more extravagant consumption than anything yet seen. In this sense, poverty is the ally of wealth, just as the rich have become not enemies, but supposed friends of the poor.

Inequality has, meanwhile, been tolerated, because it has grown in a context in which everybody was becoming better off. This serene progression has been interrupted recently, not least by the exorbitances of wealth, which now appear dishonourable in a global economy in a state of crisis. Worsening inequality has illuminated the delusion underpinning globalism. The coexistence of showy and extravagant fortunes with the hunger-stricken conflicts between agriculturists and nomads in Central Africa, the water-stressed regions of the world and the turbulent mega-cities of Asia demonstrates defects in the theory that indefinite growth is the guarantor of social harmony.

These are some of the ways in which inequality has been transformed from a manageable and subordinate problem into a great evil. Whether or not the United Nations Millennium Development Goals on poverty are achievable,[1] the problem of poverty now appears more tractable than that of inequality. It is not only the injustice of inequality that has created the crisis: it is the limits of the biosphere to carry the system we have created, and to which there have been, until lately, few dissenters. Equity becomes more salient once the establishment of limits has been accepted. The heroic age of consumption is surely over. Eventual curbs on consumption, the result of an omnivorous and accelerating depletion of the natural world are inevitable. This will bring to the fore the issue of distributive justice once more. The economic freedom to exploit the planet and its people will come to seem as archaic as slavery, apartheid or other totalising ideologies that tempted peoples in the age of industrialism.

If we want seriously to address inequality, we have to look at the divergent and incompatible interests of the unequal. In this respect, another myth needs to be destroyed – that which claims it is impossible to distribute wealth that has not been made. Of course we would like to help the poor, the rich have protested, but you have to allow us to make the money first. The proponents of this theory have had a good run over the past generation or more. And this version of economic freedom has brought us to the brink of ecological ruin. The apparently conflict-free proposition that if everyone is getting richer, no one will notice the disparities between rich and poor, is no longer tenable. The disparities have become too glaring. Nor should it be imagined that the current financial crisis and recession are going to alter the distribution of wealth. Despite the present resentment of 'fat cats' and the odium in which bankers and financial manipulators are now held, agreement is almost universal that what is most urgently needed is to 'get the economy back to normal' – a normality that will involve a customarily uneven allocation of rewards.

Rediscovering humanity

It is significant that much of the modest security enjoyed by the people depended on public goods – healthcare, social security, unemployment and sickness pay and old age pensions. The welfare state laid down the basis for the compromise. And inequality was indeed reduced in the early post-war period. The growth in private affluence was dependent on the promise and premise of freedom from want guaranteed by the welfare state. The entertainment, fashion and other consumer industries could scarcely have grown if significant numbers of people had remained prey to Beveridge's five 'giant evils': want, idleness, disease, squalor and ignorance.

But older ideologies were only sleeping, biding their time until the moment of resurrection presented itself. The 1970s showed the limits of a Labourism characterised by high public spending and high taxation, where the trades unions were believed to have gained too much power. The coming of Margaret Thatcher made explicit what was actually happening in a world in which globalisation was already in train. The working class vanished almost overnight. The labour movement was demoted from being the primary agent of change into just another interest group, along with evangelists, chambers of commerce, ratepayers, spiritualists, sporting clubs and antiquarians. In place of the erased vanguard of the future arose a new focus for hope. The rich who, in an earlier ideological iconography, had been exploiters and bloodsuckers were transformed into the idealised model for all human aspiration and ambition. Their showy lifestyle, their munificence, their desire for luxury and inventive spending patterns became the supreme object of emulation and striving.

It is impossible to overestimate the consequences of this change. At a stroke, the rich were rehabilitated; their excesses became prowess, their heroic capacity for consumption became an inspiration to the world. This has led directly to the cult of celebrity, fame, wealth and power. These have displaced any archaic notions carried by a suffering and impoverished population who demanded only a secure sufficiency for themselves and their families. For now, the sky is the limit, and no one any longer knows what would constitute 'enough' for a human life. Indeed, in a world of perpetual economic growth, the word itself is a kind of secular blasphemy.

This shift, underpinned by policies of liberalisation and deregulation, and combined with the weakening of supports for the most vulnerable, has set in train the extremes of inequality we see in most countries. According to the United Nations in 2005 the richest 50 individuals in the world had a combined income greater than that of the poorest 416 million. The 2.5 billion people living on less than $2 a day – 40% of the world's population – received only 5% of global income, while 54% went to the richest 10% (UNDP, 2005).

International institutions, charities, humanitarian organisations and non-governmental organisations (NGOs) regularly publish such figures. Yet this does nothing to dent the perception that it is only by the energetic endeavours of the generators of wealth that the poor and the unequal can expect their situation to improve. The poor have been demobilised in the struggle of remedying their own poverty. This onerous task has now been entrusted to global wealth creators, their agents and representatives who have shown that it is they who are now in charge of the noble mission of alleviating poverty.

These changes are bound to lead to both paralysis and impotence. Tenderness for the poor increases and inequality is universally deplored; yet the global economy continues to reward those it favours without regard to justice, while governments vainly try to repair the damage. No matter how much they spend on tax credits, compensatory payments, benefits and handouts, this can never match the prodigious sums deployed by the well-to-do. Tax havens – rest homes for the most reclusive creature on earth, money – continue to play host to the most secretive fortunes. The pressure from the super-rich and transnational companies on governments to decrease the 'burden' of tax, with the threat that they will otherwise depart for more welcoming shores, undercuts any serious will to confront the widening gulf.

It is not in the realm of government policy making, the representations of NGOs, or charitable activity that change will be found. The myth that wealth is the supreme purpose of human striving on earth needs to be attacked head-on. It is an ideological struggle. While the rich are revered and regarded as universal role models, while celebrity and fame are sycophantically admired, as long as what money will buy continues to be exalted over what it cannot, nothing will happen. One story can be contested only with another. A different narrative is required. We need to hear the story of quiet satisfactions and contentment with sufficiency that celebrates the heroism of the everyday and draws on the ample storehouse of human rather than material resources.

Recognising wealth as the problem

What can be done is intensely political, yet it has nothing to do with the sterile quarrels between existing political formations. It may be that the people of the world are not susceptible to the possibility of a secure sustenance for all. It may be that the ancient imagery of wealth – jewels, yachts, fur coats and sequestered mansions – retains a stronger hold over the popular imagination. It may be hard to paint the exorbitant and disproportionate consumers of the world's treasures as monsters of egotism, to be scorned for their vacuity. But maybe not.

There is a widespread sense of dissatisfaction in the world. People are hungry for the opportunity to be effective actors and to shape the society which also shapes them. That means not so much a change of heart as a change of perception. All the conventions that declare wealth as progress, and money the source of all hope, have to be subject to question and scrutiny. Poverty is not the problem in a world of such abundance, wealth is. 'Give me neither riches nor poverty,' sang the prophet Isaiah, 'but enough for my sustenance.' 'There is no wealth but life,' wrote John Ruskin in 1980. Without some such reappraisal, the people of the world will continue to be wasted, either by excess – of which the 56 million people in the US who are obese are a powerful image – or by want – of which the world's 900 million malnourished are the emblem. The stigmata of inequality are borne in the bodies of actually existing human beings.

It may be that a more gentle myth than the violence of wealth creation fails. Perhaps the ideologues of accumulation without limits are right, and greed and selfishness really are attributes of human nature rather than aspects of the nature of capitalism. Perhaps efforts to rectify inequality really are doomed. But that is scarcely a reason to abandon the attempt. On the contrary, it makes our efforts all the more poignant and necessary.

> *It is dawn in a glass and steel tower in the city of London. A cleaner is already at work, moving her polisher noiselessly over the marble floor, between unidentifiable plants, vegetation known to no other global climatic zone than the arid spaces of office blocks. The cleaner has probably not calculated that she will have to work 50 weeks a year for a century and a half to earn as much as the Chief Executive Officer of the company receives as annual income.*

Note

[1] The eight Millennium Development Goals formulated by the United Nations include, by 2015, halving the proportion of people suffering from hunger, ensuring primary education for all children and eliminating the gender disparity in education, reducing by two thirds the mortality rate of children under five, and by three quarters the maternal mortality rate, reversing the spread of HIV/AIDS, ensuring environmental sustainability and developing a global partnership for development.

Reference

Ruskin, J. (1860) *Unto this last*, 'Ad valorem', Chapter IV, *Cornhill Magazine*.

UNDP (United Nations Development Programme) (2005) *Human development report 2005: International co-operation at a crossroads: Aid, trade and security in an unequal world*, New York: UNDP.

SECTION 3

Reflections

18

Reflections on social evils and human nature

Matthew Taylor

It would I suppose be surprising if a project on the new social evils were to conclude that there weren't any. But was it inevitable that there would be such agreement about what Zygmunt Bauman (Chapter 12) calls 'the withdrawal of society'? Most of the public and most of the intellectuals consulted by the Joseph Rowntree Foundation spoke with one voice; the greatest evil is society's retreat in the face of rampant individualism.

It is in the explanations for this phenomenon, and the emphasis put on its different manifestations, that can be traced to familiar dividing lines. The starting point for writers from the Left, like Neal Lawson (Chapter 13), is the decline of social solidarity, the widening of inequality, the labelling and punishing of the disadvantaged. For thinkers from the Right, like Anthony Browne (Chapter 7), the dilution of behavioural norms and the loss of a shared sense of identity lie behind our sense of social malaise.

On the whole, the public leans towards behavioural rather than structural accounts of social fragmentation, with the poorest – perhaps reflecting their own day-to-day experiences – most inclined to highlight pathologies like criminality, drug use and family breakdown.

All this confirms that we are living in a time of profound social pessimism. Opinion polls show an ever-widening gulf between our view of ourselves and our view of society at large. A major recent BBC poll found that more than nine in ten of us are optimistic about our family's prospects (up from 40 years ago) while an ever-smaller minority (fewer than one in five) shares this optimism about other people.

The contemporary feeling of social unease is undeniable; the dark seam exposed by the JRF is the same one mined by David Cameron in his talk of a 'broken society'. Yet as A.C. Grayling (Chapter 8) reminds us, a latter-day Harold Macmillan would have every reason for proclaiming that we have never had it so good (this, of course, before the credit crunch, of which more later).

Nor is it simply that we live longer, earn more, travel more and relax more than our parents or grandparents. We are also today more tolerant, better educated and more compassionate, certainly, than our Victorian counterparts. And the last few years have seen serious and successful attempts to reverse the baleful legacy of both 1970s planning and the abandonment of the public sphere in the 1980s.

Take the hard case of Birmingham. Fifteen years ago the city centre lived up to the West Midlands' image of unloved and unlovable utilitarian grimness. Scuttling nervously through dank, gloomy subways – the planners' churlish concession to pedestrians in the age of the car – lifelong Brummies were found to be ignorant of the topology of the city's remaining historic buildings. The city was not only ugly and barren; it had also become illegible.

Go now and you can walk from New Street station (the last relic of 1970s subterraneanism and itself earmarked for replacement) to the refurbished canals at the back of the International Convention Centre without seeing a car. Instead, you stroll along pedestrianised streets past the restored glories of Victorian municipalism and multiplying examples of the new wave of public art. That locals have affectionately renamed the magnificent sculpture and fountain in Victoria Square 'the Floozie in the Jacuzzi' is testament to how they feel at home again in their city. And, yes, there are lots of new shops. But these too can be engaging, attractive places where people of all races and backgrounds rub shoulders.

A similar story of town centre renewal can be repeated in cities across the UK. Maybe this seems anecdotal, but is it any less so than most of the examples of social decay paraded before us by media commentators and opposition politicians? Whether we are relying on dry statistics or vivid stories, it is as easy to say that things are good and getting better as to assert the opposite.

One way to resolve this apparent paradox is simply to choose one view of reality over the other. So, from one side of the argument, social pessimism is seen as an aspect of modernity only to the extent that we now have higher expectations and the opportunity to wallow in our doubts. The gloomy findings of opinion polls on the state of the world can be questioned on the reasonable grounds that they invite us to speculate on issues we hardly ever consider and that the framing of the questions invites negativity.

The converse position says that what matters is what we feel. Not only do we suffer social pessimism, but also our aggregate levels of life satisfaction have not risen with higher levels of affluence. We are, it is said, twice as rich as our grandparents but no more content. What is the point of all these improvements in our material circumstances if we don't feel happier in ourselves or more hopeful about society?

A more fruitful line of thought may be to explore, at a number of levels, what it is about the way things have got better that makes us feel worse. In what follows I will explore three ways of answering this question: first, a theory of affluence and its discontents; second, a theory of human development and transition; and third, an account of the fundamental forms of social relations.

Affluence and its discontents

A convincing account of the detrimental impact of affluence on human contentment and social relations has been developed by Avner Offer (2006) in his seminal work *The challenge of affluence*. Offer does us the favour of summing up his argument and the wealth of evidence on which it is based, in the first few words of his book: '[A]ffluence breeds impatience and impatience undermines well-being' (2006, p 1). Offer means by this that affluence undermines the material and emotional case for those social norms, conventions and institutions that encouraged us to look to our own and society's long-term interests. He calls these aspects 'commitment devices' and includes among them marriage, the welfare state, but also regulations and social norms that encourage deferred gratification by, for example, incentivising saving and discouraging debt. The weakening of these commitment devices has been cause and effect in the rise of a culture of instant gratification, inauthentic communication (for example, advertising, public relations, spin doctoring) and unearned entitlements.

Offer maintains that it is impossible for society to thrive and for most of us to get what we want without commitment devices. Indeed, it proves to be impossible even for the market to work without both trust and regulation. The idea that we can always get what we want whether in our relationships, at work or in collective decision making is a myth, as is the notion that the short-term choices we make are always fully informed or wise even in narrowly self-interested terms. (This, by the way, is the myth that more than anything else blinded us to the crisis brewing in the financial services.) People don't work like this and society can't work like this. For example, it leads to the suboptimal solution to the classic 'Prisoners' Dilemma'[1] (both betray) and makes it impossible for us to develop the optimal learned solution (both cooperate). Affluence encourages us both to believe and to live by myth. Without a change of direction we are doomed to be disappointed and for society to be eviscerated.

Offer's book was a powerful critique of consumer capitalism and neoliberal politics even before the economic turmoil through which we are now living. Polly Toynbee and David Walker (2008) recognised their debt to Offer in their more trenchant and policy-oriented book *Unjust rewards*. But now, as we see the full folly of an under-regulated banking system, a political class in thrall to free-market fundamentalism and a populace that had come to take ever-greater debt-fuelled affluence for granted (regardless of its wider social consequences), Offer moves from siren to prophet.

Offer is an economic historian and to explain why we have succumbed to the challenge of affluence, he relies on an economist's explanation. Technological innovation fuelling economic growth and rising living standards (in the developed world) has simply changed the incentives we face. Instead of being held back by commitment devices we are now free to pursue blind short-termism. In tracing our problems to our hardwired limitations, Offer's theory reminds us of the joke about the previously obedient dog, who when given a £50 note to perform his usual trick of buying milk from a store is later found by his owner *in flagrante* with a poodle, blind drunk and penniless. "But you never did this before!" says the dismayed owner. "Ah yes," slurs the dog, "but you never gave me £50 before."

For many on the Left, the problems Offer describes are not an accident. The powerful combination of neoliberal ideology, financial globalisation and consumer capitalism was created and maintained by those who most clearly benefited from it. This is true. The politics and economics of the bubble relied on an ideology that portrayed something human-made and precarious (the cocktail of consumer debt and financial speculation) as a force of nature. It is more evidence of collective delusion that many of these who were champions of deregulation and debt-fuelled finance are now queuing up to say they had misgivings about the Emperor's new clothes all along: "We all knew the bankers weren't wearing anything, but it was just too embarrassing to say it."

Society in transition

But Offer's analysis prompts a different question. Human beings are not simply driven by short-term desires (for Offer to be arguing this would put him in the camp of the neoliberals). We can make collective judgements and adapt. Why have we proven so susceptible to attitudes and behaviours that did little to increase our well-being in the short term and about which we clearly felt major misgivings? True, this party is now over but it was not because we chose to call time. One answer is that society is going through an acute period of transition. In this period we are particularly prone to confusion and social pessimism. As well as explaining our current malaise, transition theory offers the hope of human beings attaining a higher stage of development.

Offer suggests that we cannot cope with plenty. Historians argue that past civilisations have collapsed in part because the elite in those civilisations – the only ones who lived with plenty – succumbed to self-indulgence and a loss of vitality and authority. Today, three quarters of the UK's population has more disposable income than it needs, not only to survive, but also to enjoy good health and the opportunities for leisure and self-development. But rather than growing from this opportunity, some would say, we are exhibiting a kind of mass version of the decadence that history has taught us to associate with the fall of the Roman Empire. If this sounds far-fetched, try going out to an English city centre on a Friday evening, watch the chemically enhanced mood swings of the entertainment classes or witness politicians turning a blind eye to the big, hard, long-term issues while pandering to the demands for middle-class tax cuts.

There is a 'chickens coming home to roost' feel in much commentary about the economic downturn. Public concerns about excess, whether drugs, food or alcohol, about the decline of social relations, about the lack of political leadership mean that we cannot help feeling we had it coming to us.

But could it be that the period of hyper-consumerism was transitional? Human beings have, after all, spent most of their existence with only just enough; indeed, being hardwired to expect no more than that. Those who live among the top two thirds of the people of the rich countries have now found that plenty creates as many problems as it solves. So will we start to ask a different question: what do we truly need to live the good life? This is after all what we tend eventually to do in our own lives; to crave something we are denied, to over consume it when we have unlimited access and then to realise that (in my grandmother's favourite phrase) 'enough is as good as a feast'.

If we imagine a timeline labelled 'material need and consumption', might it be possible to trace a transition from subsistence, through excess, to a balanced and sustainable way of thinking and living? It would be a strange line as the first stage lasts 200,000 years and the second, in the rich world at least, a few decades. But there are other areas of human endeavour – most notably science and technology – that have seen a similarly rapid acceleration of development in modern times. Other important facets of the human condition (and sources of discontent) can be traced on to this crudely Hegelian account of human progress. Thus, current worries about identity, community cohesion and religious extremism can be seen to reflect a transitional stage of unease and disturbance between our long history of social segregation and homogeneity and our emergence into a higher stage of cultural plurality, global citizenship and freedom of expression. Similarly, in our political culture we can be said to be moving from a long history of deference (or, at least, obedience) to tradition – and to earth and then sky Gods – to hereditary and finally democratic authority. The goal for human development is creative self-government. But sadly, we are currently stuck, surly and disengaged; unwilling to be governed, not yet willing or able to govern ourselves.

From the perspective of transition theory, our vulnerability to the challenge of affluence, and our susceptibility to social pessimism, reflect not just the power of new technology and the allure of its consumer goods, but also a more general frailty as we go through what some have caricaturised as the adolescence of enlightenment man. This is an attractive argument. It suggests that we might grow out of our current weaknesses and ascend to a higher level than a promiscuous canine. The adolescent metaphor also helps us explain the coincidence in modern character of folly and self-obsession with an impressive capacity for inventiveness and growth (just ask any parent of a teenager).

There are those who argue strongly for the possibility, indeed the necessity, of human beings attaining a qualitatively higher state of functioning and consciousness. Many of these thinkers – for example, Henryk Skolimowski (1994), author of *The participatory mind* and Ken Wilber (2000), author of *A theory of everything* – have been heavily influenced by Buddhist practice and teachings.

Maybe it is just that the attainment of Nirvana is beyond me, but I fear few of us can hope to transcend human nature. Notwithstanding the change of heart needed to transform us from 'shopaholics' to truth seekers, it is difficult to see how one might reconcile the disciplines of personal enlightenment with the concrete challenges of running a complex society. Who will make the trains run on time when we are all in a state of meditative bliss?

Social change, cultural theory and human nature

Progress is possible. Otherwise we would still have an average life expectancy of 29. But progress does not take place down a linear or inevitable path. Instead, social change results from the enduring contest between fundamentally different ways of seeing and acting upon the world. This is the perspective offered by cultural theory. It is based on the work of the classic French sociologist Emile Durkheim French and the research of the distinguished anthropologist Mary Douglas (1992), as taken forward by scholars like Christopher Hood (1988) and Michael Thompson and colleagues (1990). Cultural theory suggests four fundamental ways of viewing and managing social relations. These ways are:

- the *hierarchical*, in which change is driven from the top down through authority, expertise and rules;
- the *egalitarian*, in which change is driven bottom up through strong group membership, shared values and solidarity;
- the *individualistic*, in which change is the result of free individuals pursuing their own self-interest; and
- the *fatalistic*, in which change is seen as illusory or random.

(Thompson et al, 1990, add a fifth category – *the hermit* – but things are complicated enough.)

Cultural theory is analytical and normative, arguing not only that these ways of seeing and acting are ubiquitous, but also that engaging with each of them is necessary to enable the emergence of what they call 'clumsy solutions'. The theory is evidenced by solutions that were doomed by their failure to engage with one or more of the ways of conducting social relations. For example, cultural theorists predicted the limited impact of the Kyoto accord due to its reliance on hierarchy and its failure to engage individualism or be realistic about fatalism.

Is it possible that cultural theory offers us a way of understanding not only our social pessimism but also the unfolding of the credit crunch? To do so requires us to add history and technology to the theory. The argument is that at certain times the reinforcing combination of socioeconomic context and emerging techniques fosters a particular cultural orientation. Thus, the conditions between the end of the Depression and the end of the Second World War created the right context and encouraged the right techniques for a hierarchical orientation to become dominant in the succeeding decades. This expressed itself through the centralised corporation (both private and public sector), national planning and corporatism, and a confidence in the scope for socially benevolent expertise (in science, economics, social policy) to drive social progress. The norms and methods of post-war hierarchism generated real gains for society but, like all systems that systematically privilege one orientation to social relations, it contained the seeds of its own destruction. While hierarchy was arguably compatible with fatalism (those happy to follow orders and be the cogs in systems), egalitarian and individualist dynamics were marginalised. Their fight back came through the combination of the radical anti-establishmentarianism of the 1960s and 1970s, and the neoliberal individualism that triumphed in the late 1970s and 1980s. The build-up of both an egalitarian (Left) and individualist (Right) critique of the post-war settlement may help explain the apparent paradox that the revolutionary politics in culture, universities and trades unions broadly coincided with the triumph of neoliberal political economy.

Continuing to paint with the broadest of brushes, the last 20 years can be seen as a period of hegemonic individualism favoured both by historical circumstance – the perceived failure of corporatism and the big state, the collapse of communism – and by the emergence of powerful techniques of individualism – personalised consumerism, focus group politics, the internet. The culture of the City represents the most extreme version of individualism triumphant. All that mattered in the City was individual ambition. There was no egalitarian belief in a wider social or moral purpose for banking, nor was there any effective hierarchy as the rules didn't work. Those notionally in charge were on a merry-go-round they could not get off (even if they wanted to) and no one even really understood how the system worked. Finally – and crucially – there was no fatalism, which cultural theorists see as playing an important role in social order and change. Every banker believed they had an unlimited capacity to generate wealth and increase their earnings. To have a major area of activity so dominated by a single framing of human relations is rare. To then give those in that area the power to influence the well-being of billions of citizens is – as we have now come to understand – a disastrous error.

As individualism stumbles, we are seeing the reassertion of other ways of thinking. Hierarchy will be rehabilitated as world leaders rediscover the idea of global leadership, coordination and regulation. Egalitarians who were already gathering strength at the margins through the growth of downsizing, alternative living and environmental movements will be emboldened to question the values and outcomes of the free market. Advocates of individualism will have to adapt their message and means to new times or accept being out of fashion. And if we enter into a prolonged period of economic stagnation we will all be more prone to (and possibly comforted by) fatalism.

Perhaps this is simply an evolutionary cycle, a dialectic of memes (cultural traits) in which dominant patterns emerge, dominate and decay. Most people will find a way of adapting to the prevailing cultural atmosphere, others will resist. Like politicians we can sail with the wind. Or like record collectors we can be out and proud when our tunes are in fashion, retreating to a small circle of true believers when our music is considered naff. But what about those of us who have found something of interest in very different political platforms (and much to deprecate in them all); those who like the fatalism of Joni Mitchell, the egalitarianism of the Clash and the individualism of Kanye West? We have been encouraged to see our eclecticism as weak and woolly minded. Yet, if individualism, egalitarianism, hierarchism and fatalism and the inherent competition between them are inevitable, should we not be looking for solutions that harness (or at least recognise) them all? Should we not favour accounts of society, types of organisation and ways of managing that speak to these different perspectives?

With the rise and rise of neuroscience, one fruitful new area of research may be to explore ways in which the schemas of cultural theory might map onto brain activity. Reduced to its simplest, the four ways of seeing social relations can be expressed as 'I will do what I want', 'I will do what the group does', 'I will do what I'm told' and 'It doesn't matter what I do'. Do these responses involve particular cognitive processes? Recent research has distinguished between the brain processes involved in learning through experience (which are likely to be linked to individualistic and fatalistic responses) and those involved in learning through advice (which are more likely to be associated with egalitarian and hierarchical responses).

Having, at last, left behind the baleful myth of selfish, separate, rational humankind, can we demand of attempts to explain human action that they are at least credible at three levels: the social, the behavioural and the physiological? We are a long way from 'a theory of everything' but it would be good to start looking in the right places. More practically, are there examples of the kind of approach that cultural theory implicitly advocates? How about social enterprises, which combine clear goals and strong management with shared values among employees and the space for individuals to express themselves and grow? Or for those who despair of politics, how about the brave and holistic account of the problem of race given by Barack Obama in March 2008?

President Obama, as he became, called for solutions that require leadership, overcoming group victimhood and promoting personal responsibility. Aren't the best schools the ones with visionary and strong leaders, that want their pupils to thrive as individuals and which create a strong sense of community and pride in the institution? No solution is perfect, and cultural theory insists that each paradigm of social relations gains its strength from competing for power and adherents with the others (selfish memes to go with our selfish genes). But we can at least distinguish solutions doomed to failure from those that might at least provide the right framework for progress.

The human race has made great strides, especially in the last few hundred years. But progress has been interspersed with error and tragedy. By privileging one way of thinking over others – as we have recently done with individualism – we at best squander human potential and at worst risk disaster. We could achieve more and be happier about it if our ways of thinking and acting engaged with all the ways in which we are human.

Note

[1] The Prisoner's Dilemma, first framed in the 1950s, suggests that two suspects are arrested without sufficient evidence for a conviction. The police separately offer each the same deal. If one testifies against the other and the other remains silent, the betrayer goes free and the accomplice receives a 10-year sentence. If both remain silent, they are sentenced to six months in prison for a minor charge. If each betrays the other, they receive a five-year sentence. Each prisoner must choose to betray the other or to remain silent.

References

Douglas, M. (1992) *Risk and blame: Essays in cultural theory*, London: Routledge.

Hood, C. (1988) *The art of the state: Culture, rhetoric, and public management*, Oxford: Clarendon Press.

Offer, A. (2006) *The challenge of affluence: Self control and well-being in the United States and Britain since 1950*, Oxford: Oxford University Press.

Skolimowski, H. (1994) *The participatory mind: A new theory of knowledge and of the universe*, London: Penguin.

Thompson, M., Ellis, R.J. and Wildavsky, A. (1990) *Cultural theory*, Boulder, CO: Westview Press.

Toynbee, P. and Walker, D. (2008) *Unjust rewards: Exposing greed and inequality in Britain today*, London: Granta Books.

Wilber, K. (2000) *A theory of everything: An integral vision for business, politics, science and spirituality*, Boston, MA: Shambhala.

19

Afterword

David Utting

To those familiar with the work of the Joseph Rowntree Foundation (JRF), but unaware of its history, this book on contemporary social evils may come as something of a surprise. Like some respondents to the public online consultation, they may feel uncomfortable that a moral dimension has been so overtly acknowledged to the factual study of social disadvantage and its consequences. Yet anyone who pauses to consider the meaning of a social policy term like 'poverty' – among the most consistent areas of the JRF's research interests – can hardly fail to recognise the implications of moral unacceptability, demanding that 'something be done' (Piachaud, 1987; Roll, 1992). No less importantly, there is the desire that Joseph Rowntree, successful manufacturer and Quaker philanthropist, expressed for the trusts he endowed a century ago to search out the underlying causes of "weakness and evil" in society.

The question of how its founder's wishes, expressed in splendid Edwardian language, should be interpreted in the 21st century is of self-evident interest to the JRF, which commissioned this work. But what this book and the consultations that preceded it have demonstrated is that the concept of 'social evil' is of much more general concern. It has been proved fully capable of provoking impassioned debate about the issues of our own time in a way that less pejorative language could not achieve. The social evils project has allowed a much-needed space for these discussions to take place. It is also a reminder of how an historical perspective can so often enrich and enlighten our understanding of contemporary research discoveries and issues. Jose Harris (Chapter 2) describes the coincidence of an international recession, a government fiscal crisis and the aftermath of an unpopular foreign war that served as the stimulus for national soul-searching amid economic and social pessimism. She is, however, referring to the opening decade of the last century, not our own. Her description of the regional differences that made experiences of the 1930s depression so variable are, likewise, a reminder of how geography may relate to different perceptions of contemporary problems, including a very urban emphasis on gun and knife crime.

She also demonstrates how perceptions of social evil have shifted with the tide of events, as they did during two world wars, mass inter-war unemployment and the post-war 'culture of contentment' (Galbraith, 1958) whose hallmark was increased private affluence at the arguable expense of communal prosperity. This, most of all, can be seen to resonate with the anxieties raised in the public, online consultations and a repeated emphasis among the essayists in Section 2 on the rise of individualism and a decline in community spirit and collective action. There is also a strong sense of the warning repeated by several authors that periods of widespread 'moral panic' are not uncommon in history and have proved apt to dispel in the light of more dispassionate investigation.

Matthew Taylor (Chapter 18), responding to the debate, rightly highlights the level of consensus that emerged concerning the evil consequences of personal greed and lost social solidarity. This is eloquently and trenchantly expressed by Zygmunt Bauman (Chapter 12). But readers will also have discovered that consensus does not always prevail, and that there is more than enough tension elsewhere between the various viewpoints to add salt (and occasionally acid) to the discussion. Some, like Anthony Browne (Chapter 7) and Shaun Bailey (Chapter 10), maintain that a loss of communal, family and parental regulation has accelerated our moral decline at a time of excessive emphasis on individuals' rights as citizens rather than their responsibilities. Others, including Anna Minton (Chapter 11) and Neal Lawson (Chapter 13), direct their fire at growing insecurity and a malign sense that those who experience social disadvantage are not only to blame for their own problems but also pose a threat to the prosperous majority.

Julia Neuberger (Chapter 9) and Ferdinand Mount (Chapter 16), spanning both arguments in their different ways, regret a loss of mutual obligation in society and call for the restoration of personal trust, participation and altruism. Stephen Thake (Chapter 14) is more optimistic that investment in civil society and social enterprise can provide a much-needed step in the right direction. At a visceral as well as an intellectual level, readers may have felt challenged by A.C. Grayling's assertion that inequality, within reason, is a price worth paying in a liberal democracy where the real contemporary social evil is poverty (Chapter 8). Likewise by Jeremy Seabrook's attack on politicians who espouse 'equality of opportunity'; and by his call for 'a more gentle myth' to replace an obsession with accumulating wealth (Chapter 17).

The range of thought and expression that these contributions represent is considerable. They extend from Shaun Bailey and Anna Minton's accounts of street life in London and Liverpool (Chapters 10 and 11) to Matthew Taylor's elucidation of the ways that cultural theory can help us to understand the slide into social pessimism and the credit crunch (Chapter 18). But beyond that we have the many perspectives contributed by the wider public, which are set out in Section 1. These include the online consultation whose 3,500 respondents, while not a representative sample of opinion, gave vent to an even wider variety of views concerning social evils, both tangible and abstract.

The same themes emerged repeatedly throughout the online public consultation, albeit without any obvious consensus regarding where the responsibility might lie for perceived social evils such as family breakdown, or incivility and youth crime. Widely shared, however, were feelings of unease about the sheer pace of social change in recent years and concern that particular values relating to community cohesion and social responsibility have, somehow, been left behind. Whether talking about individualism, consumerism and greed, or about poverty, crime and drug misuse, there was a genuine sense of fear expressed in the face of complex national and international trends over which people felt they had no sense of control. The pervasive level of anxiety displayed in the online consultation is, perhaps, all the more remarkable for having been apparent a full year before Britain entered economic recession, when the consumer boom was still in full swing.

No less compelling were the reports from workshops and discussion groups initiated to gather the views of socially disadvantaged groups (such as young homeless people, carers, people with learning difficulties, unemployed people and ex-offenders) who were thought especially unlikely to access an online consultation. The themes that emerged from the first series of discussions, in which participants were asked to identify today's social evils, were in many respects similar to those highlighted by the website consultation. They included poverty, crime, family breakdown and a declining sense of community, as well as a common (although misplaced) perception that refugees and asylum seekers are treated more favourably than British citizens. It is also worth noting that this exercise – like previous research in socially disadvantaged neighbourhoods (see, for example, Heath, 1992) – helps to rebut the notion that an 'underclass' exists in Britain, excluded not only by poverty, but also by differing, deviant attitudes.

Even more striking was the way in which people described their personal experiences of many of the social problems they identified. As is evident from Chris Creegan's viewpoint (Chapter 15), these discussions left a profound impression on the researchers who organised them. They were prompted to coin the term 'truncated opportunities' to describe the way that the social evils revealed in people's personal histories were threaded with the deadening evidence of surrendered potential at every stage of their lives. Most potent of all, however, were the 'unheard voices' of people who took part in a second phase of consultations, when they were asked to describe their day-to-day experiences of coping with social disadvantage and various social evils. It was here that we encountered the young residents of a homeless hostel who were determined to stay positive and to believe that their lives would improve despite their lack of money, qualifications and family support. Some cited religious faith, or made favourable comparisons between their own situation and that of people in the developing world. Others spoke of living for the day and deliberately suppressing their emotions, even the wish to cry.

Here, too, we met the carers, unemployed people and ex-offenders whose distractions from their everyday difficulties extended from sitting down with a good book or taking physical exercise to seeking a temporary escape from reality through drugs or alcohol. Darker, more extreme responses were also cited, including resorts to self-harm, violence and crime. Yet the value of external help, through friends and family where available, and from non-judgemental, accessible support services were also apparent. It is no disrespect to other contributors to say that people's fragmented accounts of their daily struggles to preserve dignity in the face of adversity are as impressive, touching and salutary as anything else that this book contains.

By its very nature, the consultation was more successful in achieving its primary goal of obtaining views of contemporary social evils than in surfacing ideas about potential solutions. Nevertheless, individual authors in this book have contributed ideas and proposals for remedying the problems they identify. These extend from specific suggested adjustments to the tax and benefits system to more general appeals for a kinder and more altruistic society.

People from disadvantaged groups were also asked, in the second round of discussions, to say what they thought could be done to address social evils. Wishes were expressed that the media, business, financial institutions and faith groups would all endeavour to play a more constructive role. As in the wider, online consultation there was a widespread view that a more responsible media should dwell less on violence, scandal and the cult of celebrity, and do more to promulgate ordinary people's success stories. Faith groups were regarded, even by declared atheists among the website respondents, as an important source of missing 'moral fibre'. Personal responsibilities, whether as individuals or parents, were also recognised.

Yet it was clear that, more than any other external institution, those in socially disadvantaged circumstances looked to government and politicians to strive more vigorously against the social evils they experienced in their daily lives. They saw roles for government as 'enforcer' tackling crime and antisocial behaviour, as 'educator' promoting positive parenting and stronger family values, and as 'distributor' achieving greater fairness in the division of wealth and opportunities. Beyond that, they wanted politicians to 'practise what they preach' and to listen. They and the machinery of government were perceived as simply too remote to understand what life was like, struggling to cope on a low income with the pressures that participants so graphically described.

What conclusions might be drawn from this project by those who continue to search for answers to the social problems of our time? One thought that contrives to be both satisfying and challenging at the same time concerns the foresight of Joseph Rowntree himself. He realised that the interpretation and extent of 'social evils' was bound to change with time and he vested his legacy in trusts that have proved fit for their continuing purposes. For example, the JRF, along with the Joseph Rowntree Housing Trust, combines search activities with the capacity to demonstrate 'real-life' solutions to problems. They can be seen to offer a multidimensional response to many facets of the social evils that the current consultation has identified. The challenge lies in knowing that, notwithstanding a century of discernable progress (see, for example, Glennerster et al, 2004; Joseph Rowntree Charitable Trust et al, 2004), there is so much still to achieve, particularly in current economic circumstances.

Jose Harris (Chapter 2) has reminded us that neither Joseph Rowntree, nor his son, the pioneering researcher Seebohm Rowntree, ever sought to distance their scientific investigations into impoverished living conditions from a moral dimension. Yet as eminently practical men, they also believed that the proper purpose of social research was less intellectual, theoretical or moral enrichment, than solid, palpable change. Examining the contributions to this book from that perspective, we might, in company with Matthew Taylor (Chapter 18), hope for a less partisan and more eclectic view of what would in future contribute to the 'good' society. Perhaps, as Ferdinand Mount

(Chapter 16) proposes, we should give more thought to the 'equality of membership' that marriage and other essentially classless institutions can provide. Maybe, as Jeremy Seabrook (Chapter 17) would have us do, we can aspire to a more global and less materialistic view of what we want from human existence, knowing that the journey may be valuable without any confident expectation of reaching the objective.

We should also acknowledge how any case for moral or attitudinal change can usually be enhanced by empirical evidence from research and by demonstrable good practice; just as it can for more concrete social advancement. Existing trends and policies must continue to be assessed and new approaches to social problems explored, not least where political leaders and public opinion perpetuate a belief in stereotypes that have a limited basis in objective fact. Independent research is needed to debunk myths that have, themselves, become a form of social evil.

It is also necessary to provide a continuing critique of the powerful and the ways they choose to exercise their power, to counteract the sense of unease with institutions and the way we are governed. With the excesses of international banking that triggered the current economic recession still vividly in mind, we may feel we have reached a peak of awareness of the socially destructive greed that flows from failure to reign in the power of market forces. Yet those with longer memories might also feel a sense of déjà vu, recalling how many lessons from previous recessions – in the early 1980s and the start of the 1990s – were quickly forgotten once 'good times' returned. The materialism deplored by so many respondents to the social evils consultation was surely no less rampant 20 years ago, when an increasingly prosperous majority discovered, too late, how insecurity and loss of social cohesion flow from a rapidly widening gap between rich and poor.[1]

Having explored the meaning of contemporary social evils, we may conclude that those who search for the underlying causes of social problems have a moral as well as objective responsibility to scrutinise the use and abuse of economic power. We should also recognise the potential for their research to be applied in ways that help empower people who lack the opportunities and resources to make their voices count. For, if there is an immediate lesson to be gleaned from this book, it concerns the value of listening to the 'unheard voices' of people whose circumstances, modesty or alienation place them beyond the reach of more conventional consultations. There is a demonstrable need for different forms of engagement. This is not to tumble into any fallacy of assuming that people with first-hand experience of problems must invariably be authorities on the solutions. Impoverished circumstances

APPENDIX

How the 'social evils' consultations were organised

Plans for the Joseph Rowntree Foundation's (JRF) programme were developed in late 2006. From the outset, the emphasis was on eliciting a wide range of views and stimulating public debate.

The online consultation

It was decided to set up a website consultation, through which it was hoped to access a large number of responses in a short period of time. This ran between July and September 2007. People were asked to write briefly about the three social evils that, in their view, caused 'the most damage to British society as a whole or the most misery to its people'. The aim was to include society-level issues as well as issues that impacted at the individual level. However, the definition was deliberately open-ended, with every care taken to avoid leading respondents in particular directions (see Chapter 3).

A total of 3,500 submissions were received via the website and a further 100 responses were sent to the JRF by post. The responses were analysed using a substantial coding process designed to capture the depth and richness of the opinions expressed.

Listening to often 'unheard' voices

It was acknowledged from the outset that relying solely on a website would exclude many people. Only 61% of UK households in 2007 had access to the internet.[1] It was also recognised that the publicity that was planned for the programme was more likely to reach some groups than others. Moreover, it was anticipated that a considerable number of people would be unlikely to participate in a website consultation even if they had access to the internet. This might reflect a lack of time and inclination, but it might also stem from personal circumstances that related directly or indirectly to the kind of excluding social problems on which the consultation was expected to focus.

It was, therefore, decided to include the views of a range of people whose voices are often neglected in such discussions. NatCen (National

Centre for Social Research), an independent social research organisation, was commissioned to capture the views of 'unheard' groups such as carers, unemployed people, young homeless people, ex-offenders and care leavers. Participants were contacted with the help of charities, agencies and community-based programmes.

Discussion groups and workshops were conducted in two waves. The first was concerned with views about what constituted 'social evils' in today's society and why (Chapter 4). The second explored people's direct experiences of living and coping with the problems that had previously been identified and seeking their perspectives on possible solutions (Chapter 5).

Note

[1] www.statistics.gov.uk/pdfdir/inta0807.pdf

Index